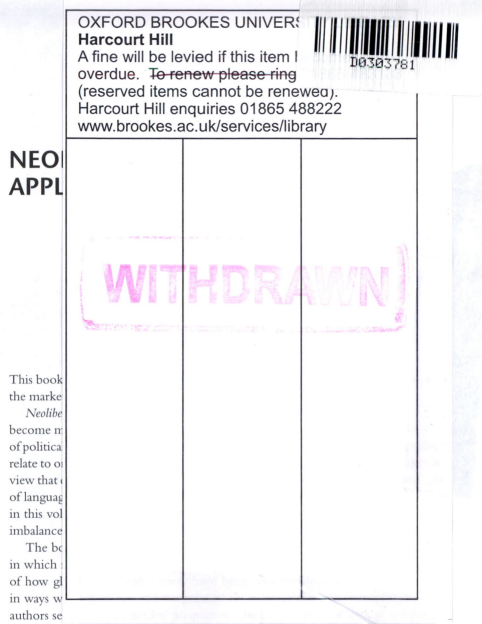

NEO
APPL

This book
the marke

Neolibe
become m
of politica
relate to o
view that
of languag
in this vol
imbalance

The bo
in which
of how gl
in ways w
authors se
the ways in which neoliberal ideology plays out in two key areas of applied linguistics
– language teaching and language teacher education.

Neoliberalism and Applied Linguistics is essential reading for advanced undergraduates,
postgraduates and researchers in Applied Linguistics.

David Block is Professor of Languages in Education at the Institute of Education,
University of London.

John Gray is Senior Lecturer in TESOL Education at the Institute of Education,
University of London.

Marnie Holborow is Lecturer in the School of Applied Language and Intercultural
Studies at Dublin City Unive

NEOLIBERALISM AND APPLIED LINGUISTICS

David Block

John Gray

Marnie Holborow

Routledge
Taylor & Francis Group

LONDON AND NEW YORK

First published 2012
by Routledge
2 Park Square, Milton Park, Abingdon, Oxon OX14 4RN

Simultaneously published in the USA and Canada
by Routledge
711 Third Avenue, New York, NY 10017

Routledge is an imprint of the Taylor & Francis Group, an informa business

British Library Cataloguing in Publication Data
A catalogue record for this book is available from the British Library

Library of Congress Cataloging in Publication Data
Block, David, 1956–
   Neoliberalism and applied linguistics / David Block, John Gray,
   Marnie Holborow.
        p. cm.
   Includes bibliographical references and index.
   1. Applied linguistics. 2. Language and languages–Study and
   teaching. 3. Neoliberalism–Social aspects. 4. Globalisation.
   I. Gray, John, 1955- II. Holborow, Marnie. III. Title.
   P129B46 2012
   306.44–dc23   2011033723

ISBN: 978-0-415-59204-8 (hbk)
ISBN: 978-0-415-59205-5 (pbk)
ISBN: 978-0-203-12812-1 (ebk)

Typeset in Bembo
by HWA Text and Data Management, London

MIX
Paper from
responsible sources
FSC® C004839

Printed and bound in Great Britain by the MPG Books Group

CONTENTS

Acknowledgements   vii

1 Introduction   1
DAVID BLOCK, JOHN GRAY AND MARNIE HOLBOROW

2 What is neoliberalism? Discourse, ideology and the real world   14
MARNIE HOLBOROW

3 Neoliberal keywords and the contradictions of an ideology   33
MARNIE HOLBOROW

4 Economising globalisation and identity in applied linguistics in
neoliberal times   56
DAVID BLOCK

5 Neoliberalism, celebrity and 'aspirational content' in English
language teaching textbooks for the global market   86
JOHN GRAY

6 The marketisation of language teacher education and
neoliberalism: characteristics, consequences and future prospects   114
JOHN GRAY AND DAVID BLOCK

Notes   144
References   147
Index   162

ACKNOWLEDGEMENTS

We would like to thank the following people for reading one or more chapters of the book and offering helpful feedback: Colin Barker, Debbie Cameron, Nigel Harwood, Adam Jaworski, Claudia Lapping, Tim McNamara, Tom Morton, Peadar O'Grady, John O'Sullivan, Siân Preece, Scott Thornbury, Cathie Wallace and Stephen Wong. Obviously, any shortcomings remaining in individual chapters and the book as a whole are down to the authors. Thanks also go to the participants in the research reported on in Chapters 5 and 6.

David and John would like to thank fellow members of their ongoing Marx reading group for providing ideas and stimulating their thinking during discussions of *Capital 1*, *The Communist Manifesto*, *The German Ideology* and other works: Melanie Cooke, John O'Regan, Siân Preece and Cathie Wallace. They would also like to thank Marnie for being a veritable fount of information regarding all matters related to political economy. Marnie would like to thank David and John for making this a truly collaborative project which was a real pleasure to be part of.

Finally, we would like to thank several key people at Routledge: Louisa Semlyen, Publisher, for being very supportive of this project from the beginning and Sophie Jaques, Senior Editorial Assistant, English Language and Linguistics, for being superb in answering questions and providing information and guidance along the way. Thanks also go to John Hodgson and Holly Knapp for their attentiveness and help with editing.

David Block, John Gray and Marnie Holborow
London and Dublin, August 2011

1

INTRODUCTION

DAVID BLOCK, JOHN GRAY AND
MARNIE HOLBOROW

During the process of writing a book, authors often have to respond to the question: 'What is your book about?'. Depending on the source of the question, the response will vary. On the one hand, it might be very didactic, as when the author feels that he/she must explain several key ideas underlying the central argument of the book if the question asker is to walk away with any idea whatsoever about the content of the book. On the other hand, when talking to peers, the author might produce the most tautological of answers. In the case of this book, *Neoliberalism and Applied Linguistics,* one of the authors (David Block) found himself answering this question by saying: 'Well, it's about neoliberalism *and* applied linguistics'. Interestingly enough, the question asker seemed happy with the response!

But such a response is clearly not very helpful and one way of improving it is to say what is meant by the two key terms in the title, 'neoliberalism' and 'applied linguistics'. Thus we begin this chapter with a discussion of applied linguistics and then follow it with a discussion of neoliberalism, showing along the way the overlap of the two. However, it should be noted that these discussions will necessarily be brief and partial. Applied linguistics is thus focused on through the prism of a key article published by Ben Rampton in 1997, in which he called for an interdisciplinary applied linguistics.[1] Rampton's suggestion has certainly been taken up if we are to judge by applied linguistic conference papers and publications which have appeared over the past decade and half.

However, as we will note, one blind spot in the interdisciplinarianism of applied linguistics has been political economy and in particular a detailed critique of neoliberalism as the ideology driving the practice of economics by governments and international organisations today. Political economy was the term used at the time of Marx and was used by him in his critique of classical economics but today it is more widely used in human geography, social and political science, anthropology and cultural studies to emphasise the interrelatedness of political and economic processes. It tends to focus on aggregate economic activity, resource allocation, capital accumulation, income inequality, globalisation and imperial power (Harvey 2005, 2010a; Dunn 2009a; Callinicos 2009, 2010; Ritzer and Atalay 2010). It can be defined or understood in two ways: first, as an academic discipline drawing on methods from economics, politics and sociology, which deals with the relationship between the individual and society and between the market and the state; and second as a pathway to interdisciplinarity which combines branches of economics and politics in order to understand how social institutions, their activities and capitalism influence each other in various ways. From our perspective, it is the latter understanding of political economy which informs our work. In short, our concern to include the social and the economic in our book naturally leads us towards the terrain of political economy which, we believe, grounds neoliberalism in the wider economic and political developments of contemporary capitalism and provides the vital political and economic dimension to issues of social identity, language and language teaching.

As indicated above, we begin this chapter with discussions of the two key terms in the title of the book, applied linguistics and neoliberalism. These discussions will be followed by descriptions of the content of the five main chapters of the book, which will shed light on the logic of their inclusion and the logic of the order in which they appear. We close the chapter with a brief account of how we came to write this book.

Applied linguistics as backdrop

In a landmark paper calling for a 'retuning' of applied linguistics, Rampton (1997) made the point that the field was not just about language teaching, as many at that time seemed to think; rather, it was better seen as '[t]he theoretical and empirical investigation of real-world problems in which language is the central issue' (Brumfit 1991: 46). For Rampton, adopting this definition meant that any linking of theories and research about language to day-to-day phenomena would have to be classified as applied linguistics. As a sociolinguist, Rampton proposed an applied linguistics associated with areas of research such as the microethnography of institutional settings, ethnographic studies of language socialisation, new literacies studies, genre theory, critical discourse analysis, speech accommodation and conversation analysis. Such an applied linguistics required a definitive move to what Hymes, writing a quarter of a decade earlier, termed a 'socially constituted linguistics'. As Hymes (1974: 196) explained, a socially constituted linguistics is based on two interrelated notions: (1) 'that social function gives form to the ways in which linguistic features are encountered in actual life'; and (2) that 'an adequate approach must begin by identifying social functions and discover ways in which linguistic features are selected and grouped together to serve them'. Thus, as was already happening in sociolinguistics at the time that Rampton was writing, the starting point for applied linguistics should be the study of culture and social structures, followed by an examination of how language plays a part in the enactment of different forms of social action as well as the constitution of second order understandings of these actions. In this case, in '[t]he theoretical and empirical investigation of real-world problems in which language is the central issue' (Brumfit 1991: 46), linguistics would come to serve social analysis, which means that linguistics would change from being, in Hymes's words, 'only a theory of grammar', to being 'concerned with social as well as referential meaning ... with language as part of communicative conduct and social action' (Hymes 1974: 196–7).

Rampton's call for an interdisciplinary applied linguistics sitting at the crossroads of sociology, education, and other social science disciplines was the natural outgrowth of several tendencies which had developed amongst academics who called themselves 'applied linguists' over the decades preceding his article. Above all, there was the general tendency towards interdisciplinarity, which had begun to gain momentum in the social sciences from the 1970s onwards, clearly linked to suggestions that economic and social orders were undergoing dramatic changes (Bell 1973; Giddens 1973). Arising from the influence of structuralism, there developed at the same time the 'discursive turn', in which social science methodologies foregrounded the importance of discourse as constitutive of social being (Laclau and Mouffe 1985), an idea which came to resonate among some sections of applied linguistics. Interdisciplinarianism meant that social scientists were more likely to base their analyses of social phenomena on literature from other disciplines. In the case of applied linguistics, this led to a move away from an overwhelming allegiance to theoretical linguistics and to a tendency to draw on social theory and current thinking in anthropology and sociology. Thus over the 1990s, we see different and more sophisticated takes on language-related issues, including the following ones:

- The entry of postcolonial frames of analysis in the study of English in the world (e.g. Canagarajah 1999; Kachru 1986; Pennycook 1994)
- The rise of critical discourse analysis, which combines critical theory with discourse analysis (e.g. Fairclough 1992, 1995; Hodge and Kress 1993)
- The rise in interest in ideology in language studies (e.g. Blommaert 1999; Joseph and Taylor 1990; Schieffelin *et al.* 1998)
- Challenges to linguistic and cognitive biases in mainstream second language learning research (e.g. Block 1996; Firth and Wagner 1997; van Lier 1994).

Rampton's call for a retuning of applied linguistics has proven to be prescient as there is little doubt by now that many applied linguists work in an interdisciplinary manner. Clear evidence of this can be found in the kinds of discussions taking place in recent texts on applied linguistics (Cook 2003; Davies 2007), as well as collections of readings on applied linguistics (Davies and Elder 2005; Kaplan 2005; Li Wei 2011; Simpson 2011), where contributors bring to bear on their topics multiple frameworks taken from a range of disciplines. Nevertheless, the fact that many applied linguists today practise a form of interdisciplinarianism in their work does not mean that they have, in effect, covered all of the possible epistemological bases. It is our view that if there is one gaping hole in the work of many applied linguists today, it is in the way that so many either ignore the economic and material bases of human activity and social life, or only deal with and incorporate these bases into their work in the most cursory of manners. As a consequence, it is our aim in this book to reorient interdisciplinarianism in applied linguistics in such a way that these economic and material bases of human activity and social life not only get a look-in, but they become central to discussions of a range of language related issues. For applied linguistics to be truly socially constituted, it must take full account of the political economy of contemporary capitalism – a political economy which encompasses both social classes and their ideologies.

At the time of writing, the world is engulfed in what people of all ideological and political persuasions seem to agree is an economic crisis. However, the exact causes of this crisis are contested, with two contrasting orientations emerging. On the one hand, there are those who would agree with the following view, outlined by Slavoj Žižek (2009: 19):

> the main task of the ruling ideology in the present crisis is to impose a narrative that will not put the blame for the meltdown on the global capitalist system as such, but on its deviations (overly lax legal regulations, the corruption of financial institutions, and so on).

On the other hand, there are those who reject the kind of thinking alluded to by Žižek, and who claim, following Marx, that such economic crises are not the result of excesses in the system but the inevitable outcome of its inner workings. Analyses which look only at the superficial workings of the economy fail to see the forces which drive the economy and therefore suggest solutions which only tinker with the model. Marx made numerous references in *Capital* to this approach to the study of economics as the purview of 'vulgar economists', that is, those 'who in their shallowness, make it a principle to worship appearances only' (Marx 1976: 679), or, in other words, those who could not see beyond the obvious and who manifested no interest whatsoever in moving backstage to pick apart the foundations and workings of capitalism. We are aware of the obvious fact that we cannot go the distance in carrying out an analytic dismantling of capitalism, but we do aim in this book to put such a project on the table, as we see it as a possible new direction for those applied linguists for whom Brumfit's 'real world problems' are clearly linked to political economy and our material existence. And if one is to understand the workings of the economy today, it is necessary to engage with the other key term in the title of this book, 'neoliberalism'.

Why neoliberalism? Why now?

Neoliberalism has become a powerful point of reference in the world today. Eclectic, indeterminate, polemical, one thing that can be agreed upon is its capacity to position the speaker vis-à-vis what is being described. *Neoliberal*, in most cases, implies a critique of the rule of the 'free' market, a counter position to the social phenomenon being described.[2] This dualism at the heart of *neoliberalism* has been present since the term first came to prominence in the early 2000s. It gained currency, in Europe and South America particularly, within the ranks of the growing anti-capitalist movement at the time. Pierre Bourdieu (2005) has noted how economic liberalism, in the first instance a theory of economic practice, had burst out of its field to become an all-embracing utopian vision of a pure and perfect market, a way of thinking with its own logic, its own chain of constraints, and whose aim was the methodical destruction of collectives. Free-market thinking, which sang the praises of the dot.com bubble and the wild speculation of financialisation, became the hymn of advanced capitalism. Its precepts were simple: 'human well-being could best be advanced by liberating individual, entrepreneurial freedoms within an institutional framework of private property rights, free markets and free trade' (Harvey 2005: 2). As governments of all political hues (from the British Conservative Party, elected in 1979, to the Australian Labour Party, elected in 1983) converted to its creed, it became 'rooted in a system of beliefs and values, an ethos and a moral view of the world, in short, an *economic common sense*' (Bourdieu 2005: 10; emphasis in the original).

More recently, Naomi Klein (2007) has added another dimension to the 'free'-market orthodoxy: the terrorising fashion in which it was sometimes imposed. As Klein explains, neoliberalism has thundered its way across the globe with 'shock and awe', through wars waged for the benefit of corporate cartels and through aggressive exploitation of natural disasters to set in train even bigger market monopolies. This terrorising approach has been studied in considerable depth with regard to the experience of Eastern Europe in the early 1990s. Stuckler, King and McKee (2009), writing in the medical journal *The Lancet*, argue convincingly that the rapid introduction of neoliberal policies and employment practices into the post-communist countries was a crucially determining factor in the rise of the mortality rate of working-age men – a phenomenon they relate, among other factors, to acute psychosocial stress. In the wake of the havoc wreaked by the shock tactics advocated by economists such as Jeffrey Sachs (1990) they conclude:

> The policy implications are clear. Great caution should be taken when macroeconomic policies seek radically to overhaul the economy without considering potential effects on the population's health. As variants of rapid reform policies are being debated in China, India, Egypt, and several other developing and middle-income countries – including Iraq – which are just beginning to privatise their large state-owned sectors, the lessons from the transitions from communism should be kept in mind.
>
> (Stuckler *et al.* 2009: 406)

In 2008, the banking crisis and recession struck, first in the US and then, via contagion, the rest of the world. The fall of Lehman Brothers in September 2008 marked the dramatic impact that the explosion of the financial bubble would have on the global economy and on peoples' lives. These events meant the final death knell for old industrial heartlands like Detroit in the US, as well as a dramatic rise in the number of foreclosures and poverty in general around the world on a scale not seen since the 1930s. The European Central Bank, the International Monetary Fund, and individual state governments, desperate to avoid economic meltdown, injected huge sums of money into supporting their own banking systems. The result was the imposition of austerity programmes on the populations of Europe, the US and the Middle East, the effects of which will stretch into the future (Mason 2009; Stiglitz 2010; Callinicos 2010). These events represented a watershed for neoliberalism. Thirty years of expanding market reforms on a global scale gave way to a severe economic crisis, itself caused by spectacular market failure.

In the aftermath of these events, references to neoliberalism have multiplied, both at a popular level and across academic disciplines. Journalists railed against the tyranny of the corrupt mythology of the market and gave voice to the profound crisis of conviction which circulated, as neoliberal ideology stood exposed as a 'collection of secrets, superstitions and non-sequiturs' invented to justify the dominance of a ruling group (Mason 2009: 119). Bankers and politicians were the 'ship of fools' that had driven the system to disaster (O'Toole 2009). A sign posted on the docklands of Dublin during the maelstrom of the crash, reading 'greed is the knife, and the scar runs deep', spontaneously expressed the level of ideological disquiet in Ireland. In academic circles, economic and human geographers observed that the fault lines of neoliberalism had been so exposed that its own failed *raison d'être* would lead to its demise (Birch and Mykhnenko 2010). Others charted the resilience of 'actually existing neoliberalism', its embeddedness in society, and its infinite capacity, even in crises, to reinvent itself and adapt (Peck 2010). Less categorical accounts have charted the fateful connection of neoliberalism to the booms and slumps of capitalism which, post-crash, became tainted as *zombieconomics*, a system unable to provide sustainable economic growth outside established centres of accumulation, let alone within the neoliberal heartlands themselves (Fine 2010; Harman 2009). Deeper anomalies in the ideology piled up as the crisis unfolded. Injections of huge amounts of state money into private banks, and the appropriation of private debt as sovereign debt, stretched to the limit belief in the hands-off state. The shifting of blame from private banking to the public sector set off an ideological debate that neoliberals still have not been able to win, highlighting the unresolved dilemma for a ruling orthodoxy that has been seen to fail (Callinicos 2010; Harvey 2010a; Žižek 2009). This ideological sprawl and turmoil, alongside dramatic economic events, forms the background for an examination of aspects of neoliberalism and applied linguistics.

Neoliberalism and applied linguistics

In the broader field of education, the impact of neoliberalism on education has been foregrounded for some time (Hill and Kumar 2009). The shift from pedagogical to market values has been widely commented on as involving a fundamental shift in educational philosophy: the abandonment of the social and cooperative ethic in favour of individualist and competitive business models. In the US, educationalists wrote of the way in which 'educational "reform", embracing the twin legacies of neoliberalism and neoconservatism, had resulted in greater social inequality, more cumbersome bureaucratic measurement and greater power for the "evaluative state"' (Apple 2004).

Neoliberal discourses, through the channels of intergovernmental organisations such as the International Monetary Fund and the Organisation for Economic Cooperation and Development, have buttressed the drive towards global privatisation of educational services, particularly in higher education, and set the priority of education to be the provider of human capital and the engine for economic growth (Spring 2008). Capturing the educational arena was judged to be of particular significance for neoliberal thinking, since schooling was both a green field for corporate designs and also an important means of inculcating market values in future generations. Saltman (2009: 55–6) describes extent of the process as follows:

> Neoliberalism appears in the now commonsense framing of education exclusively through presumed ideals of upward individual economic mobility and the social ideals of global economic competition … The 'There is No Alternative' has infected education thought as the only questions on reform agendas appear to be how to best enforce knowledge and curriculum conducive to national economic interest and the expansion of a corporately managed model of globalisation as perceived from the perspective of business.

In applied linguistics, by contrast, studies on neoliberalism have been few and far between. Phillipson (2008a) speaks of 'the linguistic imperialism of neoliberal empire' and 'the role of language in corporate-driven globalisation' but his account is more of a statement of fact than an analysis of the mechanisms by which language, language teaching and neoliberalism intersect (2008a). Critical discourse analysis, it is true, has taken a long look at the neoliberal world order and measured its effects on the construction of texts, but its purview is specifically discourse-bound and the concept of neoliberalism itself has remained relatively undertheorised within CDA. As we investigate in more detail in this book, Fairclough's understanding of neoliberalism, as both a system and a discourse, has meant that within applied linguistics, the term 'neoliberal' often comes to be used interchangeably with globalisation, globalism, or, simply, capitalism (Fairclough 1995; Blommaert 2010). However, more common within applied linguistics is an avoidance of the term altogether. Poole, for example, considers it to be an unhelpful description of the market mindset, too politically explicit, and to be referred to only in quotation marks (Poole 2010). A book entitled *Language and the Market Society* makes a brief reference to the 'neoliberal climate', but more often to 'a market ethos', 'marketisation' and a 'market society', and considers neoliberalism not to be worth an entry in the index (Mautner 2010). Perhaps this is a case of applied linguistics positioning itself – not for the first time – out of earshot of mainstream educational debates.

As regards this latter point, it may well be that one of the consequences of Rampton's argument for an expanded field – not just about language teaching but about a wide range of real-world language-related phenomena – has been that many, particularly within the field of English language teaching (ELT), have ceased to see themselves as part of applied linguistics. In the UK, for example, attendees at the annual International Association of Teachers of English as a Foreign Language (IATEFL) conference are generally not the same people as those attending the British Association for Applied Linguistics (BAAL) conference. In many ways, as the field has become more interdisciplinary, ELT has become more narrowly focused; so much so in fact that, in the words of one critic, its noticeable lack of engagement with the kind of social theory now being drawn on by many applied linguists is suggestive of 'discourse paralysis' (Kullman 2003) – an imperviousness which can be correlated, we would suggest, with the increasing commercialisation of education globally. Of course there are exceptions (e.g. Edge 2006) – but it is interesting to note that recently a number of voices have been raised to warn practitioners of the dangers inherent in the use of social theory in ELT. For example, Alan Waters (2009) has argued that the application of what he calls 'critical theory' to ELT is in effect an ideologically motivated imposition of dubious pedagogical relevance. At the same time, Colin Sowden (2008: 284), taking up arms against the use of critical pedagogy (oddly understood as a form of postmodern thinking) in ELT, argues that this is 'to politicize teaching in a way that is unnecessary and potentially harmful'. Misunderstandings of the epistemological basis of critical pedagogy aside, it will be clear that we take the view that teaching is perforce already a highly politicised activity and that ELT, and in particular commercial ELT, is profoundly imbricated in the consolidation of English as 'a crucial element of an international business class structure' (Ives 2006: 136–7).

Indeed our concerns extend beyond the use of social theory to the real-world activities of the ELT industry and UK ELT in particular. Take for example the case of Rwanda, where the government of Paul Kagame's Rwandan Patriotic Front (RPF) has recently introduced a programme of English-medium education to replace existing French-medium provision – a politically motivated change on the part of the largely Anglophone RPF (many of whom were educated in Uganda) which is being facilitated by the British Council (British Council 2010). Despite reservations about the regime's human rights record, many Western governments and the World Bank in particular are happy to support Kagame largely on account of his willingness to reform the Rwandan economy along neoliberal lines. In its *Doing Business Report 2010,* the World Bank notes with approval that Rwanda is 'the world's top reformer of business regulation, making it easier to start businesses, register property, protect investors, trade across borders, and access credit. It marks the first time a Sub-Saharan African economy is the top reformer' (World Bank 2010). And indeed the switch to English is presented by the government as a means to realign the country more firmly within a globalised economy, while ignoring the fact that the indigenous French-speaking elite is being sidelined in the process – a tactic Beth Samuelson and Sarah Freedman (2010) suggest is fraught with danger, given Rwanda's troubled past. Eddie Williams (2011: 47) too concludes that as a result of current language policy 'it is almost certain that Rwanda will generate a small English-proficient elite'. While Sowden (2008) may well be right in his assertion that there is more to life than politics, we take the view that the ELT industry is an area of applied linguistics activity in which language and political economy come together in ways that it would be unwise for the field to ignore.

It is against this backdrop that we have written this book. One might say that the conjunctural frame requires this refocus on neoliberalism and applied linguistics. A 'conjuncture', as Denning succinctly explains, was Gramsci's term for the immediate terrain of struggle (Denning 1997: 22). Gramsci, writing in a similar period of crisis and acutely aware of the role of ideology in broader movements for social change, explained that crises were often long-winded affairs, sometimes even lasting for decades.

> This exceptional duration means that incurable structural contradictions have revealed themselves (reached maturity) and that, despite this, the political forces which are struggling to conserve and defend the existing structure itself are making every effort to cure them within certain limits and to overcome them. These incessant and persistent efforts … form the terrain of the conjunctural and it is upon this terrain that the forces of opposition organise.
>
> (Gramsci 1971: 178)

Gramsci argued that, for opposing forces to triumph, they must be involved in a series of ideological polemics whose concreteness can be judged by the extent to which they are convincing and thereby shift the balance of social forces. Certainly, the present conjuncture requires that those forces which continue to proclaim the need for more radical neoliberal 'reforms' and still greater rolling back of state spending need to be challenged on the ideological front. This book, it is hoped, will form part of a renewed engagement with the ideological within applied linguistics, an engagement that we cannot afford to pass over.

The chapters

Interdisciplinarity, if it is to create new insights for the disciplines involved, must do more than simply cross-reference. It must define the parameters within which the common ground is being established and in so doing, it may shine a new light on the core concepts of the different disciplines. In the case of neoliberalism, as Chapter 2 shows, definitions, even within the field of political economy, are not agreed upon and have given rise to different interpretations of contemporary capitalism and the role of ideology. This chapter, by way of an introduction to neoliberalism, broaches the subject first as an economic theory, second as a new form of capitalism and, third how it has come to be referred to within discourse analysis. The theme of the chapter is that neoliberalism, for a variety of reasons and for our purposes here, is best understood as an ideology. The chapter makes a distinction between ideology and the real world and argues that ideology constitutes a representational mechanism, articulated on behalf of specific social interests, which precisely blurs the distinction between the two. Ideology presents itself as the 'real', as common sense, as simply the way things are – characteristics which neoliberal ideology displays in abundance. For example, it purports to advocate small government and light-touch regulation, although in practice the state remained a significant economic player and strongly interventionist throughout the neoliberal era (Harvey 2005; Harman 2007; Saad-Filho and Johnston 2005) and continues in this vein post-crash. This distinctive double-speak aspect, the chapter argues, makes it difficult to say that ideology amounts to various discourse practices, something which many discourse analysts, in different degrees, have tended to claim. Critical Discourse interpretations, for example, interpret neoliberalism as a discursive construction and often deem a loosely defined 'neoliberal discourse' to be itself constitutive of social practice in what is called 'new capitalism' (Fairclough 2002). Discourse theorists also see the articulation of discourses of authority and management as vital in the formation of new post-class identity (Laclau and Mouffe 2001). Ideologies, understood as coherent world-views emanating from a particular social class, promote specific class interests, and are examples of 'meaning in the service of power' (Thompson 1990; Eagleton 2007). Yet this chapter argues that discourse, however it is understood, can never quite acquire the cohesiveness, the link to social actors, nor the predictability of an ideology. The chapter concludes that ideology remains a core theoretical tool for understanding the intersections between neoliberalism and language.

Chapter 3 deals with a specific aspect of the relationship between neoliberal ideology and language: the way in which neoliberal meanings have come to dominate in language in the public sphere. Developing further Williams's (1976) notion of keywords, the influence of neoliberal ideology in language in the public domain is examined by noting the wider use of certain keywords from the economic field and the construction in new contexts, of a complex knot of meanings whose acceptance relies upon a specific ideological reasoning. When these keywords are transposed outside their economic sphere, ideological tensions become foregrounded and this often prevents the keywords being fully appropriated in the spontaneous speech of these new settings. These ideological tensions are examined through core words in neoliberal thinking – *deregulation, human capital, entrepreneur* – and the process of reconstitution of meaning in new contexts. Examples are taken from the Irish context and they reveal the fragility of ideology in language, refer to social relations independent of discourse and point to the connections of ideology to events in the real world, all of which have been put into sharp relief since the banking crisis in Ireland began. The analysis also highlights the attempts by the promoters of neoliberal ideology, in the face of incontrovertible market failure since the crash of 2008, to seek to reinvent and adapt the dominant ideology.

Chapter 4 takes on how many applied linguists frame globalisation and identity today against the backdrop of the current global economic crisis which has resulted from the wide-scale adoption of neoliberal policies. In the midst of this crisis, there is an opportunity to remind applied linguists who have taken a poststructuralist approach in their investigations of globalisation and identity that it is perhaps not wise to abandon, as so many have done, all grand narratives and, in particular, an economic take on the issues that they choose to research. Indeed, in ignoring economically based theories of globalisation (e.g. Wallerstein 2004), focusing exclusively on more culturally based ones, and in framing identity exclusively in terms of inscriptions such as gender, race, ethnicity, nationality and sexuality at the expense of class, many applied linguists have occupied an ideological space which neoliberalism has found easy to accommodate. In other words, a focus on globalisation processes and identity through a poststructuralist prism has been perfectly manageable in the wealthy post-industrial nation states of the world where neoliberal policies have been implemented. This chapter begins with a consideration of how globalisation has tended to be conceptualised and framed in applied linguistics, according to models of cultural forces and flows drawing heavily on the work of scholars like Appadurai (1996) and Giddens (2000). It then moves to consider a more economically driven interpretation of the phenomenon, examining the work of scholars like Wallerstein (2004) and Harvey (2005). The shift from more culturally based to economically based framings of globalisation leads necessarily to different emphases when applied linguists turn their attention to identity. Indeed, it is argued that while inscriptions such as gender, race, ethnicity, nationality and sexuality are important in any discussion and analysis of identity, they can blinker researchers as regards hard economic realities which have a great deal of explanatory potential for identity. For this reason, class needs to occupy a more central position in language and identity research.

Chapter 5 turns its attention to the multimillion-pound ELT industry and focuses in particular on UK-produced textbooks for the teaching of English as a foreign or international language. The Publishers Association, the UK publishing industry's representative body, points out in its 2010 report that 17 per cent of all books exported from the UK are ELT textbooks and that sales increased by 26 per cent from £164 million in 2005 to £207 million in 2009. The chapter takes the view that these globally disseminated artefacts merit close scrutiny, given the ways in which this lucrative industry constructs and images the language contained within their covers. It focuses in particular on the proliferation of representations of celebrity in a sample of best-selling textbooks from the late 1970s onwards – a period which largely coincides with the global boom in ELT and the arrival of neoliberal economic policies across whole swathes of the world. Beginning with an exploration of the meaning of celebrity, the chapter looks at how celebrity has been theorised particularly by those working in a variety of Marxist/neo-Marxist traditions and concludes that the manufacture of contemporary celebrity can best be understood as a species of branded individualism congruent with the values of the current phase of capitalism. The survey of the textbook sample shows how over the past three decades textbooks have been colonised by discourses of celebrity which serve to construct English as a condensation symbol of wealth, individualism and extraordinary professional success. This, the chapter argues, can be traced to ELT publishers' ideas about what they refer to as 'aspirational content' and its supposed motivational potential. Drawing on the views of a number of ELT professionals, the chapter concludes by arguing that teachers, teacher educators and applied linguists need to recognise the inherently political nature of ELT and themselves become more sociopolitically active in making the case for alternative articulations of English to those which are currently available.

The book ends with Chapter 6 which also examines the world of language teaching, this time focusing on what Donald Freeman and Karen Johnson (1998) have called the epistemological and political strands of the knowledge base for language teacher programmes. It argues that these two strands are interwoven in such a way that at any given time they constitute language teacher education as practice. The chapter begins by tracing the trajectory of teacher education from the last century onwards – from the 'craft' model to the 'applied science' model through to the currently dominant 'reflective' model which is located within a broadly sociocultural paradigm. It shows how most contemporary scholars adopt a social psychological view of teacher cognition in which the interplay of mental processes, pedagogic practices and contexts of instruction are seen as fundamental to learning to teach. However, although in general agreement with the value of and the need for a reflective model, the authors show how the supposed 'quiet revolution' (Johnson 2000: 3), which the turn to reflection is taken to represent, is in fact contradicted by teacher education as it actually occurs in two key settings – the British Postgraduate Certificate of Education (PGCE) and the ELT industry's Certificate in English Language Teaching to Adults (CELTA). This challenge is seen as motivated by the neoliberal marketisation of education whereby concepts such as 'exploratory talk' and the centrality of reflection are undermined, although lip-service continues to be paid to them. Both courses are seen as examples of disciplining and McDonaldised systems appropriate to a view of education which has the production of human capital as its goal, but which are ill-suited to the formation of genuinely reflective and theorising practitioners. The chapter concludes by arguing the need for such courses to provide trainee teachers with access to the broadly based social scientific theory that the authors believe is needed for meaningful reflection, as well as sufficient time to think, reflect and learn from the potentialities afforded by the experiential learning so valued by the reflective model, but which are currently denied under the weight of the neoliberal imperative.

Together these chapters represent what we see as an attempt to frame our areas of interest in applied linguistics in terms of political economy and specifically neoliberalism as the dominant economic ideology of our times. We are all too aware that this is a partial application of political economy to the field, as it focuses on our individual and particular interests and not others. Thus, in the chapters of this book we discuss how neoliberal ideology impacts on language, language teaching, language teacher education and how globalisation and identity are conceptualised in applied linguistics. It is our hope that readers of this book will find these chapters interesting, but we also hope that they will be encouraged to frame their own interests in similar terms. If this occurs, applied linguistics will become more interdisciplinary, more politically engaged and indeed more fit for the times in which we live.

About the authors

Although we came to the task of writing this book with a shared concern about the impact of neoliberal ideology on a range of language-related practices and issues, we are aware that we have done so from somewhat different intellectual starting points. We therefore think it important to close this introductory chapter with a brief note about who we are, how we have come to be involved in this book and what we bring to the task of writing it.

David Block comes to the writing of this book in a state of intellectual transition. If in recent years he has written extensively about identity and other issues in applied linguistics from a markedly poststructuralist perspective, he is now reading and engaging with work which is associated with a more structuralist perspective, in particular the work of Marx and recent Marxist-inspired work in political economy (e.g. Harvey). In addition, he has recently been examining critical realism as a source of epistemological inspiration, which in turn leads to a certain change in how he might understand the interrelationships between structure and agency. In the midst of all of this rethinking, he is seeking his own personal third way through structuralist and poststructuralist thought.

John Gray comes to this volume from a background in English language teaching and teacher education. In his work he has made the case for an interdisciplinary approach to researching the ELT industry and in *The Construction of English* (2010b) he examined the representational practices adopted in the mapping of linguistic and cultural terrain in textbooks aimed at the global market from a cultural studies perspective. He takes the view that the explosion in commercial ELT globally since the 1970s is concomitant with and integral to the current phase of globalisation and that it is incumbent on researchers in the field to explore the tensions inherent in this association.

Marnie Holborow first wrote about the issues of language and power, ideology, language dominance and the world order in *The Politics of English* (1999). Since then, in the context of boom and then recession in Ireland and the huge changes that both made to higher education, her writing has focused more directly on the nature of neoliberal ideology and its various manifestations in language. Her theme is that ideology, in the classical Marxist sense, has become more relevant in our troubled times and that Ireland and Irish Higher Education remains an interesting vantage point to trace the contradictions of neoliberal ideology in a market-distressed world.

2

WHAT IS NEOLIBERALISM?

DISCOURSE, IDEOLOGY AND THE REAL WORLD

MARNIE HOLBOROW

Introduction

Neoliberalism has become the stamp of our age. In less than a generation, neoliberal principles have spread across every continent and become so integral to public and private life that thinking outside their parameters is almost unthinkable. The present economic crisis, despite coming about through market failure and prompting huge state intervention in the economy, has become the occasion to promulgate even more stridently the tenets of the 'free' market, deregulated financial speculation and the need for ever greater market competitiveness. Neoliberalism, sometimes in a brazen *volte face* of its core principles, has reinvented itself to suit these turbulent times. The gap between what it proclaims and what its promoters actually do has always characterised neoliberalism, which is, no doubt, why definitions have proved so difficult. When neoliberalism coincided with what appeared to be an economic boom, from the 1990s to midway through the next decade, it was often taken to mean a whole range of phenomena: an economic doctrine, a political mindset, but also the actual working of a self-regulating market, privatisation, financial deregulation, even an entirely new phase of capitalism. Perhaps due to its widespread presence, neoliberalism seemed to stand for a social representation and a social reality at the same time. Where neoliberalism and discourse are discussed, we encounter a similar overlap. Neoliberalism, as a social system and an ideology, is said to have invaded discourse; at the same time, discourse is deemed to reproduce and cement neoliberalism. Such category confusion around neoliberalism requires a disentangling of the different definitions and interpretations in order to clarify the relationship between neoliberal ideology and language. In applied linguistics, these things have a special relevance. At least two influential strands within the discipline identify neoliberalism as central to their concerns. Critical discourse analysis argues that neoliberalism has 'colonised' discourse and that discourse constructs social relations while, from a different perspective, the theory of linguistic imperialism makes English the core social agent of the neoliberal project. Both draw on specific interpretations of neoliberalism. This chapter identifies four definitions of neoliberalism: as an economic theory, as a new form of capitalism, as a 'discourse' (including the discourse of 'Englishisation') and finally as an ideology.

Neoliberalism as an economic theory

Neoliberalism, for all its apparent sweep, is at root an economic theory. It came to prominence in the particular economic conditions of the late 1970s, and was articulated by specific social interests. Neoliberalism, in this respect, was an economic template whose dictates seemed to provide answers to a spiralling crisis and, for the controllers of capital, chimed with their need to restore profit levels. It supplanted a previous economic orthodoxy – Keynesianism – which had advocated state intervention in the market and now argued that markets themselves produced symmetry of supply and demand. Following the crises of the 1970s, neoliberalism championed the view that the state was an inefficient, cumbersome economic player and that now the supposedly untrammelled market should be left to shape the economic and social world. Less state intervention, more deregulation and widespread privatisation of public services was the way to set free market mechanisms. David Harvey, one of the first to give a full analysis in English of the origins and development of neoliberalism (2005: 2), sees it as 'a theory of political and economic practices' that proposes that 'human well-being can best be advanced by liberating individual entrepreneurial freedoms and skills' within an institutional framework of strong private property rights, free markets and free trade. It is worth pointing out here that the term is used, generally, by those who are critical of it; neoclassical economists and free marketers seldom refer to neoliberalism. We thus are in the presence of a dominant worldwide orthodoxy whose very name is contested.

Its theoretical roots go back to the Chicago School of Economics of the 1950s with Milton Friedman, who dreamed of reinstituting neoclassical economics via monetarism (or controlling the supply of money as the chief method of stabilising the economy). The theory justified governments avoiding inflation by limiting money supply and letting unemployment settle at 'natural' levels, regardless of the social hardship caused. Later, monetarism was combined with fiscal incentives in order to boost consumption and became known as Reaganomics or Thatcherism (Lapavitsas 2005). The main plank was giving the market free rein while, at least ostensibly, reining in the state, now required to withdraw to its earlier *laissez-faire* role. By the mid-1990s, neoliberalism had moved centre stage, becoming the official policy of many Western governments and, through the dictates of international financial institutions, the economic doctrine also meted out to the Global South. Smaller, slimmed-down states were now to bow to the market's invisible hand. Public services were to be tendered out to private providers, to be run along market lines and, now targeting their users as customers, to adopt the ethos of corporate enterprises.

Neoliberalism, once a marginal, sidelined, extreme economic theory suddenly came to occupy all available social space and belief in the market was embraced across the political spectrum, from neoconservatism to social democracy, which was now renamed as the pro-market Third Way (Harvey 2005: 19–24). Unleashing the market became the overriding social imperative; even the concentration of wealth amassed in fewer and fewer hands now became no more than what the market directed. Greed, as Gordon Gekko declared in the 1990s popular film, *Wall Street,* became good. Neoliberalism seemed to usher in new economic configurations, ever greater financialisation (the expansion of banking and the ballooning of credit) and intensely competitive work regimes, the result of which was to enrich shareholders and speculators and, in the eyes of some, to mark the arrival of 'capital resurgent' (Duménil and Lévy 2005).

Because neoliberalism often presents as a uniformly imposed social order, it is important to distinguish between the doctrine and what happens in practice, between what it says about economies and how economies actually develop. One of the most mystifying things about neoliberalism is the way in which it appears to merge perceptions of reality with reality itself. That its champions would seek to have it thus is hardly surprising but many critics of neoliberalism fall in behind the same step. Cultural theorist and educationalist, Henry Giroux, for example, leaves us in no doubt that the doctrine is the driving force of society, that it unleashes the most brutalising forces of capitalism and that 'it is easier to imagine the end of the world than the end of neoliberal capitalism' (Giroux 2004b). Duménil and Lévy also see the institution of neoliberalism as 'a new social order whose basic economic and political mechanisms are tightly intertwined' (Duménil and Lévy 2009). They conflate 'the rules' of the economic theory with the institution of a new neoliberal 'social order', a macroeconomic theory with a '(counter-) revolution'. Economic theory, in this scenario, mutates unproblematically into economic practice.

There is no doubt that the rise of neoliberal thinking coincided with substantial economic growth and further globalisation. While it was ascendant, world trade more than tripled and world output doubled.[1] The various intergovernmental organisations, such as the International Monetary Fund (IMF) and the World Bank, amid the debt crisis of the 1980s, managed to tie their granting of loans to the driving through of rigid market dictates, the 'Washington Consensus' as this became known. As a result, indebted countries of the Global South were forced to slash their public services and turn over their markets and resources to multinational corporations. It is true, too, that there was a shift in monetary policy by the US Federal Reserve Bank which in 1979 raised interest rates to the benefit of creditors. The financial sector, thereafter, grew to proportions unimaginable a decade before, drawing older industrial players into its complex web of financial instruments, and seeming to become the incarnation of neoliberalism itself (Callinicos 2010). The Washington Consensus and the money markets were neoliberalism's global templates and English more and more its language. English became the medium for many of the new service industries such as business process and information outsourcing, or call centres, and English was identified at the heart of globalisation itself, or in one glowing account of the brave new world, a global language 'which had come of age' (Graddol 2006).

But, even in its heyday, there were both limits to implementation of the policies and deep inconsistencies within the theory itself. Debt conditionalities applied to some countries but not to the main debtor country, the US (Mason 2009). The raising of interest rates, described as a 'neoliberal coup' by Duménil and Lévy (2005: 10–14), lured capital into the finance sector but also reflected weakness elsewhere within the system, namely the long-term decline of profits in industry (Harvey 2005; Harman 2007). The transfer of capital into derivative markets was symptomatic of the deep structural disorders of capitalism, and elaborate financial instruments were so many time bombs ready to explode, as we now know. More generally, the imposition of neoliberal policies failed to deliver significant improvements in economic performance and also encountered substantial resistance, particularly in Latin America. Even privatisation, despite continuing apace, brought about new inefficiencies. It sometimes resulted in costlier and poorer provision of services and, contrary to the theory, the creation of new, bureaucratic, monopolistic service providers (Allen 2007: 46–60; Kay 2004: 360). Furthermore, state-run economies often seemed to be doing better than privatised neoliberal ones: China's meteoric rise dramatically highlighted the value of state intervention and how spectacular growth could occur outside the one-size-fits-all (usually Western) free-market model (Saad-Fihlo 2003). Even neoliberal globalisation did not turn out to be quite the run-away success that it was made out to be. On an everyday level, it seemed that globalisation had arrived in our supermarkets, but, on the bigger scale, still the vast bulk of industrial production remained in the richest countries. Only a handful of developing economies experienced significant growth and, even in the supremely mobile world of international finance, the main centres remained concentrated within rich countries (Dunn 2009a, 2009b).

Most notably, the cornerstone of neoliberal theory – small government – remained something of a fantasy. The state, in practice, was rather more economically engaged than the theory led us to believe. Even critics of neoliberalism have tended to echo, from a different perspective, what they, too, see as the diminishing role of the nation state. Hardt and Negri (2000) claim that we are witnessing the decline of the sovereign states, and the rise of a 'deterritorialised', 'smooth space' of empire, which they see as a new form of governance with no boundaries. Sklair, too, sees 'transnationalism' as the hallmark of this era, claiming that capitalism is no longer an international system but a 'globalising system' decoupled from the nation state, within which operates a 'transnational capitalist class' (Sklair 2010). Yet, as Callinicos reminds us, capital, even when it has wide international presence, still looks to its home or regional base for labour skills, for a secure market and as the main location of investment; indeed, he argues, 'the idea that capital has broken free of its geographical moorings is a myth' (2009: 203). Footloose capital operating indeterminately across the globe ignores what drives capital accumulation – competition with other capitals – and the close ally of a nation state can provide preferential tax regimes and access to contracts that can clinch competitive advantage (Callinicos 2010).

From a different perspective, Naomi Klein has convincingly described how states play a key role, from Iraq to New Orleans, in the brutally successful capture of new markets and in corporate take-overs of local infrastructures. Her tale of what she calls the 'shock doctrine of disaster capitalism' presents a chilling account of proactive neoliberal states which seek to safeguard their own homegrown capitals (Klein 2007). Indeed, the striking thing about the neoliberal era is that, counter to the official orthodoxy, state influence amongst the Western powers, in reality, has grown quite substantially over the last decade. Some of this is due to military spending over this period (Harman 2009: 238). But state real expenditure has also increased, indicating that, in the advanced capitalist countries, economic globalisation has gone hand in hand with an increase in state power, with states remaining 'massive actors involved in a number of complex and expensive tasks' (Béland 2010: 176). While some sectors of the public services were being outsourced to private corporations, others were employing more and more people.[2] After the crash of 2008, it has become even more difficult to sustain the view that globalisation has done away with states, when the state's lifeline to capital became clear for all to see. The unimaginably huge sums of government money injected into the financial system across the US, the UK and the Eurozone (reckoned in 2009 to be a staggering $14 trilllion) have dramatically exposed the neoliberal myth of the retreating state. The post-crash state stands very much as the protector of the capitalist market, but how the uncovering of this paradox will harm the ruling 'free-market' consensus, in the long term, remains to be seen (Watkins 2010).

When neoliberalism is referred to in applied linguistics, it is often loosely defined, if at all. I have chosen to sketch the economic backcloth of neoliberalism and the broader political issues in some detail. If applied linguistics is to make the links between language and society, if it is to embrace the realm of political economy and interdisciplinarity, it has to satisfactorily describe the contours of neoliberalism. The inconsistencies I have outlined highlight the gap between neoliberal theory and reality – a gap which promoters of free-market economics may have an interest in downplaying, but whose significance those critical of neoliberalism also should not overlook. As Fairclough (2006: 40–1) remarks, the 'facts' presented by advocates of neoliberal globalism are ideologically selective. One of the reasons, perhaps, that governments, influential think-tanks, intergovernmental organisations studiously avoid referring to this wave of 'free-market' economics as neoliberalism is because to do so would be to identify their standpoint as a political world-view. Their claim is that 'free'-market economics has the status, precisely, of a natural law. Marx pointed out a long time ago that neoclassical economic theory tends to 'naturalize' the market: it presents the free market as the way the world works and the only way it can, a process independently at work in society, decidedly not an ideological construct. Free-market economics treats the appearance of society – competition in the market – not as something driven by social relations but as a machine in which individuals, like objects, are mere cogs. What Marx called 'vulgar economics' 'actually does nothing more than interpret, systematise and turn into apologetics the notions of agents trapped within bourgeois relations of production'

(Marx 1991: 956). This 'estranged form of appearance in economic relations' accepts the workings of capitalism at face value. It holds up a mirror to the world which reproduces atomised, economic behaviour as outcomes of supply and demand as if these were as much beyond human control as the weather. The real forces that run society and the social relations that underpin the specific market in question do not figure in this looking-glass.[3]

Getting behind the supposed iron law of market forces, examining the social relations of the capitalist market and laying bare what the economic theory declares and how in practice it departs from its pure form are important first steps in unpicking the appearances of capitalist society upon which the taken-for-grantedness of neoliberal ideology depends. Real-world events in the form of the crash of 2008 and the recession which followed acted as potent demystifiers: they confirmed the mismatch between the free-market, neoliberal model and reality. The certainties of neoliberalism began to break up and reminded even its critics that the free market was not quite as mesmerisingly triumphant as was claimed.

Neoliberalism and 'new capitalism'

From a slightly different perspective, neoliberalism is defined as representing a new regime of economic production, often called 'new capitalism'. An influential proponent of the free market and new capitalism, Diane Coyle, automatically accepts the identification. She describes the huge leap forward represented by new technologies, the establishment of a 'weightless' economy driven by the market and in which work supposedly is no longer place- nor nation-bound (Coyle 1997: pp. vii–viii). For her, the free-market new capitalism represents a turning point in technological innovation and a revolution in work practices, productivity and society itself (Coyle 2003).

Commentators in the area of discourse and neoliberalism tend to accept this premise, sometimes without elaboration or explanation, referring to neoliberalism and new capitalism as if they were the same thing. In a special issue of *Discourse and Society* on 'Language in New Capitalism', the claim is made that language and discourse feed into the new economic order in special ways. New capitalism, it is argued, is a new economic form emerging from contemporary transformations; it is restructured and rescaled with 'shifts in relations between different domains or fields of social life', with local and global economies interacting dialectically (Fairclough 2002). In a later piece, neoliberalism is identified as 'removing obstacles to the new economic order'. New capitalism is 'post-industrial', has displaced the old Fordist model and is 'necessary to the expansion of capitalism' (Fairclough 2004: 104). This new economic formation has involved a 'restructuring of relations between economic, political and social domains'. In an article written with Phil Graham, Fairclough describes the development as part of the current 'emergent form of capitalism', variously referred to as 'globalisation', and 'the information society' (Fairclough and Graham 2002: 185). In other words, neoliberalism appears to constitute a new form of capitalism, and language and discourse have become central components of the new system in a way that they were not before.

These notions are loosely articulated but the implication is that neoliberalism has been able to take root because of technological and structural changes in capitalism. Laclau and Mouffe, whose work is often a point of reference within discourse studies, were among the first to announce the arrival of a new social configuration in which social subjects were positioned and identified in relation to a discursive framework. Their description of social meaning filling 'floating signifiers' and the creation of new 'nodal points' reinforces the idea that society is discourse determined (Laclau and Mouffe 1985: 115; see also Jessop 2004). Manuel Castells's *The Rise of the Network Society* (2000) built on the importance of discourse and communication in society, and his vision has been influential across language and culture studies disciplines. Networks and their interconnected 'nodes' are communication structures and it is these that constitute social life (Castells 2009: 19). Discourses, according to Castells, frame the options of what networks can do and these are generated, diffused, fought over, internalised and ultimately embodied in human action in the socialised communication realm. 'Power in the network society' as he puts it, 'is communication power' (Castells 2009: 53). His identification of information technology as the creator of a new post-industrial, knowledge-based economy, the purveyor of a new social dynamic whose core social units are flexible networks is often accepted by those in the fields of cultural studies and language without reserve. Fairclough (2006: 47–50), for example, while sceptical of some assertions made for the knowledge-based economy, does accept that Castells's 'space-time relations' should be taken up in a transdisciplinary way to explore methods by which in textual analysis 'one can operationalise perspectives on space and time' (2004: 117). Principles associated with the network society have also been very influential within the broader arena of higher education and have often driven proposals to restructure institutionalised learning, towards prioritising the teaching of skills as defined by 'the knowledge-based economy'. In the field of world English, too, the significance of the knowledge economy has been much commented on. David Graddol (2006: 11), for example, speaks of a world in rapid, almost break-neck, transition, 'from the modern to the post-modern', a world in which 'global education and English will take off in a very new direction'. Hardt and Negri, somewhat influential in the field of critical linguistics, also subscribe to the view that the production landscape has been irreversibly transformed by new forms of communication. 'It is that the network has become a common form that tends to define our ways of understanding the world and acting in it … [N]etworks are the form of organisation of the cooperative and communicative relationships dictated by the immaterial paradigm of production' (2005: 142). For them, too, the informational content or 'immaterial labour' of a commodity has become a core product of modern capitalist production with information itself driving societies.

A note of caution about the brave new world of 'communication power' needs to be expressed. Unquestionably, quicker access to information and new instantaneous forms of communication have changed the way society interacts, but, perhaps, it is better understood as the continuation of a development than an entirely new one. Claims made for the network society are often more impressionistic than substantiated and, as Kevin Doogan points out, tend to inflate the actual size and role of the ICT industry in modern economies as well as traditional ones (2009: 59; see also Fuchs 2009: 101). Moreover, the frenetic quest for what is 'new' or 'post-' in society often involves latching on to immediate, surface features and missing the features of underlying continuity, as Slavoj Žižek observes (2009: 7). In this breathless embrace of the new, technology itself becomes identified as the prime mover of new social relations. There is no denying that, from railways to electricity, from the telephone to the iPhone, new inventions radically alter the rhythm and texture of people's working lives, but technological change also appears in a context, within certain social relations and as a response to the needs of capital. Ellen Woods, writing at the beginning of the new technologies expansion, uncovered the weakness of technologically deterministic explanations: 'What is new [...] about this so-called new economy is not that the new technologies represent a unique kind of epochal shift. On the contrary they simply allow the logic of the old mass production economy to be diversified and *extended*' (Woods 1998: 39). Technological developments are less about revolutionising social relations than operating within them and very often their use and extent reflect the confines of social privilege. In a discussion of the impact of Web 2.0 and the rise of cloud computing, the British Council, usually enthusiastically at the forefront of new trends, makes some cautionary remarks concerning the continued inequality of access to digital media and the web. While less than 5 per cent of Africans use the web, more than 75 per cent of the populations in the Nordic countries do. Overall in the G8 countries it was just over 50 per cent of the population in 2006 (Leadbeater 2010). Even if this figure may have risen, the exuberance of new capitalism's networkers should not allow us to forget that the information economy is certainly more transformative in some places than others. ICT and cloud computing expand and develop along existing social grooves and are used within the social structures already in place. Rather like language itself, the channels of communication cannot be seen independently of society as a whole, still less as constituting the pillars of social organisation.

From this perspective it is worth noting how little, in practice, the autonomous, 'networked' workplace has played out in the recessionary world post-2008. With unemployment a strong feature of many economies, identification with the claim of 'unprecedented autonomy for communicative subjects' enabled by the global digital age (Castells 2009: 136) is hard to sustain. The knowledge economy in which 'people work by communicating' (Fisher 2009: 34) seems rather less plausible when the huge bank of people's communication skills appear to affect not at all the number of lay-offs, nor economic growth staying obstinately close to zero. The post-crash world has reminded us that the levels of capital investment, more than language and communication, are the shapers of social power. Regrettably, new technologies have not lived up to the network revolution, nor ushered in a more egalitarian workplace. The new information industries have tended to use their sophistication for achieving higher levels of monitoring to meet centralised productivity targets rather than for enabling more democratic workplaces. Call centres may be hubs of information flows but discipline and lack of control is as much a feature of these modern-day factories as ever it was in the days of Henry Ford (Bunting 2004; Holborow 2007). Social networking may well have been a feature of communication in the political arena but, in the workplace, new communication technologies have been shaped to greater productive, not social, needs, to more stringent surveillance and more invasive micro-management, of the type we discuss in Chapter 6. Communication skills, sadly, do not make economies; they are put to use within existing production structures and their being put to use at all is dependent on events in the real economy.

Neoliberalism, discursive practices and discourse

As an extension of the idea that language and communication have a special salience and function in today's world, neoliberalism is often understood as being discourse-generated. Norman Fairclough, a leading discourse analyst and critic of neoliberalism, expresses this view. His claim is that 'new capitalism' is knowledge- or information-based and concludes that this means that the transformations of capitalism are 'discourse-led'. Globalisation is 'enacted and inculcated' through both the global language of English and a global 'order of discourse' expounded by corporations, governments and international agencies (Fairclough 2002).

For Fairclough (2006: 163), 'neoliberal globalism' is discursive in character:

> If we think about what is globalized, what the 'flows' consist of, this includes discourses, ways of representing, construing and imagining aspects of social processes. And if we think of the changes in social activity, interaction and interconnection associated with globalisation, these entail new forms of communication, or genres. So we can say (using a somewhat rough and ready distinction) that both the contents and the forms of globalisation have a discursive character.

Fairclough's work sees discourse as operating on the levels of social relations, on representations and on identities. As Phelan (2007) points out, his interdiscursive analysis rests on genres (ways of interacting that imply social relations), discourses (ways of representing social practices) and styles (ways of being or identification).

Fairclough insists there is a difficulty distinguishing between 'real globalisation and the discourses of globalisation' but his claim that there is a dialectical amalgamation between 'existing structures and successful strategies and successful discourses' (2006: 164) does little to clear up the confusion. The functions of discourse are presented as representative, misrepresentative, legitimising ideologies and achieving of hegemony. Discourse is a 'moment' of globalisation which, in a 'cultural political economy' framework, is part of social construction. In this schema, 'orders of discourse' are empowered as semiotic social practices which can recontextualise and then operationalise new social realities (2006: 168–9). Orders of discourse, understood as discourse in particular social or institutional settings, can be 'conventional or innovative' and it is the tension between the two that transforms discourse into the 'site' of a power struggle. Seeing 'globalism' as an ideology, he considers, is 'not inappropriate', since for him 'globalism' is both the condition and the means of economic activity. In a succinct blurring of the representational and the real, of action in the real and discursive acts, he claims that globalism as a neoliberal discourse creates a *space* for unconstrained and highly profitable *action* on the part of corporations (2006: 41; my emphasis).

It is undeniable that controversy, tension and interpretation exist within discourse and that all language use is potentially ideological. Language and ideology overlap but this does not mean that the two things are the same. Fairclough's ever expanding view of discourse overflows to drown the social and economic system. In this frame of reference, discourse analysis assumes the same status as social events. Discursive representations and reality *tout court* are seen as two points on a continuum. Indeed it might be said that, in practice, actual social events, such as economic crisis or social movements and their potential to challenge ruling ideology, are not the central concern for discourse analysis. Text itself lies at the heart of the Faircloughian interpretation of social practice, as his three-dimensional diagram of discourse – text, discursive practice, social practice with text placed at the centre of his schema – makes abundantly clear (Fairclough 1992: 73). Discourse thus constituted sidelines real events and implies that ideology in discourse is a structurally closed system rather than a fragile expression of the connections and tensions between ideology and the wider society. One of the difficulties in Fairclough's work is that he fails, unlike Blommaert (2005), to theorise ideology or its relationship to discourse. One has the impression that, in Fairclough's schema, ideology has simply morphed into discourse and, beyond loose references to the more 'salient' role of language in late capitalism (2002), we are not told how or why this has come about. In placing ideology in the mould of narrative or discourse, Fairclough robs ideology of its dynamic, its reference to competing social interests and its expression of a 'multiplicity of accents' (Eagleton 2007), and reconstitutes ideology as an all-enveloping discursive 'regime', out of which it seems difficult to escape. Indeed the implication in this enclosed discursive circle is that critical discourse analysis is *the* instrument of neoliberal deconstruction and thereby, potentially also, the route to social resistance and emancipation.

This leads to a second problem. Identifying neoliberal ideology as a discursive event inevitably draws Fairclough towards the analysis of individual texts and it is micro-analysis which tends to take precedence. Specific texts, from Blair when he was Prime Minister and from excerpts from public discourse in different settings, become key sites for capturing the presence of neoliberalism. This work is successful in uncovering ideological presuppositions in the selected text and is useful as far as it goes. But it suffers from a problem of scale and representation: seeing ideology through the prism of a single text can both, paradoxically, overstate its presence and trivialise its impact. This focus, as Blommaert points out, forces temporal closure through its restriction to the here and now of communication and leaves out any broader sense of history (Blommaert 2005: 37). Relying on individual texts, moreover, tends to stress in ideology what is coherent more than what is non-representative, contradictory or uncertain. A snap-shot of communication, a single text even sensitively analysed tends to freeze meaning and suspend the complexities and tensions of the ideological process. How the text is understood by the audience can only be surmised for it depends on knowing how it was received and on the wider context. These limitations amount to what some have seen as recurring blind-spots of discourse analysis (Barker 2008: 53). As Chapter 3 in this book attempts to show, ideology can be better grasped, and in greater complexity, through a more general approach to the meanings involved, rather than through analysis of a specific (written) text whose frozen character misses something of the scale and dynamics of ideology as it operates through society at large.

At a superficial level, the overlap between ideology and discourse seems logical. In everyday language, 'discourse' and 'discourses' have come to mean something which is not said explicitly or something that has a certain social currency, a 'sub-text', be they the 'discourses of colonialism', or sexist or racist discourses. At a more theoretical level, however, the replacement of ideology by discourse represents an epistemological shift which signals the displacement of the real in favour of the representational. Ideology in its Marxist sense is precisely the theoretical recognition of the interaction between the material and the representational, between class and view of the world, between what happens in society and what appears to be common sense. The foundations of ideology lie in the real. The superimposition of discourse on ideology marks a distancing of social processes from structures of expression. This step partly arises from the 'discursive turn' of structuralism and post-structuralism but the broad strokes of this pathway can be traced back to Foucault, whom many in critical theory recognise as a formative influence. Fairclough pays tribute to Foucault for his theorising of discourse, as does Pennycook within applied linguistics, specifically in his work on Englishes and transcultural flows (2007). Many other critical stances within applied linguistics have built on the Foucauldian framework[4] and so a word is needed here about his understanding of ideology.

Foucault has a particular view of power and knowledge. Power resides in knowledge and is institutionalised through inclusionary and exclusionary practices. Penal systems, knowledge systems and discursive regimes are all methods and manifestations of these practices. Foucault's emphasis is on how power and dominant ideologies come to be internalised by individuals and his objective is to map the micro-sites of power in order to reveal these processes of normalisation. In his reworking of the concept of power, Foucault is explicit about setting aside the notion of ideology. Ideology is seen as too linked with objective truth, which for Foucault does not exist, and with material class interests which he sees as increasingly secondary to discursive practices (Foucault 2002a: 119). Whereas discourses 'in themselves are neither true nor false', ideology implies a socially determined agent which Foucault rejects in favour of self-constituted subjects. For him, techniques and procedures, including discourse, allow the 'effects of power to circulate in a manner at once continuous, uninterrupted, adapted and 'individualized' throughout the entire social body' (Foucault 2002a: 120). It is not surprising that in a world where neoliberalism appeared to offer a kind of regulatory practice from a point of observation which, panopticon-like, compelled conformity, Foucault's theoretical frame has seen a resurgence in various critical analyses of neoliberalism.

For our discussion of neoliberalism, two features of Foucault's approach stand out. First is the assumption that power is a central given in discourse. For Fairclough, this means that discourse has a particular role in sustaining dominant power relations and is itself a socially creative form of practice. Language is seen to contain and reproduce power relations. However, it is difficult to accept that words do actually constitute, to paraphrase Foucault, the same 'order of things' as acts in the real.[5] Power in society and between humans, however, is an empirical question, something that actually manifests itself through various social channels, such as the control of production and institutions, social class, social relations and unequal access to education, but also through basic material means such as physical strength and many other things. Language, in spite of its outcomes being affected by social and educational inequalities, is actually inherently unpredictable, is never quite a structured form of power, and precisely something rather different to sticks and stones. Linguistic communication is two-way, potentially more egalitarian, more open-ended and, as Eagleton puts it, 'a rather weightless way of carrying the world around with us' (1996: 73). The Russian linguist, Volosinov, described the word as a bridge thrown between two people that depends for its interpretation on social context, but it is also a bridge along which everyone can walk relatively freely and in different directions. For this reason, it is difficult to speak of social relations or social practice entrapped within discourse in quite the same way that one can about other social structures and processes.

The second feature of Foucault's framework is his view that power is as much about the individual as it is about society. Regulation and regulatory practices mean that Foucauldian power relations are less something imposed on us than something dispersed through the network of relationships which make up society. Power becomes something generated by ourselves, what Foucault calls 'the government of the self by the self' (Foucault 2002a: 364). Discourse contributes to this self-regulation and it is through discourse that we constitute ourselves as social subjects. Foucault displaces events themselves into our representation of them; history is not so much what happened but what people interpret as having happened, a series of narratives and discourses. Foucault's subject is a self-regulator whose interface with external social power passes through the prism of discursive regimes – the closest one gets to ideology in Foucault's work. Discourses are about conformity to the dominant *episteme,* the body of ideas considered true at any one time, and about subjects consenting to the particular discursive regime. Subjects thus become implicated in the reproduction of power. While no ideology can be said to be hegemonic without a degree of consent, it is difficult to see how power can be exclusively viewed, not in terms of its source, but in terms of how it is received. For example, while the imperialist ideology of 'the white man's burden' may have been internalised by hundreds of British subjects, it would be perverse to claim that this was the source of its hegemony, or that it could be explained without making reference to the underpinning material factors of occupation and economic dominance. The question of material substance is important: to argue that neoliberalism ultimately prevails because we have imbibed the truth of the market seriously underestimates the social conditions in which the ideology came to dominate as well as the powerful interests that seek to promote it. With a strange twist of irony, this internalising of social power repeats in distorted fashion one of the mantras of neoliberalism itself, namely that there is no society, only individuals.

The corollary of Foucault's internalising of social control is the possibility of refusal to submit, to promote 'new forms of subjectivity through the refusal of what has been imposed on us' (Foucault 2002a: 336). Pennycook refers to socially performative vernacular voices, which in the context of hip-hop subcultures in English, he calls the route to the 'critical philosophy of transgression'. He takes this as meaning not only the adopting of a critical stance towards globalisation and English, and towards consumerist culture, but also as meaning 'thought in movement', how we can start to think and act beyond the present limits (Pennycook 2007: 43). His interesting study shows convincingly that world English never simply smothers those obliged to speak it. But he exaggerates the transformative role that performative linguistics can play, and seems to equate adopting critical stances with social change. 'Critical', now a tag given to many subjects, reflects the same concern and contains the same limitations. Position-taking, in the 'critical' framework, is not just an explicit admission of an individual's political stance, but is also judged to be the necessary first step towards making a dent in the hegemonic order, an act of 'redemptive insurgency', as Foucault might term it. It is almost as if the collective and the social cedes to the sincerity of the individual and is, perhaps, symptomatic of a profound narrowing of perspective regarding social change. Discursive 'performativity' becomes the rampart against social power and, as acts of resistance, the means to transformation. Rather obviously, this begs the question that, if discursive acts are redefined as resistance, if the individual can escape the dominant order within existing social parameters, where does that leave society?

Neoliberalism and English

Within applied linguistics, world English has often become coupled with neoliberal globalisation and therefore it is worth discussing how neoliberalism has been seen to intersect with English as a dominant language. The focus of this section will be English as the embodiment of neoliberal ideology, for it is in the context of English as a dominant world language, in applied linguistics, that neoliberalism has been most often mentioned. In a piece written in 2008, 'The linguistic imperialism of neoliberal empire', Robert Phillipson lays out a theory of language and of the dominance of English which 'situates discourses and cultural politics in the material realities of neoimperial market pressures' (2008a: 1). Language ideologies which promote English as a world language are seen as a prop for neoliberalism. Drawing on theories of imperialism and empire from Harvey, Neverdeen Pieterse, Negri and Hardt, he argues that English is part of the US empire, a representation of corporate consumerism, and that the promotion of English today is ideologically driven. TESOL's view of languages 'other' than English he sees as modern-day version of the 'civilising mission'. The 'Anglo-American Community of Purpose and Language' has enforced 'poodle behaviour' in Europe which blindly follows US economic and military expansion. Against this, he calls for full linguistic rights for minority languages, the maintenance of linguistic diversity and opposition to 'occupation physical and mental' (2008a: 39).

His substantial and important argument – that the dominance of English must be challenged – transformed the apolitical landscape of applied linguistics when he first raised it with his book *Linguistic Imperialism*. It provided a long-overdue critical analysis of world English and of its seemingly benign promoting agents, particularly the British Council and the Ford Foundation. More recently, Phillipson has extended his notion of linguistic imperialism and 'linguicism' to the neoliberal world order. He identifies a creeping neoliberalisation in Europe through the covert dominance of English, arguing that *laissez-faire* language policies allow English to be 'the cuckoo' in the nest of European languages and serve US economic interests. His claim is that English is not just an imposition but also, due to its identification with 'success, influence, consumerism and hedonism', experiences 'bottom–up' popularity. Phillipson argues that stemming the tide of English imperialism requires the concerted promotion of minority languages and these can act as a political bulwark against the Anglo-American neoliberal empire (2003). His understanding of linguistic imperialism is effectively a theory of economic neoliberalism and empire superimposed onto language. Perhaps his analogy is intended metaphorically, to drive home the extent of the dominance of English but, taken literally, the identification is difficult to accept.

To equate imperialism and linguistic imperialism, he must materialise language. Interestingly, as part of this process, he appropriates Harvey's term 'accumulation by dispossession', which is said to describe the privatisation of the public sector and the bringing into the capitalist market of services hitherto provided by the state. The process of 'linguistic capital accumulation by dispossession [...] entails, as in commerce, some combination of internal motivation and external pressure, push-and-pull factors' (Phillipson 2008a: 29). He describes how European Union higher education initiatives, such as the Bologna process, facilitate 'linguistic capital accumulation' in favour of English. His critique of the competitive, business ethos which has saturated university campuses constitutes a timely, convincing critique of the neoliberal agenda in higher education as it is ravaging university campuses across Europe.

But the theoretical tools he uses are less than satisfactory. Primitive accumulation in its Marxist version usually refers to imperial plunder. Colonies were robbed of their land, their raw materials and later their labour, and dragged forcibly and, at great human cost, into the capitalist system. Phillipson's adoption of the term may seem to be more fitting in an imperial, international context than Harvey's within an already capitalist state. But 'linguistic capital accumulation by dispossession', as a literal analogy, does not really work. A language, quite simply, cannot be the vehicle of a mode of production, any more than it can be of imperialism. English may have been the language of the empire builders, buttressed by wealth, education and means, but it also became the language of the oppressed, with unexpected outcomes. As a matter of fact, English did not manage to disseminate and instil the same thoughts about the British Empire, however much Macaulay's famous Minute on Indian Education implored it to do so. Language, as so much of post-colonial writing proves, can turn round and bite the hand that feeds it. The dominance of English does not preclude it being used to denounce Western culture (Spring 2008: 352). Phillipson concedes that languages can be used to decolonise minds (2008a: 39) but seems to exclude this taking place anywhere else except in minority languages, or Esperanto. As I have pointed out elsewhere, promotion of minority languages may not always be as emancipatory as Phillipson would lead us to believe. They can be put to use by those who have no quarrel with the neoliberal empire, who wish to deflect things into nationalist rather than radical directions and who may have the principle of language rights rather low in their priorities (Holborow 1999). Latvian in the official language position, which Phillipson cites favourably (2008a: 9), seen from the point of view of now-disempowered Russian speakers, might just be a case in point. Regarding Esperanto, taking into account sociolinguistic principles of the role of social factors in language use, it is difficult to see how it could in any way become a viable alternative as an international language. Phillipson's less than convincing alternatives reflect something of the cul-de-sac of his own linguistic determinism and the difficulties of equating of English with imperialism.

Materialising English takes another form and one that is referred to beyond Philipson's work – that of identifying language with linguistic capital. In Phillipson's neoliberal empire, 'global' English is underpinned by interlocking structures and ideologies that constitute English as linguistic capital, whose benefits privilege its users in the current world order (2008a: 5). Linguistic capital is a term borrowed from Bourdieu who has described how a national language gains legitimacy through the material and symbolic profit that it bestows on the holder of the official linguistic capital (Bourdieu 1991). The use of English across the world does not fit as neatly into the model of the rise of standard national languages. One only has to look at a potentially rich and very populous country like Nigeria, or indeed any other post-colonial country in Africa where a variety of English is spoken, to see that English *per se* affords very little linguistic or material capital in the global world order. Nigeria, on the GNP-weighted wealth levels around the world in 2005, stood at 185, near the bottom. During the decades following independence in Ireland and before the Celtic Tiger, English afforded the Irish little in terms of growth rates. In fact the only thing that English gave to the new Irish state was a quicker route to emigration. English for the Irish, post-2008, looks set to play the same role again. English for emigration, certainly in the minds of the emigrants, feels very little like linguistic imperialism.

Extending the application of capital to language, to culture, to social attributes or indeed to humans, may itself be an outcome of neoliberal thinking which converts everything into a product, as some have argued (Fine 2002). It is interesting that Phillipson and critical discourse analysis in their critiques of neoliberalism both resort to reifying language. Paradoxically, despite the appeal to the broader social forces in their analyses, both critiques end up making discourse or English more central to society in rather a narrow, language-determinist way.

Neoliberalism and ideology

Neoliberalism, we have seen, involves necessarily talking about society and capitalism, and the real world in which it circulates. Neoliberalism as an economic theory and its overlap with specific developments in capitalism makes it seem to reach beyond the purely ideological. Nevertheless, focusing on its ideological aspects does allow us to bring together, in a structured way, the relationship between its set of principles and the material and social world in which it circulates. In this last section, I shall explain why I think ideology is an indispensable theoretical tool for our analysis of neoliberalism and language.

Ideology, for the purposes of our analysis, we shall define as:

*   a one-sided representation;
*   articulated from a particular social class but constructed as a world-view;
*   part-believed and part-rejected;
*   influenced by real world events;
*   coextensive with language but distinct from it.

First, ideology is a one-sided representation. In an oft-quoted passage, Marx compared ideology to the workings of a *camera obscura* in which the image appears turned upside down (Marx and Engels 1974: 47). This notion has triggered much debate amongst theorists of ideology and language who have tended to see Marx's characterisation as too centred on the real, too focused on the illusionary nature of ideology and by extension too dismissive of the power of ideology in its own right (Thompson 1984). The metaphor of the *camera obscura*, for all its old-fashioned mechanical associations, does still capture something of the making of ideology. Ideological representation starts from the real but sees the real through a certain lens. Social class affects its take on the world and frames its distinctive rhetoric. The contradictions between what neoliberalism says and what actually happens, as we have seen, constitute what makes it an ideology. Neoliberal ideology draws a picture of the world to suit its ends; starting from the real world, it misrepresents it.

Second, the foundations of an ideology are the expression of specific social interests and in the case of neoliberalism we are dealing with a dominant ideology emanating from a dominant class. It is in the interests of the controllers of capital, in an uneasy partnership with the state, to present society as driven by an external force – the market – whose dictates must prevail. Within competing interests of capital and across governments, there may be a different emphasis between those who would like to see a complete playing out of the market (the neoconservatives) and those that seek state support for it (Democrats in the US, Social Democracy in Europe). But ultimately the ideological fundamentals remain, namely that free-market economics are the accepted framework and structural dynamic of society. Market ideology makes present-day social relations appear as the outcome of natural laws outside history. It presents itself not as ideology, nor even belief, but as simply how things are, a pervasive 'truth', and this subterfuge contributes further to what Žižek terms the 'symbolic efficiency' of today's ruling ideology. As he aptly puts it, the end of ideology has been repeatedly proclaimed but while people say they have no ideology they still practise it (Žižek 2009: 3). A world-view fashioned to suit a specific social class, like other ruling ideologies before it, neoliberal ideology disguises itself in the mask of universalism.

But even a dominant ideology does not operate a blanket control. Nor are its effects on people necessarily best described in the binary terms of acceptance or resistance (Pennycook 2007; Van Dijk 2008). An ideology, and this is our third point, may be half-accepted and half-rejected. In the case of neoliberalism, people may go along with some aspects and reject others. They can, as Gramsci pointed out, have two sets of beliefs, one which reinforces the way things are and another which looks to how things could be different, a 'critical conception' (Gramsci 1971: 334). Most of us live with competing ideas most of the time; living in capitalism, Gramsci would argue, breeds it.[6] Market maxims may seem to make sense at one level but not at another: to fit for the fixing of prices but not for the delivery of hospital care; to be seen as efficient for services such as hairdressing or taxis but not, as opinion polls continue to bear out, for water supply or for buses. Contradiction lies at the heart of both the construction of an ideology and how it is received. Taking this into account, it is not quite the case, therefore, that neoliberalism is a rule of 'terror' (Giroux 2004a); it rules only with fragility and jostles constantly with other ideas that threaten to challenge it.

Fourth, these tensions within an ideology surface with a crisis. Ideology is highly sensitive to real-world events, something that was forgotten in the decades of triumphant neoliberalism. The financial meltdown of 2008, followed by severe economic recession, unceremoniously jolted market ideology. Through 2008 and 2009, the lid on neoliberal common sense blew off and some of the certainties went into reverse. Speculators became 'spivs', bankers the barefaced beneficiaries of corporate greed, and state welfare something given to the rich. 'Faith. Belief. Trust. This economic orthodoxy was built on superstition', was how one British newspaper headline in 2008 described the scales falling from people's eyes.[7] Real-world events disrupted the smooth flow of ideology. Discursive practices, regimes of discourse and even ideological formations seemed irrelevant in the inexorable swing back to the material. The truth of Gramsci's dictum that 'it is not ideology that changes the structure but vice versa' (Gramsci 1971: 376) rang true as real-world events dislodged people's usual interpretation of the world. This did not necessarily mean that neoliberalism retreated, as we shall see in later chapters. But it did mean, at the very least, in order for the capitalist system to carry on, the dominant ideology had to readjust. This is not to discount the value of critical thinking about ideology, merely to set the standing of an ideology in a context of real-world events. As Eagleton aptly puts it, 'ideology neither legislates situations into being, nor is simply "caused" by them; rather ideology offers a set of *reasons* for such material conditions' (Eagleton 2007: 209). Those sets of reasons may have more or less acceptance depending on circumstances and on how social events unfold.

Lastly, these characteristics make ideology distinct from discourse. The characterisation outlined above may seem to contain elements not incompatible with those also identified with discourse. There are however some important differences. First, what Volosinov called the generative nature of language, the changing and adaptable sign, drew attention to the fact that signs were both sensitive to ideology but not reducible to it (Volosinov 1973). The ideological potential of language is different to ideology in the same way that language is different to literature or that numbers are different to mathematical theory. The fact that language can be the site of ideological conflict, also highlighted by Volosinov, itself points to ideology being something other than sign. Secondly, ideology seen as discursively constructed, as the filling of a 'floating signifier' (Laclau and Mouffe 1985), bestows ideology with a 'hegemonising articulation' whose power appears to derive from representational structures themselves rather than any objective interests or social agency. In this case, the adoption of the theoretical notion of discourse also includes implicitly the weakening of the link between expression and the economic foundations of society, and specifically, for Laclau and Mouffe, the rejection of the notion of social class as a key social agent (1985: 109). The value of the notion of ideology is that it links views of the world with social relations and social class and sees the source of dominant ideas not in structural terms but arising from social relations themselves.

In sum, language has the potential to be ideological but this does not mean that all language is ideological or that discourse doubles up as ideology. While language and ideology may overlap, they are not equivalent or interchangeable. Ideology is not always a verbal phenomenon, nor even confined to expression. Barthes's deciphering of myth convincingly uncovered the deeply ideological in the visual, most memorably in his analysis of a 1950s front cover of *Paris Match* showing a young black soldier wearing a French uniform and saluting a French flag (Barthes 1973). The mechanism of ideological meaning – here *la mission civilisatrice* – may appeal to discursive logic in the loosest sense, but this is not strictly language. And even if discourse is taken to be a multimodal system, there is a difficulty with constructing ideology purely as a means of expression whose coherence derives from the relationship of the various structural elements with the communicative event. The emphasis here, as Blommaert has pointed out, is on a specific set of symbolic representations, whether terms, arguments, internal logic or images, serving a specific purpose and operated by specific groups or actors. Ideology on the other hand is a general phenomenon, characterising the totality of a particular social or political system and affecting every member or actor in that system (Blommaert 2005: 158). To replace ideology by discourse is to displace the dynamic of expression from the social to the individual. It is to start philosophically from a different premise. In *The Germany Ideology,* where ideology was first theorised by Marx, he argued that the philosophical error of placing language at the centre of society was that it set out from what people say, imagine, conceive, from people as narrated, thought of, imagined, conceived, and then made suppositions about their social life. Ideology, on the other hand, is a description which retains the link between ideas and reality, between mindsets and social class: it starts from real, active people and, on the basis of their life process, shows the development of the ideological reflexes and echoes of this life process. Ideology becomes the theoretical tool to break up language as an independent realm and 'descend from language to life' (Marx 1974: 118). It is in this sense that ideology, in a way that discourse cannot, remains an important theoretical tool of social analysis.

Conclusion

This chapter has aimed to capture something of the slippery nature of neoliberalism. Our account has described neoliberalism as an economic doctrine, as part of new capitalism, as a new discourse in the contemporary world, and finally as an ideology. Neoliberalism has been found to be highly contradictory, with anomalies between the rhetoric and the reality. It is not always what it says it is, nor is it as all-embracing as it makes out and, despite appearances, all is not well within neoliberalism. The huge gulf between its wished-for world and the real one, which surfaced so dramatically during the crash of 2008, serves to reconnect ideology to the real world and allows us to glimpse more clearly the contradictory flaws of the ideology. In the case of critical discourse analysis, this connection is not satisfactorily made and, in conflating discourse with ideology, CDA effectively closes off dynamic social processes from its analysis. In a different way, in the theory of linguistic imperialism, language also acquires a static character. It fuses a dominant language with a dominant ideology, thereby lending an overly functionalist role to English in global capitalism. This underestimates the forms of opposition to neoliberal empire which may well occur in English, and which, in themselves, may have little to do with language. Finally, our analysis of neoliberalism today has highlighted the role of real-world events in the making – and the unmaking – of an ideology. The tensions and the relationship between neoliberalism and applied linguistics, we suggest, is best described in terms of how an ideology makes its appearance in language rather than collapsing ideology into discourse.

3

NEOLIBERAL KEYWORDS AND THE CONTRADICTIONS OF AN IDEOLOGY

MARNIE HOLBOROW

Introduction

The financial meltdown of 2008 seemed to deliver a blow to the dominant ideology of neoliberalism. The wondrous workings of the market, the unleashing of wealth through deregulation, the rewards of risk-taking, huge returns on speculation, the chasing of money markets all seemed like dangerous decadence in the cold light of market failure. The state, officially labelled as economically inept, now became the system's only refuge, as billions of public money were used to prop up bad debts. The 'free' market, it seemed, was to be saved by its ideological nemesis.

The crisis has revealed how much an ideology, for all its seeming timelessness and authority, is balanced precariously in the real world. It showed that ideological representations are the products of specific social actors in particular historical moments and that their degree of acceptance relies on some credible correlation with reality. Events can lay bare ideological contradictions which, at other times, remain hidden beneath apparent social stability. This fundamental connection between ideology and the social world in which it circulates seems, as described in Chapter 2, to have faded into the background in explanations of power in society. Three decades of neoliberalism triumphant may have contributed to the apparent capacity of ideology-as-discourse to 'overdetermine', to impose a framework on social interactions, to be inevitably hegemonic. Ideological apparatuses and discursive practices were made to be the very 'conditions of possibility' for what were loosely referred to as social relations. Subjects were 'interpellated', via ideology, to their social place, and social identity was formed through 'floating signifiers' and discursive practices, which now shaped reality (Althusser 2008; Fairclough 1992, 1995, 2004; Howarth 2000; Laclau and Mouffe 1985).

The view that discourse can encompass the social engagement represented by ideology seems, on the face of it, to be no more than a logical move to include language practices in the making of ideology. However, from a social theory perspective, this view blurs the distinction between real social relations and discursive practices and ascribes to ideology-laden discourse a power potential residing, not in actual social relations, but in the structures of discourse themselves. Ideology, by contrast, contains a more specific reference to power in society. The notion of ideology, as explained in Chapter 2, links ideas to class society, and is a form of social conflict in the philosophical and political terrain. In Marx's account of ideology, it is only through the conflicting relations of production in capitalism and their attendant social inequalities that ideology can be explained and its social function understood (Marx 1977).

The events of 2008 and the challenge that they made to neoliberal market ideology have brought into question the discourse-ideology intellectual scaffolding and reminded us, again, that class relations in capitalism, not discourses, constitute the hub upon which ideology turns. The way in which language, in John B. Thompson's phrase, makes an ideological meaning 'stick' (1984: 132) is true precisely with reference to social class relations and to unfolding events. It is these, as recent events have proved, which can just as easily make these meanings come unstuck, something which, in turn, forces an ideological readjustment if the meanings are to retain any sense at all.

The clash between ideology and real-world events is particularly apparent during a crisis of the system. After the crash of 1929, the self-congratulatory mindset of the American Way – motorcars, mass consumption and moralistic individualism – forged during a decade of unprecedented boom, foundered on the bitter experiences of the Depression. Radical photographers of the 1930s exploited the realism of their medium to contrast the ideological dream world with the actual social hardship of those lean years. Margaret Bourke White's now iconic photo captures deftly, and with striking relevance for today, the impact of this process. A queue of unemployed black workers, dwarfed by the advertisement which proclaims the happy fulfilment of the American (white) dream via a smiling 2.2 kids family in their own car, bears witness to how a dominant ideology is promoted by interests inimical to the majority of the population.[1]

In our times, as mountains of sovereign debt weigh on people's lives for the foreseeable future, the new American dream of neoliberalism, in the form of the self-expanding market, limitless credit and boundless financialisation, has foundered, yet again, on the rocks of economic crisis. How a dominant ideology suddenly seems to clash with events, how the world as it has been painted no longer seems to describe reality, is what I seek to explore further here. How do these moments of ideological reckoning, or disjunction, filter into public discourse? Also, how do the core concepts of a dominant ideology, suddenly under strain, adjust to the changed circumstances? What semantic mechanisms reveal these fresh ideological tensions?

In order to answer some of these questions, this chapter has chosen to analyse how ideological meaning interacts with language through the analysis of certain keywords of neoliberal ideology. A meta-analysis of this type enables a focus on specific words which, in popular consciousness, are readily identifiable with neoliberal ideology and it is an approach which avoids some of the arbitrary aspects (as identified in Chapter 2) associated with discourse analysis of specific texts. The chapter examines briefly the notion of keywords as first put forward by Williams and his contribution to understanding the presence of ideology in language. It then analyses selected keywords in public domain. These have been chosen with reference to Irish neoliberalism, where the ideology had the freest rein and where the economic shocks in the aftermath of the neoliberal era have been, correspondingly, the sharpest. It will argue that neoliberal keywords both distil and fragment neoliberal ideology and how its contradictory meanings stand revealed in a changed social world.

Williams's keywords

Raymond Williams, writing in a similar period of social upheaval, sensed the significance of another unfolding ideological turbulence. Williams's insight was that certain 'keywords' represented the hub of this ideological struggle. They encompassed both consensus and contestation as social classes and individuals, from different perspectives, grappled with social change. The 'keywords' concept, as I have described elsewhere (Holborow 2007), is rich in potential for the understanding of ideological flux in language; here I expand on these observations to show that it provides a useful perspective on some of the ideological tensions we are experiencing today.

As part of his investigation into ideology in language and communication, Williams gathered certain salient 'keywords'. These were the ideologically sensitive words whose associations and connotations were not settled and whose meanings were under negotiation. Returning to Britain from serving in the army in the Second World War, he found a changed world and a changed language. He observed that a number of indicative words had expanded beyond their usual field and now described wider areas of thought and experience. Many of the words that he selected were directly related to politics – *class, doctrinaire, bureaucracy, nationalist, progressive* – but others were words whose meaning triggered controversy – *folk, peasant, underprivileged, tradition, welfare*, for example. The words he published as a collection in 1976, and then added to in 1983, were all both ideologically significant and difficult to pin down; they reflected new concerns and new horizons of public debate in a changed social landscape. This transformation of meaning was symptomatic of the evolving nature of language itself.

> What is really happening through these critical encounters, which may be very conscious or may be felt only as a certain strangeness and unease, is a process quite central in the development of a language when in certain words tones and rhythms meanings are offered, felt for, tested, confirmed, asserted, qualified, changed.
>
> (Williams 1986: 11)

Williams notes that in periods of change this development can seem unusually rapid. One of the words that first struck him was the word *culture* whose connotation was moving beyond the literary and the artistic to the societal, adopting the meaning of *way of life* and *values* and other things besides (ibid. 12). His selection included *culture* (in its newly acquired sense) and *society*, and as a whole constituted a glossary in progress, an ongoing cultural dictionary, a contemporary snap-shot of 'a shared body of words and meanings' with their 'explicit and implicit connections'. These were 'binding words in certain activities and their interpretation; they are significant, indicative words in certain forms of thought' (ibid. 15). The issues could not be understood simply in terms of etymology or linguistic analysis. Williams refers to another evaluative dimension: the way in which meanings of words consolidate and achieve amongst their users a 'surpassing confidence' or consensus about what that meaning is. But while 'language depends on this kind of confidence', in periods of change, 'a necessary confidence and concern for clarity can quickly become brittle' (ibid. 16). Dictionary definitions tend to exclude reference to these unstable, 'inconvenient' meanings. Williams's investigation moves beyond the finding of definitive, 'proper meanings' to the

> history and complexity of meanings; conscious changes or consciously different uses; innovation, obsolescence, specialisation, extension, overlap, transfer or changes which are masked by a nominal continuity so that words which seem to have been there for centuries, with continuous general meanings, have come in fact to express radically different or radically variable yet sometimes hardly noticed meaning and implications of meaning. Industry, family, nature may jump at us from such sources; class, rational, subjective may after years of reading remain doubtful.
>
> (Ibid. 17)

The difficulty of providing fixed definitions arises from what he terms 'sense and reference', which are constructed around social norms and rules. 'These are embedded in actual relationships and [...] both meanings and relationships are typically diverse and variable within the structure of particular social orders and the processes of social and historical change' (ibid. 17–21). He makes a plea for historical semantics which he sees as the study of how meanings have evolved historically but also encompassing a changing and disputed status in the present. For Williams, this approach provides a pathway into recording the social shared in language and elements of ideological conflict:

> This recognises, as any study of language must that there is indeed community between past and present but that community [...] is not the only possible description of these relations between past and present; that there are also radical change, discontinuity and conflict and that all these are still at issue and are indeed still occurring. The vocabulary I have selected is that which seems to me to contain the key words in which both continuity and discontinuity and also deep conflicts of value and belief are in this area engaged.
>
> (Ibid. 23)

He explains that these clashes in language arise from different social experiences and different readings of that experience. Consensus about meaning is not something given which derives from deference to a natural authority; it is instead an unfinished process, an ongoing 'shaping and reshaping in real circumstances and from profoundly diverse points of view'. His exploration of the vocabulary of social and cultural terms, understood as meanings formed within definite historical and social conditions, seeks to make ideological content both conscious and critical. It amounts to 'a vocabulary to use, to find our own ways in, to change as we find it necessary to change it, as we go on making our own language and history' (ibid. 25).

What makes Williams's analysis relevant for our discussion here is that he manages to capture the presence of ideology in language, not as the predictable outcome of certain discursive practices, but as part of an ongoing process which arises from social participants in language and whose meaning shifts may, or may not, acquire 'surpassing confidence'. His entry for the keyword *management,* for example (and which seems almost quaint to us now), describes the way in which the use of this term neutralises conflict and masks class relations:

> The description of negotiations between management and men often displaces the real character of negotiations between employers and workers and further displaces the character of negotiations about relative shares of the labour product to a sense of dispute between the general 'requirements' of a process (the abstract management) and the 'demands' of actual individuals (men). The internal laws of a particular capitalist institution or system can then be presented as general, abstract of technical laws as against the merely selfish desires of individuals. This has powerful ideological effects.
>
> (Ibid. 91)

The thrust of his analysis, however, is that the intended ideological reasoning may be only partly accepted. The laying bare of the origins of ideological motives and interests origins through semantic analysis become, for Williams, critical encounters of meaning. An awareness of these deep conflicts of values and beliefs leads to the meanings becoming 'brittle' and ideologically contested. We shall return to this approach as we investigate similar semantic processes at work within certain present-day neoliberal keywords.

It is striking how Williams's interpretation of how meanings are ideologically constructed echoes the Russian Marxist linguist, Valentin Volosinov. The latter had noted that language was inherently ideological, that words could not be divorced from the concrete forms of social intercourse in which they circulated and that words carried ideological accents. 'Differently orientated accents intersect in every ideological sign. Sign becomes the arena of class struggle' (Volosinov 1973: 21–2). It was this *multiaccentuality* of the ideological sign, and the sedimentation of different evaluative accents, which lay at the root of language change and of the generative nature of language itself. For Volosinov, this dimension of language was left out of structuralist accounts, for these ignored the dynamic and unpredictable input of speakers and language as the arena of ideological struggle (Volosinov 1973).[2] Williams does not make use of a Marxist framework quite as explicitly as does Volosinov, but both writers identify ideological contention in language as arising from the actual social conflicts of its speakers and constituting a core component of language change.

An account which echoes the directions set out by Williams is given by Ruqaiya Hasan in an article which deals specifically with the significance of meaning-change brought about by neoliberal ideology (Hasan 2003). She argues that the influence of 'free market fundamentalism' on the meanings of such words as 'globalisation', 'liberalise', 'democracy' is part of the 'semiotic struggle' to control how reality is defined and results in turning accepted usages of these words upside down. Re-semanticisation, or meaning shift, is commonplace in language although, usually, this is part of a slow process of change, with various groups of speakers having an input. Such changes underline the social properties of language: that it is not only a mechanism for referring to things and events but also a resource for the creation of human relations. It is through language that social relations are expressed and attitudes, including social judgements, made. What is different about neoliberal re-semanticisation is that it is led by 'people who can enforce their will' – the CEOs of corporations and the chieftains of finance – a factor which allows the changes to be enacted 'through an intensity of use within a short period of time'. She sees this as a top-down process enabling what she calls 'neoliberal *glibspeak*' to be adopted on a global scale and across many settings. Neoliberal re-semanticisation 'only respects boundaries set by power and control on wealth'. The linguistic patterns used in this process Hasan identifies as *inherent evaluation* on the part of speakers, *inherent elasticity* of meaning which is woven into all socially situated interactions and, thirdly, the *semantic stretching* of words into different categories and fields all of which stem from speakers' ideological interventions and purposes (ibid. 438). Interestingly, like Williams, though from a more rigorous linguistic perspective, she stresses that the 'activation of a linguistic meaning-wording conjunction' and the 'semantic pressure' for change lies in the 'context of culture' which she identifies as the series of social and political events since the fall of communism in 1989. She sees actual events in the world as a vital component to meaning change in language. Her observations provide useful additions to Williams's commentary, aspects of which we shall return to later.

Williams's work has been also been expanded upon by Tony Bennet, Lawrence Grossberg and Meaghan Morris in a work entitled *New Keywords*. Their aim is to provide 'a historically grounded guide to public questions and struggles for meaning shared by those in the field of culture and society' and to include 'strong, difficult and persuasive words already in everyday use' (Bennet *et al.* 2005: p. xviii). They seek to record the cultural and ideological shifts in meaning which have taken place since Williams's ground-breaking work. These, they claim, must take account of the ways in which our sense of 'common life' and our understanding of history have changed since the 1970s. The expansion of the role and function of higher education and its overlap with other industries, which has led to a greater diversity in the fields of public and academic debate, and the broadening of these debates into a global Anglophone dimension are two changes which for them require different and more pluralistic perspectives. Their work fans out from the original cultural focus of Williams to include questions of identity, mobilisation around religion, debates around science and evolution, psychoanalysis and individualism. Their emphasis falls on the history of different meanings of a word and less on the present struggles for meaning that a word encompasses. The compilation is multi-authored and has less of the rigorous ideological analysis of Williams's text. *New Keywords* does refer to ideological contention, but more diffusely. Their entry for *market,* for example, refers to classical neoliberal economics, and makes clear that, in popular consciousness, the perception of markets is contradictory, both necessary and not to be 'trusted' (ibid. 207) but it avoids delving deeper into the ideological implications of this.

The value of Williams's original analysis is that ideological meaning in language is situated within the context of social class and contending social forces. It is not about the isolating of one ideological lexicon to replace it with another or the artificial creation of a new postmodern vocabulary in the political field, as some have championed (e.g. Negri 2008). Williams rejects the idealism of believing that language change amounts to social change. He sees language as part of wider social conflicts whose outcomes are determined by actual historical events. Ideology Williams understands in a much narrower sense. Quoting Marx, he makes a distinction between material and ideological forms and how the ideological arena is where people become conscious of the conflict (of the economic conditions of production) and fight it out (Williams 1976: 156). We see here how Williams sees ideology as a theoretical category independent of language, a representational form which is driven by social interests and whose intention is to polemicise against other views. Neither language in its narrow sense nor discourse even its broader social sense has any of this partisanship; their compass is too wide to be a predictable, combative instrument.

Furthermore, Williams's critical analysis is not driven by moral position-taking. George Lakoff has claimed that ruling ideology can be shifted primarily by logical exposure, corrected in the name of a 'higher rationality' dislodged through progressive thinking (Lakoff 2006). In contrast to these views, Williams sees language change in tandem with social change. He succeeds in providing a compelling critique of the presence of ideology in language without believing, as some discourse theorists assert, that critical methods *per se* undo the power of ideology or that text is at the centre of social practice. Williams's object is to interweave language with history rather than to make language the prime historical agent. Through a careful analysis of how some words become ideologically laden and how the struggle over meaning is resolved in the social relations of the real world, Williams manages, in an original way, to describe the truly dialectical relationship between language and social reality,

Keywords and ideology

Willliams's approach shows how the notion of keywords is useful in the examination of the relationship between language and ideology. Gerlinde Mautner has identified keywords as playing an important role in *marketisation* in discourse, and she has observed that as objects of contention they constitute part of social conflict (Mautner 2010: 85–90). Michael Stubbs also recognises that keywords are 'nodes around which ideological battles are fought', that they 'embody facts of history' and that 'they can be analysed diachronically to reveal the unconscious assumptions of their community of users' (Stubbs 2001: 88). Both of these studies have investigated the appearance of certain keywords in specific texts and, with extensive computer data, have mapped discursive profiles of their use. Mautner's study brings together useful information about the ways in which market language is used in the public domain. She sees *marketisation* as something different to *market society* but not as an ideology – a word that does not figure in her analysis. Her assessment is that *marketisation* is the 'encroaching/ seeping/creeping/infusing' colonisation and appropriation of other lifeworlds (2010: 22) and 'a threat to established values' and all the more insidious as it is incrementally adopted by institutions and individuals (ibid. 21, 30). *Marketisation*, by this definition, is best challenged through discourse for it is this that 'paves the way' for it. The aim of critical thinking is to prevent the 'discursive closure' of marketisation, to decouple 'market' from 'society' (ibid. 179–180). The assumption made here is that *marketisation* is simultaneously a mindset and a discourse practice and that, by extension, it is through these that it can be dismantled. This rather circular approach, constructed within the confines of mental and language processes, leaves out cause and agent and why society is given to such pervasive marketisation in the first place. Williams's approach avoids this pitfall by judging keywords not as constitutive of reality but, rather, with their evolving meanings and contested status, as living evidence of the dynamic interaction of the material and the representational. The examination of keywords that I provide here returns to the Williams focus which lays stress on the making and unmaking of dominant ideology with reference to wider social relations. Selected neoliberal keywords will be examined as aspects of the tensions of neoliberal ideology – tensions which turn on developments in the real world.

Williams's understanding of the dynamic of the ideological and social avoids the fusing of ideology with language (Hodge and Kress 1993), or with discourse (Fairclough 1992, 2004; Van Dijk 1998, 2008). His distinction between language as the unstable vehicle of representation and ideology as the representation itself, highlights that ideology cannot be separated from the notion of authorship in the form of a specific social actor – that of social class. It shows how unequal social relations are a crucial component of ideology, and why ideology has been aptly described as 'meaning in the service of power' (Thompson 1990: 7). A representation of the world where things appear distorted or with a slant that suits its powerful promoters is what classical Marxist interpretations of ideology have highlighted. These have often been criticized for overemphasising ideology as 'false consciousness' (Freeden 2003: 5–10; Torfing 1999: 113) or for underestimating the way in which people come to believe in the ideology themselves. However, Marx's view of ideology was rather more complex. Ideology is not simply about pulling the wool over people's eyes nor somehow duping people into believing; it is still less about winning hegemony through individual compliance. In a discussion of these issues, Blommaert notes that it is a misreading of the notion of hegemony to displace power from its broader social and political context into the subjective domain of 'internalised consent' (Blommaert 2005: 167). Distorted perceptions of the social world, according to Marx, arose from people's experience of capitalist society, in particular the way in which everything in it, including people, were treated as commodities. This was at the root of why people had an incomplete view of social life and the source of alienation. Ideas about the naturalness of the market seem superficially to correspond to how society works and they are amplified by their constant repetition through powerful communication channels. Marx's aphorism that 'the ruling ideas are those of the ruling class' was not a reference to brainwashing, but rather to the material and institutional means at the disposal of those in power for making their voice the loudest and the most repeated (Marx and Engels 1974). Hegemony, despite the overwhelming weight often attributed to the term, is not the same as full-blown acceptance. Even an apparently widely accepted ideology is never swallowed whole nor is it uniformly dominant: people may accept some aspects but reject others. They may have, as Gramsci succinctly put it, a contradictory consciousness, one in which different ideas about society exist side by side (Gramsci 1971: 333). In this view, ideology is an unstable entity, less like social cement or 'a regime of discourse' than an amalgam of contradictions whose fragility, especially in periods of social crisis, stands exposed and potentially open to challenge. Ideology can be more usefully understood as a jigsawed, inconsistent representation which may find its expression in language but which is also distinct from it; it is a one-sided set of ideas, articulated from the interests of a particular social class, which may be part believed and part rejected and whose degree of acceptance rests on its relationship to real-world events.

It is this fluctuating character of ideology that a focus on keywords can help to uncover. The identification of keywords within the articulation of neoliberal ideology may be summarised thus:

1   Neoliberal keywords have special meanings and associations within the framework of neoliberal ideology and reflect a version of reality which promotes the interests of capital.
2   Neoliberal keywords often involve a process of re-semanticisation (or meaning-stretching) which allows for the extension of semantic boundaries into new fields for ideological purposes.
3   Neoliberal keywords are subject to evaluation and multiaccentuality, formed through social standpoints and the relationship of the ideology to events in the real world.

For each of these three aspects, three terms, readily identifiable with neoliberal ideology, will be used to show how the ideology is articulated: *deregulation, human capital* and *entrepreneur.*

Keywords and neoliberal meanings and associations: deregulation

At the core of neoliberal ideology is the free market and its objective to extend the boundaries of the market and set it free from all constraints. Taking the appearances of the capitalist market for granted, it proposes a framework which supposedly provides the optimum environment for the working of the market – a 'non-interfering' state, the conversion of public services into consumer transactions, the promotion of a market ethos, a highly competitive labour market and so on. The twin pillars of the market – supply and demand – are taken in this ideal market-driven world as independent social impulses, detached from a specific mode of production. Individuals partake in this timeless market, apparently outside the very social relations that determine who is selling and who is buying. One of the first to analyse the phenomenon of neoliberalism, Pierre Bourdieu saw the defining feature of neoliberal ideology as severing the economy from social realities and constructing a sort of logical machine that presents itself as a chain of constraints regulating economic agents which are seen in purely individual terms (Bourdieu 1998). The invention of the market economy as a contrivance, running by and for itself, a self-sustaining network composed of market-driven individuals, is crucial to the making of neoliberal ideology. Its core ideas revolve around neoclassical economics but it reaches beyond purely economic theorising. It has 'pervasive effects on ways of thought to the point', David Harvey rightly notes, 'where it has become incorporated into the common-sense way many of us interpret, live in and understand the world' (Harvey 2005: 5; see also Chapter 2).

In many ways, Ireland is a good vantage point to survey neoliberal keywords. Prior to the crash of 2008 Ireland, with its soaring growth rates, was lauded as one of the world's most globalised economies and hailed as a neoliberal model. In 2004, Ireland's Celtic Tiger had been proclaimed Europe's 'shining light', an economy that had experienced a rapid transition from a basket case to one of the most successful economies in the world.[3] Foreign direct investment, above all from the homeland of neoliberalism, the US, had played a key role in Ireland's spectacular economic growth and its economy was irrevocably linked to the US boom and financial deregulation (Allen 2007; Kirby 2010; O'Toole 2009). US investment in Ireland was significant, with the amount of US capital deployed per worker seven times the EU average (Allen 2009: 34; Boucher and Collins 2003). This brought an almost uniform adoption of US corporate styles and practices. American *neoliberal speak* became English as it was spoken in official circles in Ireland. Irish public policy in the area of education, for example, repeated faithfully, indeed word for word, formulations from reports from the Organisation for Economic Cooperation and Development, with the result that neoliberal buzzwords passed seamlessly from the corporate to the public sphere (Holborow 2006). Tax policy emanating from the Irish Department of Finance bore an unexpected similarity to statements from the American Chamber of Commerce.[4] Links with the US had always been historically close, but in Ireland the Washington Consensus filtered particularly tightly and faithfully into public discourse. Ireland was also at the receiving end of a new neoliberal turn, from Europe. During the years 2005–8, the neoliberal package of privatisation, deregulation and commercialisation, originally an Anglo-American invention, increasingly found an echo in the European Union (EU). Various liberalisation measures, given official status in the Lisbon Treaty, which was finally passed in 2009, set the EU on a deregulatory path which saw Ireland propelled into the global limelight of soaring growth rates and speculative returns, becoming known as the Celtic Tiger (Allen 2009). Ireland, already a bridgehead for US corporations into Europe, became a magnet for newly deregulated EU financial activity, becoming an off-shore financial hub and tax haven for both centres of capitalism. Ironically, after the crash, it was the US and the EU acting in unison, through the International Monetary Fund and the European Central Bank, which intervened in ways which seemed to send so many of their neoliberal nostrums into reverse.

Deregulation is a keyword of neoliberal ideology. It refers to the process whereby the market can be allowed to flourish without legal or social fetters. In the early days of the neoliberal era, it became the by-word for the opening up of 'new zones of untrammelled market freedoms for powerful corporate interests' (Harvey 2005: 26). From airlines to telecommunications to finance, *deregulation* was shorthand for the unrestrained expansion of both privatisation and financial speculation. It is a neoliberal keyword that merits examination. *Deregulation* as part of the neoliberal mix was first used in the North American context in an attempt to deal with stagflation (where an economy has both high inflation and low economic growth) in the 1970s. As the neoliberal Washington Consensus model took hold, it came to be the umbrella under which an assault could be made on a whole range of 'restrictive practices': financial regulation, higher tax regimes, state provided services, established work practices in unionised workplaces. Harvey sums up its headline position in neoliberal ideology: 'privatisation and deregulation, it is claimed, combined with competition, eliminate bureaucratic red tape, increase efficiency and productivity, improve quality and reduce costs, both directly to the consumer through cheaper commodities and services and indirectly through reduction of the tax burden' (Harvey 2005: 65; see also Chapter 2 for an account of this development). *Deregulation* as a keyword of neoliberal ideology, however, is as we shall see, an ambivalent term.

Given that *regulate* customarily means to adjust, control or to bring into conformity with a rule, principle or usage, its opposite evokes an apparent freedom from constraint which is at the centre of neoliberal thinking. The interpretation of freedom here is that it exists outside the confines of government, with society now being replaced (following Thatcher's dictum) by the individual. Free choice is held to be the driver of society, now interpreted as being the mere agglomeration of individually motivated human beings. *Deregulation* becomes another step towards this individually based freedom, the enabler of greater choice on the part of individual companies. The justification of *deregulation* rests on the assumption that private ownership constitutes a central pillar of freedom and that planning and control on a societal basis amount to the denial of free enterprise (Lakoff 2006; Polyani 2001). While dictionary definitions of *deregulate* describe it as the removal of restrictions in general, over the decades of neoliberalism it has become used primarily in connection with economic policy. It collocates, according to concordance patterns compiled by the British National Corpus, with *transport services, telecommunications* and *financial markets*, sometimes with *Europe* or *Europe-wide*, and interestingly, even in mainstream media, not always with positive connotations.[5]

Deregulation, in other words, has come to stand principally for the privatisation of state services. In Ireland, *deregulation* occurs in official documents, often with reference to conformity with EU competition directives. For example, a 2005 government discussion document on the electricity market spoke of the need to make the 'transition to a deregulated energy market driven by the EU', with *deregulation* being used interchangeably with *liberalisation* (DETE 2005: 5). In the case of the airline sector, in relation to the privatisation of Ireland's national carrier, Aer Lingus, the necessary *deregulation* is also described as arising from 'competition rules' from the EU (Dept of the Taoiseach 2006, 2010). Presenting the imperative to enact *deregulation* as the necessary compliance with EU requirements may serve to reinforce the ideological force of the argument. The need to *deregulate* is imposed from outside, beyond the control of the Irish Government, an inevitable step which must be taken in order to conform to the institution of a regime which, paradoxically, allows no exceptions. *Deregulation,* as used in a paper from the Irish Government's advisory board, Forfás, is synonymous with *regulatory reform* and *good regulation,* in so far as this supports competition and is kept to a minimum (Boyle and Evans 2007: 188). *Deregulation* thus interpreted stands for not the absence of regulation but *regulation* according to certain principles.

The overlap between *deregulation* and *regulation* is ideologically significant. It uncovers a deeper contradiction: the way *deregulation* occurs. Behind *deregulation*, as Harvey notes, lies state implementation of a deregulatory regime, something which gives rise to the unstable and contradictory form of the neoliberal state (Harvey 2005: 78–9). Neoliberal states declare themselves to be non-interventionist and moving towards smaller and smaller government; however, behind the scenes it is they who spend a great deal in providing what is necessary for the 'free market' to flourish. In the Irish case, the state has implemented such a strident *deregulation* that it has been identified as the crucial enabler of what has been described as the corporate take-over of Ireland (Allen 2007) or the effective merging of corporate and state interests, policy and ethos into one indivisible entity. It is something of an irony that at the end of an era which proclaimed officially the state to be superfluous to the market, the state emerged bigger, more stridently interventionist and more closely intertwined with transnational corporations than ever before. Intel Ireland or Deloitte Touche Ireland invoked a whole panoply of state institutions behind the corporate façade.

Deregulation is also used in connection with Irish fiscal policy. The legal framework, referred to in reports as the *regulatory environment,* regarding taxes on capital and transnational companies, is one of low corporation tax rates, tax exemptions on dividends and interest payments, and a large range of bilateral tax treaties. Ireland's much publicised 12.5 per cent corporation tax rate is one-third of that prevailing in the US and in most of Western Europe. This has resulted in a large amount of US and EU companies availing themselves of the incentives provided by Ireland's International Financial Services Centre (IFSC) and registering their head offices in Ireland, which allows them to be officially domiciled in Ireland (O'Toole 2009: 128).⁶ This sector accounted for over three-quarters of Ireland's overall foreign direct investment. As the official website of the IFSC makes plain, *global deregulation* created an open door for many transnational companies and the conditions of *local regulation* meant they were able to take full advantage of this in terms of language, location, education and technology. The American Chamber of Commerce in Ireland, in similar fashion, praised what it also referred to as the 'regulatory environment' for being 'conducive to economic growth' and argued strongly against any change as being 'detrimental to our competitiveness' (American Chamber of Commerce 2007).

The ideological nature of the use of *deregulation* is revealed in the way in which the term seems to imply a free functioning of the market through the creation of untrammelled competition when in reality competitive advantage is provided, not through hands-off *deregulation,* but precisely state-imposed and preferential *regulation.* The presence of this anomaly is an expression of larger tensions and contradictions within neoliberal ideology. The state-sponsored IFSC, its tax regulatory practices and the many government-paid legal and financial experts involved, amounts to intense state intervention. Despite the founding principle of neoliberal ideology being that the state should be a mere night watchman for the economy, through preferential tax regimes and subsidies to leading market actors, the state actually acts in a way that distorts any free working of the market. It thereby stacks competitive advantage towards those corporations which are already globally dominant (Toynbee 2010). The myth of *deregulation* is that it creates a free market which is very much freer for some than for others.

After the crash of 2008, given the outcomes of these preferential tax schemes, *deregulation* reverted from positive connotation to negative and the official plea was now the need for *regulation.* In the Irish context, the claim to implement financial *regulation,* like its former counterpart *deregulation,* is ambivalent. The stated aim of the Irish Central Bank regarding regulation is as follows: 'the objective of regulation is to minimise the risk of failure by ensuring compliance with prudential and other requirements' (Central Bank 2010). *Regulation,* by this account, is not the compliance with rules and laws, but with a more vaguely defined 'prudential code'. More stringent regulation is reserved for another domain, that of the public service. The Department of the Taoiseach (Prime Minister) is explicit about the target of its newly instituted 'Better Regulation policy'. Under the banner themes of 'transparency, consistency, accountability, effectiveness, proportionality, necessity', it tells us that the aim of the website is 'to provide information on Better Regulation – an important part of the Government's drive for greater economic competitiveness and modernisation of the Public Service' (Dept of the Taoiseach 2010). *Regulation*, post-crisis, applies to what can be monitored; the public service from this point of view is infinitely more amenable to scrutiny than the banks.

Keywords and the stretching of meaning for ideological purposes: human capital

The main function of neoliberal ideology is to subsume all aspects of social life into the frame of free-market economics. From an ideological perspective, this process involves the displacement of definite social relations into the timeless arena of the market, whose supposed ultimate equilibrium is the fulcrum upon which society turns.

Others have already highlighted, from different perspectives, the degree to which business terms have 'colonised' communication in the public sector, and particularly higher education (Fairclough 2006; Holborow 2007; Mautner 2005, 2010). The distinctive characteristic of keywords in neoliberal ideology is that they extend meanings which originally pertained to economics to other social fields such as education, health, social service provision. Examples of keywords of this type which have been noted are *customer, entrepreneur, commercialisation, intellectual property.* However, one keyword less commented on in this context is *human capital.*[7] Official government documents, economic reports, educational policy statements, mission statements of institutions of higher education, in the US, the UK and increasingly within the EU, consider 'human capital' to be essential for economic growth and competitiveness. It is a term widely used though, as we shall see, mainly in official texts. The term has a long history and is identified, through Gary Becker's work, with Milton Friedman and the Chicago School of Economics, itself a precursor of modern-day neoliberalism. The reasons that inspired Becker to take up the *human capital* theme, despite its being first seen as a debasing term, was that it allowed economists to take full account of individual behaviour within an economy, particularly individual decisions to invest in their own skill improvement, and these have continued to set the tone for subsequent use of the term, as we shall see (Becker 1962; see also Klein 2007: 49–52). An analysis of its metaphorical framing, and the connotations it evokes, is particularly revealing for the workings of neoliberal ideology in language.

Lakoff and Johnson remarked more than 35 years ago, in their landmark work on the role of metaphors in the making of mindsets, that the treating of labour as a commodity, as *human resources,* was already part of conflict-effacing managerial discourse. They noted how the human resources metaphor places labour on a level with raw materials, whose price, like oil or coffee, society prefers to see coming down (Lakoff and Johnson 2003: 65–8). The analogy between work and a resource became widely adopted: personnel departments became human resources departments, with workforces and employees becoming just another unit cost calculation in the overall production or service process.

Human capital takes this process further with some significant ideological effects. The term coalesces around the twin concepts of the skills that people bring to bear in the economy and the need for capital investment in these. An organisation which has a defining influence on government policy in Ireland, the Organisation for Economic Cooperation and Development (OECD) defines human capital as 'the knowledge, skills and competences and other attributes embodied in individuals that are relevant to economic activity'. Lo Bianco notes a wider definition by the same organisation: the knowledge that individuals acquire during their lives and which is used to produce goods and services or ideas, in market and non-market circumstances (Lo Bianco 1999: 21). The term now replaces words such as 'labour force', 'skilled personnel', 'skilled workers', 'highly educated workforce', as well as more broadly, 'investment in education at all levels'. As noted by Schuller, there is international political consensus about the human capital message – that skills, knowledges and competences will determine levels of prosperity, even if ways in which it can be measured remain less than clear (Schuller 2000).

In Ireland *human capital* has quickly come to be a keyword in official reports and government development plans. In Ireland's National Development Plan 2007–13, the principal social and economic policy document for the republic, a whole chapter is devoted to 'Human Capital'. In the executive summary of this document, under chapter 9 'Human Capital', we read:

> Investment under the Human Capital Priority is indicatively estimated at €25.8 billion. Investment in education, training and upskilling is broadly termed as human capital. Ireland has an excellent track record in this area which has been fundamental to our economic success. In the past Ireland proved adept at harnessing European Social Funds, Human capital funding in this plan will be derived from our own resources. There is a strong linkage between the availability and quality of human capital and regional competitiveness…
>
> (NDP 2007)

So accepted is the notion of *human capital,* that, even when it is first referred to, no definition is considered necessary. The term flits across many official reports, its accepted meaning apparently taken for granted. A document from the American Chamber of Commerce which appeared six months before the national development plan emphasised the value of investment and use of *human capital* and its value for economic performance in virtually the same terms. Under the heading of 'Human Capital investment aligned to Economic growth' we read:

> By 2020 we see Ireland as a leading global economy that has secured its position on the basis of significant investment in human capital resulting in a vibrant base of global industry, research and global enterprise.
>
> (American Chamber of Commerce Ireland 2007: 8)

Leaving aside the unpropitious optimism which assumed that Ireland's vibrant economic base would continue, *human capital* stretches meaning in interesting ways. *Human capital* is a metaphor in the sense that humans are likened to capital but it also comes to stand for two other terms – labour and investment in education. This process of metonymy allows for the binding of individual knowledge and expertise and human thought to their function and value in the economy. In a process of re-semanticisation or semantic field stretching, knowledge becomes thus reclassified as an economic category. Human knowledge and skill potential now become measurable in terms of returns on investment. This is part of a wider process, which Lo Bianco notes seeks to make 'invisible capital (i.e. human beings and what we know) visible to the gaze of accountants and economists' (Lo Bianco 1999: 23). Human capital makes human labour a quantifiable item which can be priced and bought on the market, a commodity in which companies can invest subject to there being adequate returns. *Human capital* is the reckoning of a person's knowledge and skills as an economic unit and the greater its productive outcomes, the greater its value.

The metaphor involves some quite specific ideological evaluations. The concept treats labour as part of the means of production and links human work more closely into the overall configuration of economic forces. Through its emphasis on education and training, it also lays emphasis on skill differentiation in the labour force and thereby indirectly contributes to greater competition in the labour market. Furthermore, the metaphor, by portraying human knowledge and educational and skill achievements as units of economic wealth, also brings other social institutions such as schools, colleges and universities within the ambit of the economy (Bowles and Gintis 1975). Where education was a social activity in the cultural sphere, it now becomes a feeder activity to the economy. *Human capital* thus becomes a pivotal keyword for the reconfiguration of society as 'a market state of economic actors' (Lynch 2006). In government discourse in Ireland, this economic functionalism is adopted enthusiastically, with economic expediency, apparently, outweighing political considerations. For example, the state's national development plan aims to speak directly to its citizens, as its subtitle – 'Towards a Better Quality of Life for All' – suggested. Yet the authors apparently see no irony in labelling the people to whom it is speaking – potentially those from whom it will seek a vote – as *human capital*. This would seem to be a striking example of ideological overkill (NDP 2007).[8]

The placing of education and knowledge within the general economy is not a new phenomenon. Education systems, as well as knowledge and science, have always been developed in parallel with the needs of capitalism. But education was deemed, from different ideological standpoints, to be relatively autonomous from the economy, with its own traditions, independent goals and styles; education 'for life itself', in Dewey's phrase. Classical liberal views took pride in the independence of the educational sphere from 'the greasy till' of commercial interest, indeed sometimes making much of placing scientific and artistic endeavour in a lofty world of its own. This view became, in practice, the justification for higher education being reserved for a cultured elite, since this kind of education was considered to provide the best background for members of the ruling class. Neoliberal ideology, in its reshaping of the society around the workings of the market, charts a different role for higher education. It is now charged with being the skills provider for an increasingly complex capitalist economy. This has involved a strong focus on learning outcomes, a euphemism for measurable skills which are needed by potential employers in the 'knowledge economy'. Perhaps never has higher education become so blatantly an outgrowth of the economy. The residues of the social value of education, of what Harvey calls 'embedded liberalism', have been stripped away and all social institutions, and most particularly education, bent to the needs of capitalist accumulation (Harvey 2005: 181). *Human capital* encapsulates, in the world of education, this capitalist homogenisation.

But if the connotations of *human capital* were simply this, its widespread adoption would be limited. The term has arisen in the context of a reinterpretation of the term *capital* as well, a compact re-sematicisation which achieves an ideological leap from the social to the individual. *Human capital* has re-emerged alongside other terms also measured as *capital,* particularly *social capital, cultural capital* and *linguistic capital. Capital* on the face of it would seem an unlikely candidate for the measurement of human qualities and skills. Capital deployed in production, in land, in finance, 'a process in which money is perpetually sent in search of more money' (Harvey 2010a: 40), has an inescapably physical, structural dimension, even if it is also a social relation. It has been argued that *social capitals* used in various texts today find their origins in Bourdieu (Fine 2002; Schuller 2000), although Bourdieu used the term in the context of the economic infrastructure and with reference to social groups and classes rather than individuals (Bourdieu 1986). In *social capital,* Bourdieu sees a resource groups can use in social relations. Some have seen the adoption of these words into management discourse as the attempt to incorporate autonomy and individual fulfilment into otherwise increasingly dull and streamlined workplaces (Boltanski and Chiapello 2007). *Human capital,* in theory, contains something of this appeal to individual self fulfilment through the acquisition of greater knowledge. But the extreme functionality of the term both limits its use and restricts its effectiveness. In objectifying and measuring human potential, the subject of human capital is obscured. Rather than personalising or bestowing individual ownership on what humans can acquire, *human capital* actually depersonalises the process, making human effort seem like just another cog in an economic wheel. These restrictions mean that the term fails to leave the arena of official reports and acquires the remote status of an official jargon, a kind of 'officialese'. Who, indeed, would describe themselves as 'human capital'? This semantic reformulation falls into the overarching scheme of things in which the market 'runs' society and in which everything, including humans, must fall in step behind. But the extension of fields from the general to the economic, as represented by *human capital,* also means that identification with the term is restricted, and its use is correspondingly confined to top-down communication.

While in a period of boom, when the potential to use human skills seems greater, the anomalies of *human capital* may remain beneath the surface: in an economic recession, however, the term evokes a new set of contradictions. Science Foundation

CAPITAL **QUALITY OUTPUT** GLOBAL REPUTATION KNOWLEDGE TRANSFER QUALITY OUTPUT GLOBAL REPUTATION KNOWLEDGE TRANSFER HUMAN CAPITAL QUALITY OUTPUT GLOBAL REPUTATION KNOWLEDGE TRANSFER KNOWLEDGE TRANSFER **HUMAN CAPITAL** QUALITY OUTPUT **GLOBAL REPUTATION** KNOWLEDGE HUMAN CAPITAL QUALITY OUTPUT GLOBAL REPUTATION HUMAN CAPITAL QUALITY OUTPUT GLOBAL REPUTATION KNOWLEDGE TRANSFER HUMAN CAPITAL QUALITY OUTPUT GLOBAL REPUTATION KNOWLEDGE TRANSFER QUALITY OUTPUT GLOBAL REPUTATION **KNOWLEDGE TRANSFER** HUMAN CAPITAL QUALITY OUTPUT KNOWLEDGE TRANSFER KNOWLEDGE TRANSFER HUMAN CAPITAL QUALITY OUTPUT GLOBAL

FIGURE 3.1   The power of neoliberal keywords: text as used to decorate the front cover of the report 'Powering the Smart Economy' (SFI 2009)

Ireland's document 'Powering the Smart Economy' (see Figure 3.1) was drawn up in 2009, before the extent of the recession in Ireland had become apparent. During a boom, the aspiration to a Smart Economy, particularly when graduates were needed in large numbers in communications industries, and the potential of *human capital* could perhaps be invoked with some credibility. Indeed placing such keywords in sequence and repetition seemed to reinforce their associative power. However, when *quality outputs, knowledge transfer* and *global reputation* continue, in changed economic circumstances, to adorn the websites of government and government agencies, the meaning of 'Powering the Smart Economy' with *human capital* becomes 'ideologically brittle', to use Williams's phrase. High levels of unemployment and negative growth rates challenge the inclusive, optimistic assumptions of a *smart economy,* especially as large swathes of *human capital* lie idle and discarded.

From this analysis, it can be seen that *human capital* as a neoliberal keyword, while superficially seeming to build on individualism, fails to speak directly to the individual. This contradiction, already latent in the over-functionalism of the term, rises to the surface more starkly in recessionary times. *Human capital*, lauded in the context of a booming economy, today as labour either leaves Irish shores or is unemployed, has lost its rhetorical force, and comes to highlight the gap between human potential and human devastation.

Keywords and ideological evaluation: entrepreneur

Entrepreneur, over the decades of neoliberalism, has been a pivotal keyword. *Entrepreneur* itself has undergone changes in meaning since it first translated into English, in the eighteenth century, as 'merchant', 'adventurer', 'employer', from the more precise French meaning of 'undertaker of a project'. An eighteenth-century Irish-French economist Richard Cantillon, known in his lifetime as 'the Irish Banker', is credited with having popularised the meaning of *entrepreneur* as risk-taker in his *An Essay on Economic Theory* (McNally 2010; Murphy 1986: 60). It became something of a defining term within the different strands of neoclassical political economy: Joseph Schumpeter defined *entrepreneurs* as prime movers of the economy and Friedrich Hayek, often claimed as the founding father of neoliberalism, rated individual *entrepreneurs* as the drivers of the market process (Kuper and Kuper 2004). During the neoliberal era, it became the omnipresent tag which symbolised risk-taking, innovation and accumulating wealth.

Prestigious *entrepreneur* competitions, sponsored by global corporations, proliferated into unexpected domains: nursing, technological invention, protection of the environment and 'smarter planet' strategies, and philanthropy, proving again how the economic/business semantic field had now become the point of reference for so many others. One of the most famous global awards was the Ernst & Young 'Entrepreneur of the Year®' – the patent indicative of the significant corporate sponsorship it attracted. Its website defined *entrepreneurship* in direct, self-seeking terms, as 'the pursuit of opportunity beyond the resources you currently control'. The award would enable entrepreneurs to 'be encouraged and nurtured – led out – through recognition, through leadership, networking and education, broadly defined' (Ernst & Young 2006). The Ernst & Young Entrepreneur of the Year awards, in Ireland, have a quasi-official status, with the current Minister for Finance usually in attendance, as guest of honour. Speeches made at these events figure prominently on the website of the (renamed) Department of Enterprise, Trade and Innovation. Minister Micheál Martin at the 2006 Entrepreneur Awards, for example, stressed 'the positive culture, which celebrates and recognises the achievement of our entrepreneurs' (DETI 2006). The Irish *Business and Finance* magazine has a similar annual award for the 'achievements and enterprising spirit of business across Ireland'. The awards, *Business and Finance* reports, are 'the longest running and the most coveted in Ireland' and are sponsored and judged by 'the most innovative and creative entrepreneurs in the country' (*Business and Finance* 2007). In 2002 the then chief executive of the Anglo Irish Bank, Sean Fitzpatrick, won this prestigious award (Ross 2009: 62).

Universities, in similar vein, were exhorted to become *entrepreneurial*. Irish universities were to see themselves as 'economic actors' in a global market (Lynch 2006). Universities were now in competition with each other, locally and globally, both in the selling of their undergraduate and postgraduate places and in accessing funding, whose totals, when secured, proudly adorned faculty and department websites. Research itself became *entrepreneurially* orientated, with its commercial potential now seen as highly desirable. Dublin City University's *Commercialisation Handbook*, which proclaimed to its researchers the need 'to transform knowledge into commercial success', 'for personal gain and revenue generation', was doing no more than hundreds of other universities across the Western world (DCU 2004; Holborow 2006). In retrospect, what was surprising was that academics, normally dismissive of uniformity of expression, accepted so readily the blanket rewriting of academic endeavour as entrepreneurial activity, including its assessment in terms of the amount of revenue it could attract. Effectively, as Mautner notes, the *entrepreneurial university* became the 'buzzword' in higher education and variations of it were reproduced across a wide range of academic settings (Mautner 2005).

Entrepreneurial universities were prioritised for two reasons: their facilities were needed for research with commercial applications and they were to be the showcase for the transformation of the public sector (Allen 2007: 133–59). It is no exaggeration to say that universities became *de facto* the privileged communication channels of neoliberalism. They coined a new set of keywords around *academic entrepreneurship* which marked the ever-closer business/academic overlap, now proclaimed to represent the future of university education. Academic capitalism had apparently arrived, just when public funding seemed less secure (Slaughter and Leslie 1997; see also Evans 2004; Harman 2003; Holborow 2007; Vally 2007). In Ireland, this development seemed, at first, to be following North American practice; however, after the passing of the Lisbon Treaty, it became the European Union which championed the neoliberal framework for higher education. In particular, the EU's Bologna process, alongside the emphasis on quantifiable skills and learning as outcomes, began also to focus on entrepreneurial activities, on intellectual property rights and universities as incubators for commercial patents. My own university, Dublin City University (DCU), on its webpage assumed, in 2011, the title of *Ireland's 'University of Enterprise'*. It announced, in a rather shrill example of neoliberal-speak, its own Enterprise Advisory Board whose mission was to enhance DCU's ability to deliver on 'optimising industry-academic synergistic relationships' and to identify 'emerging enterprise trends and/or "grand challenges", which would inform DCU's research agenda and thereby maintain it at the cutting edge internationally'. All universities were taking the same tack: former bastions of classical European liberalism were also adopting the view that in Europe now 'knowledge is produced and then traded' (Keeling 2006: 209). Phillipson's account of European higher education, now seeing itself as in direct competition with North America for students, for funding, for economic advantage and for global marketable English, reiterates the same point (Phillipson 2003: 85, 2008b, 2009a). The extent to which academics spontaneously, away from the limelight of PR, identify themselves as *entrepreneurs*, however, remains open to question. One study found that public and private stances on this differed quite considerably, with many academics feeling uncomfortable in the new regime (Deem and Brehony 2005). It may well be that there is a certain disparity between official prescriptions and individual academic practice and styles. *Entrepreneur* in the higher education domain, when it first appeared, remained confined to the official *glibspeak* of the institution (Hasan 2003). It was a keyword used by management rather than academics themselves, an indication, perhaps, that neoliberal marketisation might not have quite gained the internalised consent that its dominance in official channels would imply.

After the crash of 2008, and the deep recession which followed, *entrepreneurship* experienced in Ireland something of a bumpy ride. Ernst & Young now began to define their Entrepreneur of the Year with a different emphasis. For their 2009 award, *entrepreneurs* needed to become not 'masters of success' but 'navigators' of unknown depths. Risk-taking, rather than economic success, is now the entrepreneurial hallmark, translating, in Ernst & Young speak, into 'a blue ocean of unexplored value-enriched opportunity … away from the eye of conventional market thinking'. Post-crash, *social entrepreneurship* has been added to the entrepreneurial mix, with an *entrepreneur* expanding to include 'applying practical, innovative and market-oriented approaches to benefit the marginalised and the poor'. The newly coined *social entrepreneur* is defined as 'one who has created and leads an organization, whether for-profit or not, that is aimed at catalyzing large scale and systemic social change through the introduction of new ideas, methodologies and changes in attitude' (Ernst & Young 2010). *Entrepreneur,* now no longer solely linked to economic success, re-semanticises into new and unexpected fields, including social work and personal development.

It is in the post-crash perceptions of Irish bankers that esteem for the entrepreneurial spirit has sunk the lowest. The names of formerly feted *entrepreneurs* such as Sean Fitzpatrick, Head of the Anglo Irish Bank, now disgraced and bankrupt, have been removed from Entrepreneur of the Year webpages. Books which dealt with the Irish banking crisis, and which became overnight bestsellers, carrying front covers which cried out against the *banksters* and *zombie profligates,* marked a sharp reversal in public opinion. The entrepreneurial heroes of the boom became renamed as *chancers* abetted by *buffoons,* referring to the former Financial Regulator, the Minister for Finance and the Taoiseach himself (Murphy and Devlin 2009). Murphy and Devlin's use of *banksters,* the merging of banker and gangster, as the title of their book, reinvented a term which had first been used for the American speculators who had brought about the Crash of 1929. *Zombie,* too, had been used previously, to describe, in the 1990s, the insolvent state of Japanese financial institutions, deemed too big to fail but too full of toxic debts to provide credit. The *Irish Times,* not usually given to sensationalism, liberally used the term. From October 2008 to February 2009, the *Irish Times* used *zombie* to describe the six Irish main lending banks, the banking industry, companies, the Anglo Irish Bank, and even the government itself. Another daily, the *Irish Independent,* with a larger circulation and usually considered to be the voice of the business community, similarly joined in the chorus against Ireland's fallen entrepreneurs. On 30 March 2010, it carried the headline, 'the rise and fall of fearless entrepreneur Quinn', which documented the fall of another Anglo Irish investor, Sean Quinn, owner of the most profitable company in Ireland, now mired in fraud and illegal off-loading of worthless bank shares. It also pointed out that his banking misdemeanors were being lavishly supported by the public purse.[9] But public bitterness about the banks' malpractices, their refusal to disclose the extent of their toxic debts and the sheer waste of huge sums of money was best summed up by the monthly periodical, *Village.* The cover of February–March 2009 carried a close-up picture of rats running among rubbish, with the headline 'The Celtic Rats: dealing with the rats that killed the Tiger' and with mention in smaller print of articles covering 'explosive corruption allegations' against wealthy magnates of the boom including the former Finance Minister, Charlie McCreevy. The editorial spoke of Ireland's 'predatory' and 'aggressive' economic policy, backed by 'seductive grants', which needed to be dealt with. 'Now was the time to bring back the common good'. Ireland's esteemed *entrepreneurs* had become Celtic Rats and the *Village's* outspokenness deftly expressed the spectacular image reversal of Ireland's business community.

Even as economic crisis becomes the new normality, the significance of the ideological about-turn that the negative evaluation of all things to do with the banks and their entrepreneurial exuberance represents should not be lost. Its arrival after 30 decades of the hegemonic discourse of neoliberalism marks an interlude, however tentative, in the fortunes of the dominant model and, in the absence of a convincing replacement, has created something of an ideological vacuum.

Conclusion

If we understand neoliberal ideology as being promoted by certain sections of the capitalist class in order to both justify its role in society and also address the flaws in the system (Harman 2007), the keywords analysis here has uncovered some of the anomalies and limits of the ideological project. Promotion of the market as the prime mover of society, while seeming superficially to be true, attempts to mask the social relations behind the workings of the capitalist market. The result is a contradictory and partial ideological construction whose ideological keywords, this analysis has shown, encapsulate these contradictions and tensions. Keywords, while seeming superficially to cement ideological meaning in language, when examined in their contexts and their actual use, emerge as rather faltering ideological representations. *Deregulate* is not in fact about the state stepping back, *human capital* does not have the appeal to individual potential that it claims, and *entrepreneurship* hinges less on individual skills than the booms and slumps of capitalism. The analysis highlights how specific lexical items can be ideologically dense but also represent the bundling together of irreconcilable meanings, wherein lies the potential for ideological contestation.

In the years when neoliberal ideology coincided with a boom, it was easy to assume that neoliberal common sense had 'colonised' civil society and that its influence was unstoppable. Interpretations which focused on neoliberal hegemony *ultra,* on neoliberal ideology entrapped in discursive structures and the 'strong discourse' of neoliberalism, reflected something of this fatalism. They tended to underestimate the unevenness and heterogeneity of ideology and the fact that elements of even a dominant ideology exist alongside other contradictory elements. Neoliberal ideology, regarding the market, the state, choice and the individual, represents a cluster of contradictory notions that may prevent the 'strong' version of the ideology achieving hegemony and popular consensus. In times of economic recession and spiralling crisis, the flaws of the ideology surface, especially when the contradictions of its core values are so publicly prised open. Institutions and governments, having believed zealously in the unfettered market, after the crisis of 2008, changed their official policy and embraced the greatest wave of nationalisations that our modern world has seen. The Irish state and its ruling elite, riding highest on the crest of neoliberalism, enacted more dramatically this ideological reversal. Their huge commitment of the equivalent of three times Ireland's GNP to prop up six Irish banks and then the injection of further vast sums of state money to bail out the banks' bad debts could not but crack open the fault lines of Irish neoliberalism.

Our analysis of neoliberal keywords has pointed to some of the signs of this ideological turmoil, whose origins lie in the lived experience of capitalist society and real-world events which lay bare, however fleetingly, the inconsistencies of the ideology.

   Ideological crisis however does not automatically lead to ideological reversal. The economic crisis represents, to employ a Gramscian term, a historical conjuncture in which ideological battles become sharper and more polarised. The reworking of neoliberal ideology – as we have seen with the re-semanticisation in economic crisis of *entrepreneur* – is an attempt to restore market ideology to its dominant position, to reassert its hegemony in changed circumstances. In Ireland, that process is already under way and, given the extent and social dislocation of the crisis, the neoliberal template is being summoned again, with even greater determination. Some of the ideological conflict revolves around which keywords gain consensus, which is why discussions of the meanings of neoliberal ideology can have political significance. How successful the demystifying and remaking of neoliberal ideology is, however, depends on larger social forces – whether the capitalist crisis can recover, the duration and effects of the recession and whether credible alternatives to neoliberalism become available.

4

ECONOMISING GLOBALISATION AND IDENTITY IN APPLIED LINGUISTICS IN NEOLIBERAL TIMES

DAVID BLOCK

Introduction

In February 2009, by which time there was good reason to believe that there was a worldwide economic recession, a group of workers picketed outside the Lindsey oil refinery in north-eastern England. The workers, all British nationals, were protesting against the employment of several hundred Italian and Portuguese workers in an area of high unemployment. The oil refinery in question was owned by Total, an American oil company, which had employed Jacobs, an American engineering company, which then subcontracted to an Italian firm, IREM, which then found it more economical to employ its own labour force, consisting of Italian and Portuguese workers. The latter were EU (European Union) nationals and therefore entitled to work in the UK according to legislation related to the Maastricht Treaty of 1993, which guarantees the free movement of people, goods, services and capital across the geographical borders of EU member states. Thus Total, the company ultimately being protested against, was acting within EU law when it subcontracted to companies that further subcontracted and eventually employed Italian and Portuguese workers and not British workers. In the midst of these protests, the then British Prime Minster Gordon Brown was reminded of a declaration he had made in June 2007 – 'British jobs for British workers' – whilst championing, as he always had, neoliberal economic policies which allow, and even encourage, the kinds of activities which Total was engaging in.

Nevertheless, upon critical examination, we may see this state of affairs as problematic, not for the reasons that the picketing workers might adduce; nor even for anything that Gordon Brown might have said during his three years as Prime Minister. Rather, the issue is that the particular jobs in contention did not really constitute 'British jobs'. I say this for the simple reason that, despite their physical location on British soil, they were not and had never been, strictly speaking, 'British jobs'. They were Total jobs, and therefore the kind of jobs which have no geographic territoriality, existing as they did against the backdrop of apparently footloose capitalism in the globalised economy. And as if to make this point more empathically, the Italian and Portuguese workers in question did not actually live on British soil; rather, they lived on a ship which remained docked a short distance off-shore.

The story ran in the British press for a period of time, with different parties picking it up and presenting it according to disparate interests, often with self-contradictory results. For example, some took the side of the British workers against 'Johnny foreigner' and thus infused the debate with a dose of xenophobia. Add to this that most of the media in Britain are anti-EU and we have yet another example of British sovereignty being trampled on: 'Everything is legal by European law and we can't do a thing about it!' But what is evident in such arguments is that, while nationalism and a dose of xenophobia are brought in to trump working-class as an identity inscription, the same media protesting about foreigners and the EU have generally shown themselves to be enthusiastic supporters of the kind of neoliberal economic policies that have disregarded local workers' rights and made possible the kind of deterritorialised employment central to the Lindsey oil refinery affair.

In other media circles, such as the so-called 'liberal' press, there were portrayals of the picketing workers as a group of xenophobes who were showing their tribal, nationalistic and even racist impulses. Though different from the previously cited versions of events, these portrayals once again showed a tendency to frame the issue as anything but a protest against the dictates and consequences of neoliberal policies and practices by working-class people.

Meanwhile, on the ground, the views expressed by the protesters themselves varied. To be sure, there were some very blatant declarations that can only be termed xenophobic and racist. However, a stronger current among the protesters was to see the issue in more universal terms, as a problem with neoliberalism as the dominant economic ideology in the world today. This view, reasonable as it was, was not given much publicity by the press, long since resigned to the adage that there is no alternative to neoliberalism (see Chapter 2).

This story, one of neoliberalism and its effects, led me to think about two constructs essential in my own and other applied linguists' work. On the one hand, there is globalisation: the world today is immersed in a multitude of globalising processes in which it is becoming ever more, and ever more intensively, interconnected. And although these global processes are to a great extent about the movement of people, culture and flows of ideas and information, they are also, at root, economic in nature. On the other hand, there is identity: who we are in a range of contexts in an increasingly globalised world. And although who we are is to a great extent about what Nancy Fraser (2003) calls 'recognition' (recognition in terms of gender, ethnicity, race and so on), it is also linked to stratification and where we stand in social, political and, importantly, the economic orders in which we operate. In this chapter, my aim is to think aloud about these two key terms – globalisation and identity – and to do so in a way that is critical of general understandings of them in applied linguistics. I begin with the idea of a globalisation, focusing on what is meant by the term and how cultural globalisation has been the most common way to view the phenomenon in applied linguistics. I then move to consider more economically grounded views of globalisation – views which are critical of the dominant neoliberal ideology – before working my way towards a consideration of class as the identity inscription too often marginalised in applied linguistics research. I end with some thoughts on future directions for identity-based research in applied linguistics in the light of what I have written.

Globalisation

In discussions of globalisation over the years (e.g. Albrow 1996; Giddens 2000; Held *et al.* 1999; Ritzer 2007a, 2010; Sassen 2007; Scholte 2000), the phenomenon is generally conceptualised as an ongoing and ever-evolving process, as opposed to a point in history which has definitively been reached. This process involves the increasingly extended and intensified interconnectedness of economic, political, social and cultural phenomena, seen in human activity taking place across time and space related scales. On the one hand, there is an emphasis on how in the world today time has become compressed, such that, for example, activities and processes which previously took long periods to carry out and unfold now occur much more quickly, often in a fraction of a second (Castells 1996; Giddens 2000; Harvey 1989). On the other hand, spatial scales, ranging from the household up to the global, are today interrelated to a degree that is unprecedented in history. Thus, what happens on a global scale both shapes and is shaped by what happens at more local levels and this recursive shaping can occur within very small timescales (Held *et al.* 1999). In addition, there is a sense that the globalising world is dynamic, or in the words of Arjun Appadurai (1990, 1996), it is a 'complex, overlapping and disjunctive order' made up of different but interrelated forces and flows. Appadurai famously has termed these forces and flows 'scapes', which he puts into five categories: (1) ethnoscapes or flows of people (e.g. migrants, asylum seekers, exiles, tourists); (2) technoscapes or flows of technology (e.g. hardware components, technical know-how); (3) financescapes or flows of money (e.g. national stock exchanges, commodity speculations); (4) mediascapes or flows of information (e.g. newspapers, magazines, satellite television channels, websites); and (5) ideoscapes or flows of ideas (e.g. human rights, environmentalism, free trade movements, fear of terrorism). While none of these scapes can be viewed in isolation, given that they occur simultaneously as overlapping processes, globalisation theorists often foreground one scape over the other. Thus, migration theorists would tend to prioritise ethnoscapes, even if they link these to the other scapes, in particular financescapes (e.g. Castles and Miller 2009).

Amidst the myriad forces and flows of globalisation, there has been a good deal of discussion about whether or not, or to what extent, globalisation means greater homogenisation of the world, in terms of economic, political, social and cultural phenomena, or greater diversity and heterogenisation of these phenomena. In the midst of such discussions, there has emerged an interest in notions taken from postcolonial literature, such as hybridity (Bhabha 1994). Hybridity has moved beyond its roots in agriculture and animal breeding, where it signified the mixing of two sources leading to a 50-50 mix, to its current use among social theorists to refer to varieties of mixing. This mixing emerges in different areas of life, including human contact (inter-ethnic/racial/national relationships), leisure activities (e.g. music, the visual arts, fashion, literature and cuisine), social institutions (e.g. religious fusions, new academic disciplines), the world of work (e.g. private public financial initiatives, mixed management styles in industry), government institutions (traditional governments interacting with ONGs and lobbies), and so on (Nederveen Pieterse 2009). Hybridity thus becomes a master construct for understanding a great deal of social and cultural activity in the world today. For Nederveen Pieterse, the processual form of the word – hybridisation – is ideal for understanding the times in which we live, serving as an antidote to essentialisms, such as those related to nationalism and ethnicity. He explains:

> Hybridisation is an antidote to the cultural differentialism of racial and nationalist doctrines because it takes as its point of departure precisely these experiences that have been banished, marginalised, tabooed in cultural differentialism. It subverts nationalism because it privileges border crossing. It subverts identity politics such as ethnic or other claims to purity and authenticity because it starts out from fuzziness of boundaries. If modernity stands for an ethos of order and neat separation by tight boundaries, hybridisation reflects a postmodern sensibility of cut'n'mix, transgression, subversion.
>
> (Nederveen Pieterse 2009: 55)

However, not everyone would agree that hybridity is always an appropriate and useful term (e.g. Kalra *et al.* 2005), given that its use is too often accompanied by a certain wide-eyed romantic fascination with what otherwise might be seen simply as the diversification that necessarily comes with the day-to-day evolution of a range of social and cultural phenomena and activities. Thus, it may be best to frame discussions of social and cultural forms in the global age in terms of ever-increasing diversification rather than hybridity. Nevertheless, discussing the state of world in terms of diversity as opposed to hybridity is not, in and of itself, a solution to the romantic fascination problem. Indeed, with so much talk about 'super-diversity' (Vertovec 2009) and the increasing number of researchers who are beginning to use it as a central organising construct in their work, it would seem that, at least to some extent, wide-eyed romantic fascination has a guaranteed future.

In addition, because increasing social and cultural diversification emerges at the crossroads of global and local phenomena, there has been a great deal of interest in another term meant to capture the idea of mixing, *glocalisation*. In the social sciences, glocalisation is associated with the cultural theorist Roland Robertson and it is used to capture the idea that the global does not merely overwhelm or swallow the local; rather, syntheses emerge from contacts between the global and the local. In fact, glocalisation did not originate in the social sciences; rather, it was taken from the world of business in Japan, where it means marketing goods and services on a global basis by catering to local particularities. Robertson reinvents the term for the contexts which interest him – cultures in contact – and uses it to signify what he calls the 'interpenetrating' of the 'particular' and the 'universal' (Robertson 1995: 30). Importantly, glocalisation entails a synergetic relationship between the global and the local as opposed to the dominance of the former over the latter and the homogenisation which would result from such dominance. As Giulianotti and Robertson (2007) put it,

> Theorists of glocalisation typically challenge the assumption that globalisation processes always endanger the local. Rather, glocalisation both highlights how local cultures may critically adapt or resist 'global' phenomena, and reveals the way in which the very creation of localities is a standard component of globalization. There is now a universal normalization of 'locality', in the sense that 'local' cultures are assumed to arise constantly and particularize themselves vis-a-vis other specific cultures ... The related concept of 'relativization' helps to detail the increasingly reflexive contrasts that arise between 'local' cultures, bringing these entities into sharper comparative focus and forcing them to respond to each other in an ever-amplifying manner. The 'glocalization projects' of these local cultures are characterized by intensified differentiation in terms of meaning and identity ... as well as in the increasing significance of quotidian comparison among socio-cultural units.
>
> (Giulianotti and Robertson 2007: 134)

Notwithstanding the status of glocalisation as a corrective to oversimplified notions of the global swallowing up or over-running the local, it is probably a good idea not to lose sight of the concept's roots in the business world. In this quotation, I detect a kind of residual business culture along with a dose of instrumental individualisation. Thus, there is a market of local cultures in competition being described – '"local" cultures are assumed to arise constantly and particularise themselves vis-a-vis other specific cultures' – as well as the very instrumental and individualistic sounding 'glocalisation projects', which involve 'intensified differentiation in terms of meaning and identity'. In addition, it seems that those who embrace glocalisation have a tendency to stack the odds too much in favour of the local. Indeed, it has become almost canonical to eulogise the authenticity of the local in contrast to the illegitimacy of the global. This stance often seems to be more one of wishful thinking, based on an idealisation of the indigenous acting against outside forces which threaten to destroy it. And who is not against this happening? However, just because we desire resistance to certain globalising forces does not mean that we must see as *fact* that the local shapes the global more than the global shapes the local. Thus, glocalisation, itself originally formulated as a way of balancing views of the relative influence of the global and the local, by now needs to undergo a process whereby the two poles which constitute it are recalibrated and rebalanced.

Globalisation and applied linguistics

In applied linguistics, researchers have drawn heavily on the ideas described above. Thus there has been a great deal of interest in what Giddens (2000) has termed the 'runaway world' of late modernity, a world of time and space compressions. There is also an affinity to the dynamism of Appadurai's scapes, with the most attention going to ethnoscapes, the flows of people around the world, and mediascapes, in particular the internet and flows of music and other cultural forms. There is a great deal of interest in – and often celebration of – the ever more diverse and complex social and cultural forms which emerge as result of global processes. And finally, the importance of the local and the glocal in globalisation processes is generally emphasised. All of this has meant that what has emerged in applied linguistics is a view of globalisation which is almost exclusively about culture. This development is no doubt due to the importance of culture in the foundations of what has become over the years an interdisciplinary field of academic enquiry (see Chapter 1). Yet, it is a partial view of globalisation, as it relegates political economy to a brief mention or even no mention at all. It has led to a certain fascination with – and often a celebration of – notions associated with postmodernism, such as diaspora, interstices, heterogeneity, translation, flexibility, intertextuality, hybridity, fluidity, fragmentation, instability, liquidity, turbulence and so on. However, it has served to marginalise the more material aspects of our existence, which from a Marxist perspective of base and superstructure, are foundational to culture.[1]

For example, in his ground-breaking book examining the global spread of English via the global spread of hip-hop, Alistair Pennycook (2007) begins his discussion of globalisation with a brief coverage of the economics-based view of the phenomenon. Pennycook makes mention of the policies associated with neoliberalism – 'cuts in government spending, privatisation of public institutions, removal of subsidies and the opening up of the economy to transnational corporations' (p. 24) – which he calls 'corporatization'. However, he very quickly shifts from this discussion of the global spread of free-market fundamentalism, to his preferred view that 'globalization is not only about economic processes, but political, technological and cultural processes as well' (Pennycook 2007: 24). And it is these political, technological and cultural processes which become the prisms through which he elaborates a fascinating and detailed analysis of hip-hop around the world as dynamic, diverse and glocalised.

Elsewhere, Angel Lin (2008a) closes her edited volume, *Problematising Identity: Struggles in Language, Culture, and Education*, with a discussion of the current era of globalisation. Similar to Pennycook, she makes clear her post-structuralist and social constructivist foundations. Thus after rejecting modernity-linked 'master narratives' outright, she cites Appadurai's dynamic model of globalisation (see above). She makes the point that the two most distinctive features of globalisation today are migration and the ever more sophisticated technological mediation of our day-to-day activities, such that we are moving as never before whilst living deterritorialised lives around a wide array of electronically mediated virtual realities. Lin does add to this portrayal of twenty-first-century life a paragraph about how 'global capitalism has made electronic mass media a powerful tool of shaping people's imagination of possible lives and possible identities' (Lin 2008a: 210). However, there is no sustained discussion of globalisation as an economic phenomenon driven by neoliberal ideology.

In briefly and only very partially touching on Pennycook and Lin's work, I by no means wish to single them out as uniquely culturalist in their approach to globalisation. Rather, I would say that their views on globalisation are to be found across a range of publications appearing over the past 20 years. Indeed, I have myself adopted a culturalist view of globalisation in previous publications, most notably in *Multilingual Identities in a Global City: London Stories* (Block 2006). I begin that book by making the case that the study of globalisation is multidimensional, citing models such as Appadurai's five scapes. This is followed by a self-positioning statement: 'while all the different aspects of globalisation are important, it is the processes and flows of people around the world, that is migration, which is the key area of focus' (Block 2006: 6). I then proceed, in subsequent chapters, to discuss the stories of migrants in London in terms of time and space compression and ever more diverse and complex social forms. An economics-based model of globalisation never really appears.

There is surely nothing wrong with taking a culturalist or culture-centred approach to globalisation in one's work. Indeed, how can one discuss the spread of hip-hop around the world, or problematise identity, or discuss the lives of migrants in a global city, or investigate any number of other issues falling under the general heading of applied linguistics, without bringing culture into the discussion? However, the point I wish to make here is one put forward by Paul Bruthiaux (2008), who sees this near exclusive fixation on cultural globalisation as a problem if applied linguists see themselves as having an impact on the growing inequality in today's globalised world. As he explains:

> the reluctance of many applied linguists to consider the economic dimension of globalization and the tendency for discussions of that dimension to be cursory and one-sided severely limit the contribution the field might make to key contemporary debate. ... In the end, it undermines the credibility of applied linguists and makes it unlikely they will play a significant role in solving the social injustices they so rightly deplore.
>
> (Bruthiaux 2008: 20)

Of course, there are exceptions to this general trend as authors such as Razool (2007), Phillipson (2009) and Heller (2011) include in their analytical frameworks references to current economics-informed views of globalisation. However, this work ultimateely shifts to an emphasis on language and identity, which restores the dominance of culture over economics.

Apart from these culture-centric takes on globalisation, I also detect in applied linguistics publications a general assumption that the times in which we live are unique. In short, there is the message – sometimes implicit, sometimes explicit – that we are living in an era like no other in the history of humanity. Thus, while it might be accepted and even argued that globalisation existed five centuries ago, the view is that due to advanced technologies and the accumulated knowledge bases that exist today, the globalisation of decades and centuries in the past was nothing like the current one. Such a position is notably presentist in outlook, to say nothing of being ahistorical, and in order to contest it, applied linguists need to take not only economics seriously when discussing globalisation, but also history. Were they to do so, many who currently claim to be doing 'critical' work would be in a better position to argue that their work is indeed 'critical'. Their work would not just be respectful of diversity (important, as I will argue below) and even 'cool', but oppositional to the current neoliberal order of things and resistant to the processes which constitute this order. In the next section, I examine more economic and historically informed approaches to globalisation.

A more economically/historically grounded view of globalisation

Despite seemingly convincing arguments around notions such as interconnectedness, time-space compression and scapes, there are (and always have been) social scientists with serious reservations about the extent to which we are living in an era like no other in the history of the world. In addition, they retain a healthy scepticism about literature on globalisation which devotes little attention to the struggles related to global capitalism and ideas that shape collective and individual actions in the world today. These voices accept that societies and the world in general are changing at a fast pace and that we live in a world of ever greater human and cultural diversity, but they frame current events in very different ways, for example, in terms of the continued global spread of capitalism, albeit by more sophisticated and technologically advanced means. Proponents of this more economically grounded view (e.g. Arrighi 2010; Harvey 2006; Hirst and Thompson 2009; Smith 1997; Wallerstein 2004) tend to stress economic issues in their discussions, often adopting Marxist or neo-Marxist analytical frameworks, as they argue that the current stage in history is still closely linked to the modern era and that international capitalism, the nation state and national cultures are still very much intact. After all, Marx and Engels actually did provide a both thorough and prescient definition of globalisation in the *Communist Manifesto*:

> The bourgeoisie has through its exploitation of the world market given a cosmopolitan character to production and consumption in every country. … it has drawn from under the feet of industry the national ground on which it stood. All old-established national industries have been destroyed or are daily being destroyed. They are dislodged by new industries, whose introduction becomes a life and death question for all civilised nations, by industries that no longer work up indigenous raw material, but raw material drawn from the remotest zones; industries whose products are consumed, not only at home, but in every quarter of the globe. In place of the old wants, satisfied by the production of the country, we find new wants, requiring for their satisfaction the products of distant lands and climes. In place of the old local and national seclusion and self-sufficiency, we have intercourse in every direction, universal inter-dependence of nations.
>
> (Marx and Engels 1967: 83–4)

This view of globalisation and indeed Marxism as a general analytical frame have certainly been foundational to the work of scholars like Immanuel Wallerstein and Giovanni Arrrighi in their development of world systems analysis (WSA) over the past five decades. Wallerstein has consciously avoided using the term 'globalisation'; indeed, he has been very dismissive of it, as the following glossary entry from one of his books shows:

> This term was invented in the 1980s. It is usually thought to refer to a reconfiguration of the world-economy that has only recently come into existence, in which pressures on all governments to open their frontiers to the free movement of goods and capital is unusually strong. This is the result, it is argued, of technological advances, especially in the field of informatics. The term is as much a prescription as a description. For world systems analysts, what is described as something new (relatively open frontiers) has in fact been a cyclical occurrence throughout the history of the modern world system.
>
> (Wallerstein 2004: 9)

Wallerstein's negative take on globalisation must be understood in the broader context of his WSA, which takes a long-term look at the history and development of the modern world, contemplating centuries, epochs and cycles rather than limiting itself to timeframes defined in decades or years. Wallerstein draws heavily on the earlier work of Fernand Braudel (1972), a member of the famous French *Annales* school of 'total history', who believed that history must be studied in terms of geography, climatology, religion, navigation, literature and other areas of academic inquiry and thought. This interdisciplinary approach was accompanied by an important reconceptualisation of time in the study of history, whereby for Braudel and his associates, a history confined to events or episodes would inevitably miss what is necessary to any well-developed explanation of social phenomena, that is, a consideration of how events are episodes embedded in longer term processes and trends spanning the past, present and future. Braudel's key construct was the *longue durée* – the long term. Taking Braudel's ideas forward, Wallerstein suggests that, in addition to focusing on events (wars, assassinations, natural disasters, stock market collapses) as the main components of history, historians (and indeed all social scientists) need to a focus on 'structural time' – that is, the basic formations and principles underlying long-term historical developments – which unfolds in frames generally spanning several decades or even centuries. In addition, there is a need to focus on cyclical processes, or shorter term trends, such as economic cycles (the post-Second World War economic boom in the developed capitalist states which began to come apart with the first global oil crisis of 1973) or political cycles (the spread of Soviet-style communism in the post-Second World War era, which began to unravel from the late 1980s onwards) or cultural cycles (e.g. the rise of global online communication networks from the mid-1990s to the present). Bringing these views into the realm of sociolinguistics, Jan Blommaert makes the following observation:

> We have a tendency to perceive only what manifests itself synchronically, but this synchronicity hides the fact that features operate on different levels and scales, have different origins, offer different opportunities and generate different effects. Synchronicity, in other words, combines elements that are of a different order, but tends to obscure these fundamental differences.
>
> (Blommaert 2005: 128–9)

The heavily historical approach to globalisation, suggested by Braudel, Wallerstein, Arrighi, Blommaert and others, is a useful antidote to such synchronic biases, or 'presentist' thinking, which, as I argued above, seem to underlie much current research on social phenomena under the general heading of globalisation. The latter work foregrounds the here-and-now and postmodern concepts like those cited in the previous section, or those beginning with the prefixes 'de' and 'trans': on the one hand, decentring, destabilisation, deterritorialisation and so on; on the other hand, transnationalism, transculturalism, transtextuality, translation and so on (see Chapter 2).

For world systems analysts, nation states and societies are important; however, the basic unit of analysis is the capitalist world-economy, in which nation states and societies reside. This world capitalist system is 'a large geographic zone within which there is a division of labor and hence significant internal exchange of basic goods as well as flows of capital and labor' (Wallerstein 2004: 23). It is a stratified system, framed in terms of the core and periphery status of production processes around the world. The interconnected centres of economic power and dynamism – Western Europe, North America, and more recently, East Asia – are most associated with the core, while the poorer nation states of the world, for example, most of Africa and much of Central and South America, are identified as periphery. As Wallerstein explains:

> What we mean by core-periphery is the degree of profitability of the production processes. Since profitability is directly related to the degree of monopolisation, what we essentially mean by core-like production processes is those that are controlled by quasi-monopolies. Peripheral processes then are those that are truly competitive. When exchange occurs, competitive products are in a weak position and quasi-monopolized products are in a strong position. As a result, there is a constant flow of surplus value from the producers of peripheral products to the producers of core-like products. This has been called unequal exchange.
>
> (Wallerstein 2004: 28)

Given its interdisciplinary roots in Braudel's original thinking and the resulting complexity which goes with such intersdisciplinarity, WSA, not surprisingly, has attracted a fair amount of criticism over the years. Brenner (1977), for example, dissects WSA, aligning it with Adam Smith's notion that the rise of capitalism derived from the development of a world market and the division of labour. A stricter Marxist interpretation would see capitalism arising in the evolving relations of economic actors – the capitalist class and working class – to property and the means of production. In addition, the aforementioned core and periphery processes have been seen by some as entirely too rigid, indeed as static and reified, which led Giddens (1985: 167; cited in Lee 2010: 8) to describe WSA as 'an uncomfortable amalgam of functionalism and economic reductionism'. There has also been an ongoing critique of WSA as overly Eurocentric, and as unable to keep up with recent developments such as the rise of China as a key economic force. Finally, the issue of culture often arises in critiques of WSA, generally as the accusation that Wallerstein's world-view, too big and too 'economist', cannot engage with cultural phenomena and therefore the daily practices of individuals and collectives on the ground. Space does not allow a thorough discussion of these issues, although it is worth noting that in more recent work over the past two decades, Wallerstein and his associates have taken on the latter three (see Arrighi 2007; Wallerstein 2004). There is, therefore, more explicit engagement with cultural issues, an explicit rejection of Eurocentricism and the inclusion of the recent changes in world economic order in WSA-inspired analyses. As for the fourth critique, which focuses on the macro and economist nature of WSA, I would say two things: first, that WSA is simply about such matters, that is, it is unapologetically about economics and it takes a macro perspective; and second, that because of this clear macro and economic perspective, it serves as a useful antidote to some of the overly culturalist and overly localist thinking which I discussed above.

Arrighi (2010) notes how this world state system of core and periphery emerged over centuries via the cyclical ups and downs of capitalism. There was first of all capitalism as relatively localised sets of practices in the north Italian city-states in the fifteenth–sixteenth centuries. However, there then ensued what Arrighi calls 'three hegemonies of historical capitalism': the Dutch in the seventeenth century, the British in the eighteenth–nineteenth centuries and the USA in the twentieth century. He explains his concept of 'world hegemony', and what each distinguishable hegemony meant, as follows:

> The concept of 'world hegemony' adopted here … refers specifically to the power of the state to exercise functions of leadership and governance over a system of sovereign states. In principle, this power may involve just the ordinary management of such a system as instituted at a given time. Historically, however, the government of a system of sovereign states has always involved some kind of transformative action, which changed the mode of operation of the system in a fundamental way.
>
> (Arrighi 2010: 28)

Here Arrighi draws on the work of Antonio Gramsci (1971: 57–8) who conceived hegemony as operative at the nation-state level, via two routes: 'domination', the threat or actual use of physical force, what Machiavelli would have called 'coercion'; and 'intellectual and moral leadership', the seduction or winning over of potentially antagonistic groups, what Machiavelli would have called 'consent'. However, Arrighi reconfigures Gramsci's distinction such that domination refers to coercion while hegemony refers to consent. And consent is further understood in terms of whether or not the leadership exercised by one nation-state is recognised and received as being in the interest of a group of nation-states at a given point in history. As Arrighi puts it, '[a] dominant state exercises a hegemonic function if it leads the *system* of states in a desired direction and, in doing so, is perceived as pursuing a general interest' (Arrighi 2010: 30).

Arrighi goes on to examine in great detail the exact nature of the 'transformative actions' of the three hegemonies of historical capitalism. The first hegemony was the rise of the Dutch nation state in parallel with its emergent role as the centre of international trade. In addition, there was its status as a military power that could provide military protection for its capitalist class while expending operations beyond Western Europe at the beginning of the era of colonisation. The British era began when Britain was already well established as a nation state which was also a colonial and imperial power. Most important was the fact that Britain was the first Western European nation state to industrialise and therefore it came to world dominance not just due to its role as a centre of international trade but also because of its status as the 'workshop of the world' (Rubinstein 1977: 112–13; cited in Arrighi 2010: 180).

The third hegemony of historical capital is that which Arrighi calls the 'short twentieth century' of US pre-eminence and dominance. This era emerged in the wake of the collapse of British hegemony, which was precipitated from the late nineteenth century onwards by the existence of ever more powerful rivals in Europe, especially Germany. But more importantly, there was simple fact that, as the twentieth century began, the USA simply overtook Britain both as a centre of trade and as an industrial powerhouse. As Arrighi explains:

> The capacity of the United Kingdom to hold the center of the capitalist world-economy was being undermined by the emergence of a new national economy of greater wealth, size, and resources than its own. This was the United States, which developed into a sort of 'black hole' with a power of attraction for the labor, capital, and entrepreneurship of Europe with which the United Kingdom, let alone less wealthy and powerful states, had few chances of competing.
>
> (Arrighi 2010: 60)

The unique and transformative element in the rise of American hegemony was its status as 'a continental military-industrial complex with the power to provide effective protection for [not only] itself but also its allies and to make credible threats of economic strangulation or military annihilation towards its enemies' (Arrighi 2010: 376). In addition, the USA could engineer territorial expansion as it expanded its nation-state borders in accordance with its conquest of great swathes of North America. It did, after all, have an entire continent to absorb its rapidly growing population, that is vastly more territory than any individual European nation state. And this rapidly growing population was to a great extent down to immigration, another option not available to the European powers, which, indeed, were exporting parts of their populations to the USA.

Thus over the long twentieth century, beginning with the First World War and lasting to the present, the USA has risen to a position of dominance in the world system of nation states. And notwithstanding suggestions, generally very convincing, that it has entered a period of slow and gradual decline (Todd 2003; Arrighi 2010), and that China alone or BRIC (Brazil, Russia, India and China) hold the key to the future, there is still little doubt that in 2011, the USA operates as the world's biggest and most important economic player. This has been and continues to be the case because the US 'state managers', as Callinicos (2009) calls them, have continued to show a great deal of diplomatic *chutzpah* in (1) keeping Europe divided (with the UK playing its traditional role of veritable Trojan horse); (2) managing to advance their military presence deep into Eurasia (with NATO bases now on the Russian border); (3) encircling the most feared future rival, China, with allies (both strong – Japan – and less strong – India); and (4) managing to keep in relative isolation emerging global players such as Russia (linked to Europe as a provider of gas, but kept at arm's length diplomatically) and Brazil (rising as a powerhouse in South America, but not yet able to become a political hegemon to match the USA).

In addition, there is little doubt that the USA has been in the past, and continues to be in the present, the origin of many cultural ideas and forms (Appadurai's ideoscapes and mediascapes) which have come to be seen as normal and have been indigenised around the world (Ritzer 2011). There are the obvious examples of American dominance in cinema and popular music, which for decades now have been exported from the USA and are received and consumed in all but a few corners of the world. And not withstanding some independence displayed by industries such as Bollywood (Gokulsing and Dissanayake 2004) and the reconfiguration of a music form like hip-hop in local contexts around the world (Pennycook 2007), the most pervasive cinematic genres worldwide and the heart of hip-hop are resolutely American. In addition, there is the impact of the American ways of doing things. For example, the USA is the prototype and exporter of consumerism, and more importantly what Ritzer (2007b: 171) calls the 'new means of consumption'. For example, the following by-now global forms of consumerism all had their origins in the US: shopping malls (1956), superstores (1957), franchising of fast food restaurants (1955), cruise ships (1966), theme parks (1955), home shopping television (1985) and cyber shopping (1995).

Still, if (and when and where) clever diplomacy and cultural influence are not enough, the USA can rely on a more traditional means of maintaining dominance, the threat of violence. In the past, and in the present, the USA has maintained and continues to maintain a clear advantage over any potential rivals on the world stage, in particular China. Thus, according to the Stockholm International Peace Research Institute (2010), the US surpassed China in military expenditure in 2010, both in absolute terms – $698,000 million to $119,000 million, respectively – and as a proportion of GDP – 4.8 per cent to 2.1 per cent, respectively. The upshot of these numbers, along with the geopolitical strategies outlined by Callinicos and the prevalence of American cultural imperialism outlined above, is that American imperialism, the exercise of hegemony and dominance in the world, continues to exist as a tangible and ever-present force in the world system.

The new imperialism and neoliberalism

As David Harvey (2003, 2005, 2006) notes, imperialism has traditionally followed the logic of territorial dominance: nation states have endeavoured to obtain more power than other nation states, always taking into account their economic, human and military resources and the fact that they are bound to and by specific and unmovable physical locations. Although some social scientists have tended to see the traditional logic of territorial dominance working hand in hand with the logic of capitalism (e.g. Smith 1997), Harvey argues that this has not necessarily been the case. Among other things, the logic of capitalism means many things that are antithetical to imperialism, such as territorial dominance. Thus, the main individual and collective agents of capitalism need have no loyalty to any nation state, which means they do not have to take into account the economic, human and military resources of their own nation state. This idea is consistent with Robert Reich's (1991) discussion of the new elites of the new economy of the 1980s and 1990s, the so-called 'symbolic analysts'. These are professionals skilled in new technologies-driven literacy practices (the written word, new technologies, numeracy), who owe their allegiance not to the nation states in which they were born and nurtured, but to whatever affiliations have got them to the position they hold at present. In addition, they are not bound by space and time dimensions, as territorially based agents are.

Indeed, traditional nation-state territoriality and its interrelationships with capitalism and imperialism have been questioned over the past three decades with ever more conviction. One of the best-known examples of this kind of thinking is to be found in the work of Hardt and Negri (2000) and their notion of empire:

> The passage to Empire emerges from the twilight of modern sovereignty. In contrast to imperialism, Empire establishes no territorial center of power and does not rely on fixed boundaries or barriers. It is a decentered and deterritorialising apparatus of rule that progressively incorporates the entire global realm within its open, expanding frontiers. Empire manages hybrid identities, flexible hierarchies, and plural exchanges through modulating networks of command. The distinct national colors of the imperialist map of the world have merged and blended in the imperial global rainbow.
>
> (Hardt and Negri 2000: pp. xii–xiii)

Harvey agrees that there is a new imperialism at work in the world today, but he does not understand it in terms of 'decentering', and 'imperial global rainbows'. Instead he argues that it is about the accumulation of economic capital, aided and abetted by governments of the wealthiest nation states who look after their national elites seeking to consolidate their class power at home whilst engaging more and more with individuals like themselves in globalised financial spaces. It should be noted, however, that these national elites may be either old or new. Thus, in some cases, the acquisition of class power is about traditional elites recovering what they once had decades and even centuries before the rise of the post-Second World War economies of the developed world, which to varying degrees worked more equitably for all classes via the relatively strong presence of social democratic policies. In other cases, it is about individuals and collectives gaining class power for the first time. Thus, politicians like Margaret Thatcher in Britain were not the unconditional friends of old money. As Harvey explains:

> Margaret Thatcher … attacked some of the entrenched forms of class power in Britain. She went against the aristocratic tradition that dominated in the military, the judiciary, and the financial elite in the City of London and many segments of industry, and sided with the brash entrepreneurs and the nouveaux riche … While neoliberalism may have been about the restoration of class power, it has not necessarily meant the restoration of economic power to the same people.
>
> (Harvey 2005: 31)

The new imperialism depends on the destruction of the welfare state and the emblematic social democratic model of Western Europe and North America in the post-Second World War era and an embrace of the Washington Consensus, an amalgam of measures meant to 'liberalise' economies. As explained in Chapter 2, this state of affairs has over the past three decades become the dominant economic ideology in the world, imposed on nation states, both rich and poor, via organisations such as the World Bank and the International Monetary Fund, with successive US governments orchestrating matters in the background. In the wake of the collapse of communism, a waning faith in social democracy in the face of economic stagnation on the world stage and the rise of the so-called new economy, which represented a shift from production-led to demand-led economies, the Washington Consensus has been sold to the world under the banner of TINA – There Is No Alternative (see Chapter 2). As I noted in the introduction to this chapter, the world has now begun to feel the full impact of this state of affairs, which serves to demonstrate how the weight of this ideology cannot be understood without direct reference to the political economic context in which it circulates.

Neoliberalism and class

Significantly, in a long list of nation states in which the preceding policies have been adopted (with varying degrees of intensity and enthusiasm, it must be added), there has been a marginalisation of class as an identity inscription. And this at a time when identity has come to the fore as a key construct in academic and in lay understandings of contemporary life (Block 2007). In the public sphere in Britain, the marginalisation of class, an identity inscription associated with collectivism, is best exemplified by bold public declarations made over the years, extolling the virtues of individualism. As we have observed throughout this book, individualism is a key element in neoliberal ideology. Thus, in 1987, when Margaret Thatcher was interviewed by the magazine *Women's Own* (no. 987, 23 Sept.), she famously uttered the following words: '… who is society? There is no such thing! There are individual men and women and there are families …'. Ten years later, Tony Blair became Prime Minister and argued, apparently *contra* Thatcher, that there was a society. Nevertheless he aligned himself with the philosophy of individualism which undergirded Thatcher's original declaration, as he plumped for a 'meritocracy', based on individual development and achievement. At the time of writing, the Conservative/Liberal Democrat government coalition, led by David Cameron, has introduced the notion of the 'Big Society', which in the midst of massive cuts to public spending means that individuals – or individuals organised into niche, organised collectives – are expected to do many of the things that governments previously did. With such leadership from the top, it is little wonder that in the public sphere in Britain today the identity inscription most associated with economics and stratification – class – has been marginalised.

On the other hand, in the past decade well-known journalists in the UK, such as Polly Toynbee, Julie Burchill and Nick Cohen, have brought class into their writing, although it should be added that the latter two have done so to attack what they deem to be the hypocrisy of middle-class 'liberals' for actions such as opposing the war in Iraq, which they rather bizarrely have supported (e.g. Cohen 2007). On a more serious plane are Michael Collins's (2004) *The Likes of Us*, Ferdinand Mount's (2004) *Mind the Gap: Class in Britain Now* and more recently, Owen Jones's (2011) *Chavs*, all three interesting reflections on class in British society. However, for every book of this kind, there are hundreds of public admonitions that those who wish to invoke class in discussion of British society today are guilty of going backwards and practising 'class war' when it is no longer relevant. And, of course there are the constant reminders across a wide range of media of the unique globalised times in which we live. How relevant can a class-based analysis of society be when the main topics of discussion are social networking and new forms of social organisation, now horizontal as opposed to vertical (Hardt and Negri 2005)? Given this situation, it is useful to wonder why and indeed how class has gone away or at least been pushed to the sidelines in much social sciences research in recent years.

Why class went away

In an in-depth and thought-provoking discussion of class, Ben Rampton explains why the construct has been marginalised in much social research in recent years:

> The analytic utility and the cultural salience of social class appears to be diminishing, undermined by a wider range of factors; the social and economic changes associated with globalisation, the decline of traditional collectivist politics, the emergence of gender, race and ethnicity as political issues, and the ascendance of the individual as consumer.
>
> (Rampton 2006: 216)

This view, which Rampton goes on to reject, is elaborated in great detail in the 1996 book by Jan Pakulski and John Waters, *The Death of Class*, in which the authors sustain that as of the 1990s, class had become inappropriate as a useful construct for understanding how industrialised societies are organised and how citizens live their lives, not least because these societies have changed during the last century. They argue that, in the 'less developed countries', class may still make sense. The move in the advanced industrialised societies has been from 'economic-class society', in which conflicts arise between economically determined groups (property owners and labourers), to 'organised-class society', in which there is a political/bureaucratic battle for power, and finally, to a culture-driven society, the 'status-conventional society', in which lifestyle, consumerism and identity politics drive society as the nation state is weakened and occupational stratification becomes more complex.

That modern societies have changed since the 1960s, when class analysis was practically synonymous with sociology in the UK (Savage 2000), is indisputable. The Thatcher years in the UK are a clear example of a reconfiguration of class relations via the destruction of the social bases on which the working class had drawn for decades, if not centuries. In effect, by closing down factories and entire industries, Thatcherite economic policies were effective in undermining the glue holding together a constellation of practices which could be deemed as constitutive of class in many parts of Britain. Long terms of employment translated, collaterally, into life-changing disruptions, such as broken marriages, movement away from old neighbourhoods and different types of employment. In the latter case, there has been in Britain a rise in self-employment, an individualistic approach to work antithetical to organized work, such as employment in a factory.

Nevertheless, and despite these real changes in the world of work in Britain and other industrialised countries, are social scientists still justified in marginalising class in favour of other constructs in their attempts to understand identity in late modern societies? A survey of research on identity in applied linguistics publications shows that the vast majority of applied linguists have come to the conclusion that they are. Thus while there is a great deal of work on gender, race, ethnicity, nationality, religion and sexuality, class rarely gets a look in and when it does it is merely mentioned but not problematised or actually used to frame analysis and discussion. Thus in a journal which has identity as its main focus, the *Journal of Language, Identity and Education*, there has not been a single article in which class figures as the central construct in analysis and discussion in its more than a decade of existence (as of October 2011). The same applies across a range of other applied linguistics journals in which articles focusing on identity have been published.[2] Edited collections (e.g. de Fina *et al.* 2006; Omoniyi and White 2006; Caldas-Coulthard and Iedema 2008; Lin 2008b; Nunan and Choi 2010; Higgins 2011) show a similar tendency, as even where 'class' or 'social class' appears in the index, there is no definition provided, nor much in the way of class-based analysis. An exception in these collections is a piece by Beverley Skeggs in Lin (2008b), although it should be noted that Skeggs is a sociologist and not an applied linguist. Elsewhere, Llamas and Watt's (2010) *Language and Identities* contains several chapters in which class is discussed in terms of accent, following a tradition begun by Labov (1966) decades ago. However apart from a chapter by Ben Rampton, class is not explored in much detail where it is brought in. I will have more to say about Rampton's work in the final section of this chapter.

Observing a similar trend towards class blindness in the social sciences in general, Harvey offers the following explanation for why this trend has become so pervasive:

> The neo-liberal state emphasizes the importance of personal and individual freedom, liberty and responsibility, particularly in the market place. ... Opposition within the rules of the neo-liberal state is typically confined to questions of individual human rights and 'rights discourses' of all kinds have, as a result, blossomed since 1980 or so as a primary site of 'radical' and oppositional politics.
>
> (Harvey 2006: 27–8)

Harvey's words chime with those of Michael Halliday over 20 years ago, produced in a position paper on the present and future of applied linguistics. Halliday commented on the absence of class as a central construct in a wide range of areas of applied linguistics, from language policy to language teaching. He described how in Australia Ruqaiya Hasan (1990) had been praised for her work on language and sexism but ignored when her work examined how class differences were reproduced in mother–children conversations. As Halliday notes, 'she is criticized on the grounds that there are no such things as social classes, and (somewhat self-contradictorily) that anyway mothers and children do not belong to them' (Halliday 1990: 17). Halliday then delivered the following damning indictment – prescient as it happens – on how, by ignoring class, applied linguistics did very little to take on materially based power structures in late modern societies:

> It is acceptable to show up sexism – as it is to show up racism – because to eliminate sexual and racial bias would pose no threat to the existing social order: capitalist society could thrive perfectly well without sexual discrimination and without racial discrimination. But it is not acceptable to show up classism, especially by objective linguistics analysis as Hasan has done; because capitalist society could not exist without discrimination between classes. Such work could, ultimately, threaten the order of society.
>
> (Halliday 1990: 17)

From this perspective, it is easy to understand how during the neoliberal era – from the late 1970s to the present –there has been a remarkable increase in debates and discussions around multiculturalism and identity politics. These have occurred both inside academia (including in applied linguistics) and outside and they have been framed in terms of gender, race, ethnicity, nationality and sexuality, while celebrating difference and diversity. Meanwhile, class has disappeared off the radar or has been invoked only to make clear its irrelevance in the new global village. Put another way, neoliberalism, because of its emphasis on individualism and its capacity to commodify increasing domains of human activity and being (see Chapter 5), may be seen to allow – and even facilitate as an epiphenomenon – the rise of identity politics and multiculturalism. And to make matters, worse, as O'Neil noted a decade ago, 'the fragmentation of social citizenship is now accelerated by the New Right's curious adoption of left cultural relativism' which could lead to the left 'winning cultural battles but losing the class war' (O'Neil 2001: 82).

All of this could make for somewhat unpleasant reading for those of us who have drunk from the trough of postmodernism and been interested in identity in terms of difference and diversity in our research. However, the discussion thus far should be understood as a call for more attention to class and not as an all-encompassing critique or disavowal of all research and thinking on difference along gendered, racial, ethnic, national and sexual lines. Indeed, none of the above-cited authors, nor the author of this chapter, would argue that the rise of identity politics in the post-Second World War era and the parallel focus in academic circles on issues around gender, race, ethnicity, nationality and sexuality have been a bad thing. Rather, they would argue that the collapse of empires and the increased production and consumption that typified the latter half of the twentieth century could not have happened without a concomitant radical shake-up of the life conditions of women and people of colour around the world. And they would also acknowledge that the theory and practice of identity politics have had positive effects and have improved the life conditions of these same people.

More to the point, my discussion thus far in this chapter should be taken as a challenge to what has perhaps become ingrained thinking about (and against) all notions related to modernity and derivative constructs such as structuralism. Indeed, reading this discussion, whilst observing events in the world today, one might be forgiven for thinking that not all grand narratives are bad and that the jettisoning of all that suggests universalism is necessarily a wise move. Thus, in addition to a rigorous focus on cultural flows – transnational, transcultural and so on – there needs to be a close examination of the economic backdrop that shapes them and the economic factors that help to configure them. And there needs to be some consideration of the different historical scales that Braudel and Wallerstein have introduced into the social sciences lexicon. This means, in part, greater attention to political economy, in particular the details of economics in society, past and present, as well as ideologies – economic, cultural and so on – which impact on social practices, including education. But importantly, it means a greater consideration of the one identity inscription most associated with economic matters, class.

What is class?

In the previous section, I discussed the marginalisation of class in the social sciences, and applied linguistics in particular, while not saying what I mean by class. In this section, I will take on this definitional task. I start with an explanation from the work of Bourdieu:

class … is defined not only by its position in the relations of production, as identified through indices such as occupation, income, or even educational level, but also by a certain sex-ratio, a certain distribution in geographical space (which is never socially neutral) and by a whole set of subsidiary characteristics which may function, in the form of tacit requirements, as real principles of selection or exclusion without ever being formally stated (this is the case with ethnic origin and sex). A number of official criteria: for example, the requiring of a given diploma can be a way of demanding a particular social origin.

(Bourdieu 1984: 102)

In his examination of class in 1960s and 1970s France, Bourdieu makes the very good and by now the generally accepted point that class must be conceptualised in terms which move beyond traditional notions of income, occupation and education. But how do Bourdieu and other scholars who share his views on class come to this conclusion?

One way to answer this question is to construct an archaeology of thinking about class, an archaeology which will serve to retrace what surely were the steps followed by Bourdieu in his intellectual formation in 1950s France. The starting point is one adopted by many for whom class is a central construct, that is, the foundational work of Karl Marx and Max Weber. In the work of Marx, class is not so much a construct to be defined clearly but an emergent idea. Thus, as Erik Olin Wright notes, '[w]hile Marx never systematically answered the question [what constitutes class?], his work is filled with class analysis' (Wright 1985: 6). It is through this analysis that the reader comes to understand both how class relations emerge from particular ways of organising production, the actual processes of production and how individuals living within class structures come to organise as they engage in class struggle. Marx thus describes the economic conditions which render class both necessary and real. In addition, it is possible to extract a myriad of class positionings (or in any case, terms which are, to varying degrees glossed) just by combing through a section of the *Communist Manifesto* (see Marx and Engels 1967: 79–94). There we find references to the patricians, knights, plebeians and slaves of ancient Rome; the feudal lords, vassals, guild-masters, journeymen, apprentices and serfs of the Middle Ages; and eventually to the bourgeois class (or capitalist class), the proletariat (or wage-labourers), the petty bourgeoisie (small shopkeepers and trades and crafts people) and finally, the lumpenproletariat (those with no means of subsistence). However, ultimately for Marx, it was not these and a multitude of other positions in a stratified class system which were important; rather, it was the broader relational positions occupied by individuals with regard to the means of production and the ownership of land which merited attention. And so there was a division along three general class lines: the proletariat (wage-labourers), the bourgeoisie (capitalists) and landowners (aristocracy), although it was the former two which became central to Marx's writing about capitalism.

It is this move from multiple class positionings to few in Marx's writing, lined up against the ever more complex nature of stratification in modern societies, which has led to a situation in which '[m]ost Marxist scholars ... have pulled back from the grandiose explanatory claims of historical materialism (if not necessarily from all of its explanatory aspirations) ' (Wright 2005: 4). Indeed social scientists in general – Marxists, ex-Marxists or otherwise – have tended to seek ideas for how to understand social stratification and class elsewhere. Some have looked to the work of Emile Durkheim, in particular his classic text *The Division of Labour in Society* (1984). Here Durkheim writes against Marx, questioning whether class conflict must always follow capitalism. As David Grusky and Gabriela Galescu note, he also anticipated how industrialised societies might adapt to and ultimately absorb (or co-opt) organised labour movements and how individualism would come to the fore on the back of social mobility:

> Durkheim ... argued that class conflict in the early industrial period would ultimately dissipate because (a) the growth of the state occupational regulation should impose moral control on the conflict of its interests (i.e. the 'institutionalization' of conflict), and (b) the rise of achievement-based mobility should legitimate inequalities of outcome by making them increasingly attributable to differential talent, capacities, and investments rather than differential opportunities (i.e. the rise of 'equal opportunity').
>
> (Grusky and Galescu 2005: 54)

These ideas and many others appear in the slightly later work of Max Weber, the one scholar who most stands out as an alternative to Marx. This is especially the case as regards his argument that it is not just the economic bases of societies and individuals' relationships to the means of production which are determinant in social stratification; rather, there are other forces at work. Living and writing several decades after Marx, by which time Europe, North America, East Asia and other parts of the world had become more industrialised, Weber was better able to see how stratification in modern societies had become more nuanced and complex as opposed to divided along two or perhaps three large class categories. In his mammoth *Economy and Society*, Weber defined class and class situation as follows:

> 'Class situation' and 'class' refer only to the same (or similar) interests which an individual shares with others. In principle, the various controls over consumer goods, means of production, assets, resources and skills each constitute a particular class situation. A uniform class situation prevails only when completely unskilled and propertyless persons are dependent on irregular employment. Mobility among, and stability of, class positions differs greatly; hence, the unity of a social class is highly variable.
>
> (Weber 1968: 302)

This definition inserts into analysis a series of factors which individuals are deemed to control – means of production, consumer goods, resources and skills – to varying degrees. It is this variability of control that determines the class positionings of individuals and with whom they are grouped as class members and with whom they are not. In addition, like Durkheim (1984), Weber introduces mobility across class positions as a phenomenon alongside the reproduction (stability) of class positions. Above all, Weber's view addresses more levels of social activity than Marx's, which was heavily based on production, but did not include any detailed attention to the possession of consumer goods or skills and resources or instability in the class system and social mobility, all characteristics of modern societies which were to become increasingly prevalent as the twentieth century unfolded.

Because he was not so exclusively bound to production as the single most important organising principle of societies, Weber also saw the need to introduce status and status situation as a way of making sense of stratification based not just on material conditions but also on abstract notions like honour. And when discussing 'status groups', Weber moved into the realm of behaviours as a mark of distinction, rather presciently introducing the term 'stylization':

> status groups are the specific bearers of all conventions. In whatever way it may be manifest, all stylization of life either originates in status groups or is at least conserved by them.
>
> (Weber 1968: 935–6)

To conclude, Weber distinguished class from status groups as follows:

> With some over-simplification, one might thus say that classes are stratified according to their relations to the production and acquisition of goods; whereas, status groups are stratified according to the principles of their consumption of goods as represented by special styles of life.
>
> (Weber 1968: 937)

Although much has been written against Marx from a Weberian perspective and against Weber from a Marxist perspective, it is probably more helpful first of all to understand how the two scholars were different. Eric Olin Wright sums up their differences as follows:

> The typical characterization is that Weber adopts a definition of classes based on market or exchange relations, whereas Marx adopts a production relations definition. The real difference is subtler. Both Marx and Weber adopt production-based definitions in that they define classes with respect to the effective ownership of production assets: capital, raw labour power and skills in Weber; capital and labour power (for the analysis of capitalism) in Marx. The difference between them is that Weber views production from the vantage

point of the market exchanges in which those assets are traded, whereas Marx views production from the vantage point of the exploitation it generates, and this in turn ... reflects the fundamental difference between a cultural and materialist theory of society.

(Wright 1985: 107)

In his thinking about class, Bourdieu owes much to the two scholars, despite the fact that Marx and Weber are cited very sparingly in his work. Equally missing are explicit links to two British scholars, Raymond Williams and E. P. Thompson, both of whom would identify themselves as Marxists, but who, like Bourdieu, have tended to show at least some concern for Weberian thinking, incorporating notions such as status into their work. Above all, they have focused on those aspects of Marxism which allow for the generation of change and not just an impervious-to-culture cycle of reproduction. Thus, in his classic volume, *The Making of the English Working Class*, Thompson defines class as follows:

> By class I understand a historical phenomenon, unifying a number of disparate and seemingly unconnected events, both in the raw material of experience and in consciousness. ... I do not see class as a 'structure', nor even as a 'category', but as something which in fact happens (and can be shown to have happened) in human relationships. ... And class happens when some men, as a result of common experiences (inherited or shared), feel and articulate the identity of their interests as between themselves, and as against other men whose interests are different from (and generally opposed to) theirs. The class experience is largely determined by the productive relations into which men are born – or enter involuntarily. Class-consciousness is the way in which these experiences are handled in cultural terms; embodied in traditions, value systems, ideas, and institutional forms. If the experience appears as determined, class consciousness does not.
>
> (Thompson 1980: 8–9)

Here class is framed as a social relation and as emergent in the day-to-day activities of human beings. There is in Thompson's thinking an experiential and reflexive side which makes it a cultural as much as economic phenomenon. And this experiential and reflexive side of class, the class consciousness of individuals who form part of a class, may be linked to Marx's famous maxim that '[m]en make their own history' (Marx 1972: 437). However, just as Marx's wink in the direction of agency is mitigated by the rejoinder – 'but they do not make it just as they please; they do not make it under circumstances chosen by themselves, but under circumstances directly found, given and transmitted from the past' (Marx 1972: 437) – so Thompson reminds the reader that historically based social structure is a given backdrop to all social activity when he states that '[t]he class experience is largely determined by the productive relations into which men are born – or enter involuntarily'.

As I stated previously, Bourdieu does not engage with Thompson as a source of ideas in his work. However, his theorisation of class is certainly consistent with Thompson's attention to history and culture, and above all class-consciousness and its embodiment in behaviour, traditions, value systems, ideas and institutional forms. In this sense, two key constructs fundamental to Bourdieu's approach to class – habitus and field – are foregrounded by history and culture and involve embodiment of the dimensions listed by Thompson. The first of these constructs, habitus, has been written about exhaustively over the years, and may be described as the individual's internalised dispositions, formulated out of engagement in situated social practices and shaped by institutions as well as larger social structures, such as global economic forces. Meanwhile, fields are spaces of social activity with evolving legitimate ways of thinking and acting, in which individuals occupy positions of inferiority, equality and superiority which are dependent on the individual's symbolic capital (more on this in a moment) in relation to other participants in the social activity. Crucially, they are sites of both the reproduction and reformulation of sociocultural hierarchies, as well as processes in which individuality and agency interact with the collective and social structure. No two people are the same, but if two people engage in more or less the same situated practices in more less the same fields, then these two people will come to structure and/or reproduce and/or strengthen their class position in similar ways.

As Karl Maton (2008) notes, it should be emphasised that habitus and field are inextricably linked. However, this link is not, strictly speaking, completely and equally reciprocal; rather, it is more processual in nature. Thus, a particular field may be seen to structure an associated habitus through instances of an individual's engagement with that field. However, the habitus does not structure the field in a reciprocal manner. Rather, the habitus structures the field *cognitively* inside the individual and thus serves as both a structured and a generative template with which and against which exemplars of practice within the field take place. Practice, at the same time, is reducible neither to habitus (or any other notion of individual agency) nor to field (as social conditioner and shaper of activity).

Articulating with habitus and field in the constitution of class are symbolic resources or symbolic capital, which are the socioculturally shaped, value-laden products of habitus-mediated activity in social fields. In Bourdieu's metaphorology, there are three types of capital (Bourdieu 1984, 1986). The first, economic capital, relates to a traditional index of class, personal material wealth (the income of an individual, as well as all property and assets) relative to the field in which one is operating. Second, there is cultural capital, which may be understood as possession of the right cultural resources and assets in a field, which create particular class effects (e.g. the right or wrong accent, body movements, manifestations of taste or attitude in a particular setting); as an association with particular artefacts (e.g. art objects, music, books, qualifications); and as a connection to certain institutions (e.g. professional associations). Third and finally, there is social capital, which relates directly to these institutional contacts. Social capital is about connections to and relationships with equally or more powerful others. The greater the cultural capital of these others, the greater the social capital accrued by associating with them.

Bourdieu's notions of habitus, field and symbolic capital together offer a framework that helps us understand class as emergent in practice in a variety of settings. However, not everyone agrees about the usefulness of Bourdieusian theory and indeed, there has been perhaps as much debate about the meaning of Bourdieu's metaphorology as there has been in-depth use of it in analysis in different settings (see Albright 2008, for a discussion). For example, Bourdieu is often positioned as an 'old-style' structuralist with a deterministic model that does not allow for individual agency or the prospect of social change. However, as I note elsewhere (Block 2012a), Bourdieu's work over the years may be seen as a serious attempt to find a way between determinism and an overemphasis on individual agency. He therefore rejects with equal emphasis mechanistic, rules-based models of social activity and notions of individuals acting as free and rational agents:

> Because the habitus is an endless capacity to engender products – thoughts, perceptions, expressions, actions – whose limits are set by the historically and socially situated conditions of its productions, the conditioned freedom it secures is as remote from creation of unpredictable novelty as it is from a simple mechanical reproduction of the initial conditionings.
>
> (Bourdieu 1977: 95)

In summary, for Bourdieu, class is relational and emergent. It stands at the crossroads of sociohistorically situated life trajectories and dispositions, on the one hand, and situated activities with others taking place in a wide variety of physical, social and psychological contexts, on the other. The latter – physical, social and psychological contexts – are, in turn, organised in scalar fashion (across levels or fields) as the lives of individuals unfold. From this perspective, perhaps what we are talking about could be called class positionings, as emergent in practice. However, following scholars like Williams and Thompson, these class positionings are historically and socially shaped, and following Marx (and Weber), they are ultimately grounded in economic realities even if these are not the be-all and end-all of class formation in individuals and collectives.

In the light of the previous discussion of globalisation, and specifically how the world in which we live is capitalism-as-usual plus constant and fast-paced social change, sociologists interested in class have shown a tendency in recent years to frame the construct as multidimensional and complex (e.g. Bottero 2005; Burkitt 2008; Crompton 2008; Wright 2005). It is thus not just about income and education, or income and occupation; rather, it has become a convenient working label in the social sciences (as well as in society in general) for a number of dimensions. These include: wealth (an individual's possessions and disposable money); occupation (manual labour, unskilled service jobs, low-level information-based jobs, professional labour, etc.); place of residence (a working-class neighbourhood, a middle-class neighbourhood, an area undergoing gentrification), education (the educational level attained by an individual by early adulthood); social networking (middle-class people tend to socialise with middle-class people, working-class people with working-class people, and so on); consumption patterns (buying food at a supermarket that positions itself as 'cost-cutting' vs. buying food at one that sells 'healthy' and organic products); and symbolic behaviour (e.g. how one moves one's body, the clothes one wears, the way one speaks, how one eats, the kinds of pastimes one engages in, etc.). However, no one of these dimensions ever offers an airtight means of defining people in terms of class, especially when viewed relationally, with respect to other dimensions. Thus, wealth might be associated with a particular type of employment, for example, so-called white-collar work, as well as educational level (university degrees). However, in many cases individuals who work with their hands and have relatively low academic qualifications can amass greater fortunes over both short and long periods of time. Nowhere has this been more evident than in the construction and decorating business which has flourished in Britain and elsewhere in the world over the past two decades. Individuals who most likely would be termed working class (in their upbringing, in their symbolic behaviour, in the kinds of activities they engage in, etc.) have reached earnings levels beyond many who have traditionally been classified as middle class (e.g. teachers). And where working-class people – and indeed the poor – have not reached higher income levels, they have nevertheless found that the financialisation of economies in the neoliberal era has meant easy credit, which in turn has meant that it has been easy to borrow the money necessary to buy consumer products.

All of this reminds us that, in the neoliberal era, some rules of engagement have changed and that we may have to revise some of our ingrained ideas about how things function in societies. One trend which has emerged over the past several decades has been to argue that everyone is becoming middle class in the advanced industrial/ post-industrial societies of the world. Indeed, as Owen Jones (2011) notes, this idea was propagated by former British Prime Minister Tony Blair during his ten years in power (1997–2007). In British sociology, such thinking arose several decades ago, coming to be known as the 'embourgeosiment thesis'. In an early discussion of this thesis, Goldthorpe and Lockwood (1963; cited in Bottomore 1965: 29) suggested that 'a picture has been built up – and it is one which would be generally accepted – of a system of stratification becoming increasingly fine in its gradations and at the same time somewhat less extreme and less rigid'. According to this thesis, the 1950s and 1960s brought full employment, a fully functioning welfare state and higher salaries to working-class people in Britain. These people, in turn, began to live their lives in ways previously deemed the preserve of the middle class (more spacious housing, car ownership, appliance ownership and so on).

However, there is still reason to be careful, if not sceptical, about the embourgeosiment thesis. Thus while there have been changes along the lines of those outlined above, it nevertheless remains the case that over the past 50-odd years, class-related income inequalities have remained remarkably stable and even become more pronounced (Harvey 2006). In addition, Roberts makes a good point when he argues that 'whenever the working class has improved income levels and living standards, the middle class has advanced in line, so there has been no catching up' (Roberts 2001: 13), although it would be wise to remind ourselves that class categories are not clearly defined containers into which people simply slot themselves. Nevertheless, the point here is that class still matters, and if we are to judge by how easily class comes to the fore in the media – for example, in the form of reality programmes ridiculing individuals positioned as 'working class' (Skeggs 2004) – then we have every reason to believe that class remains a viable and useful construct in attempts to understand a wide range of social phenomena.

Conclusion

In Chapter 1, reference was made to the conjunctural frame in which we live today and how it requires us to rethink the scope of applied linguistics so as to take on board thinking and ideas from political economy. In this chapter, I have focused on how we need to reframe globalisation and identity. As regards globalisation, my suggestion is a simple one. As noted in the introduction to this book, and as I have argued throughout this chapter, applied linguists have tended to adopt a culturalist model of globalisation, one concerned with flows of people, flows of technology and flows of a range of cultural forms (in particular music). All of this is fine as there can be no doubt that a big part of globalisation is human mobility and cultural dynamism. However, given the paucity of work which has engaged in depth and in detail with debates and research on political economy, there is a need to redress what is surely an imbalance, and to foreground neoliberalism as the dominant economic ideology today with repercussions for all manners of activity in which we engage.

As regards identity-based research in applied linguistics, I have argued that class has been marginalised. My view is that it needs to be brought more to the fore as an identity inscription which interrelates with other identity inscriptions such as gender, race, ethnicity, nationality and sexuality. Indeed, there has been something of a blind-spot in language identity research when it comes to political economy and how it impacts on all social activity, including language practices. With this latter thought in mind, I propose to end this chapter with a discussion of work in sociolinguistics which does put class at the centre of analysis, noting how it may serve as a template of sorts for future language and identity research.

Ben Rampton is not identified readily as a language and identity researcher, although his work does provide food for thought for language and identity researchers, who often cite him in their work. In the context of this chapter, his work is relevant because he is one of the few applied linguists to have put class at the centre of his work in recent years, and he is the only scholar to have produced a sustained discussion of what class might mean for the purposes of his research (Rampton 2006: Chs 6–9; 2010). Rampton embeds what he does in sociolinguistics and therefore carefully charts his course through and around trends in sociolinguistic research which might be relevant to his enterprise. He thus acknowledges a tradition in sociolinguistics, going back to William Labov (1966) and later taken up by scholars such as Peter Trudgill (1974), whereby class and stratification are dealt with in quantitative terms. These early researchers sought to quantify variation across speakers and groups, focusing for example on the amount and frequency of linguistic variables, such as the pronunciation of particular vowels.

Additional influence comes from Basil Bernstein's early work (e.g. 1971) and Shirley Brice Heath's ethnographic research (1983). The former is important because Bernstein's 'analysis of language and class starts with macro-social structure and the division of labour, moves into the institutional organisation of family and education, homes in on interactional practices deemed critical in socialisation, and from there looks for links to the communicative disposition of individuals and their impact on school achievement' (Rampton 2010: 5). This is quite an enterprise, involving as it does 'most of the levels where researchers have located class processes – the economy, the community, occupations, families, activity, discourse, language, consciousness and school careers' (Rampton 2010: 5). Nevertheless, while Bernstein certainly provided later researchers with much food for thought, especially as regards his code theory, his work is seen by Rampton as limited for several reasons. First, class is not discussed in terms of or as interrelated with other identity inscriptions, such as gender and ethnicity. Second, although class struggle is alluded to, there is no sustained discussion of power in terms of ideology or activity, such as resistance. Third and finally, there is a lack of detail in his analysis of language data and overall Bernstein did not work extensively or systematically enough to be considered an ethnographer. It would be the task of researchers like Heath to fill in some of the gaps in Bernstein's work, particularly the third one.

Working in the USA, Heath famously examined in detail the different language practices at the community and family levels, with a view to linking these practices to eventual school performance. Her basic motives and interests were very similar to Bernstein's. However, she was far more an anthropologist by training than Bernstein was, far more in-the-field than in-the-armchair, and her most famous work, *Ways with Words*, proved to be a master class in how to conduct what today would be called linguistic ethnography. As Rampton notes, while Heath 'describes people in their individual and contextual particularity' (Rampton 2010: 8), bringing to the fore the 'literacy event' as a key construct, Bernstein's work seems somewhat stuck in a deductive, generative model which is fairly one-dimensional, despite its internal complexity. Rampton speculates about how things might have been different had the latter been thinking about class and language socialisation a decade or two later:

> Maybe if the ethnography of communication had been fully invented when Bernstein did his work on language and class … or if he had been less attracted to models of knowledge production propounded in formal linguistics, we would have had something like Ways with Words in England in the 1970s and 1980s.
>
> (Rampton 2010: 9)

While Bernstein and Heath have been important influences on his work, an equally important source of ideas has been the work of John Gumperz (1982) and the notion that 'the reality of people's circumstances is actively shaped by the ways in which they interpret and respond to them; and in line with this, it lays a good deal of emphasis on the cultural politics of imagery and representation' (Rampton 2006: 232). For Rampton, it is in interaction and practice that class emerges, arises or is enacted:

> If … class is seen as a process in which people negotiate and struggle for position, affiliation and advantage within unevenly receptive institutional systems that have a significant impact on their destinies, then style shifting stops being the range of variability that is respective (acceptable or authentic) for someone belonging at a particular social level, and instead becomes an index of each individual's structured moving alignment with 'high' and 'low', 'lower' and 'higher'.
>
> (Rampton 2006: 274–5)

Drawing on a range of scholars, including Raymond Williams, Edward Thompson and Michel Foucault, Rampton proposes a distinction between:

> 1. material conditions, ordinary experience, and everyday discourses, activities and practices – the 'primary realities' of practical activity which are experienced differently by different people in different times, places and networks; and
> 2. secondary or 'meta-level' representations: ideologies, images, and discourses about social groups, about the relations of power between them, and about their different experiences of material conditions and practical activity.
>
> (Rampton 2006: 222–3)

Rampton documents the everyday experiences and practices of a cohort of London secondary school students, accessed via recordings of their classroom activities. In particular, he examines their use of 'posh' and 'Cockney' voices or stylisations.[3] He notes how switching back and forth between these different voices is significant as each voice switch marks a shift from insider (Cockney) to outsider (posh), even if boundaries are fuzzy depending on the contexts of their uses. More importantly, the students are deemed to inhabit working-class subjectivities as they use both voices: talking as working-class youth when using Cockney; positioning middle-class people as 'other' when using posh. Further to this point, there are several features of Rampton's research which are important. First, he situates his research in what scholars ranging from Bernstein to Bourdieu have identified as one of the key sites (or fields) of the reproduction of and struggles over class: the educational system and schools in particular. He describes in detail how activity mediated by teachers, students and curriculum serves to reproduce class positioning. In addition, these class positionings are presented to the reader as effects created by the uses of communicative resources (linguistic and other semiotic modes) during participation in activities. However, it should be noted that these effects are not just willy-nilly created on the spot; rather, Rampton is careful to argue that the actual class positionings being reproduced exist independently of the activity reproducing them. He opts for what he calls an 'ontological realism', whereby there is assumed to be a reality outside of the researcher's ability to describe, analyse or interpret it.

Another point of interest arising for Rampton's research is how class is not explicitly evoked very often by teachers or students, that while there may be class *in itself*, there is not necessarily class *for itself* (Marx 1995). And where it is invoked, this is done with negative connotations, as when the teacher warns students about 'dropping their h's' during a university entrance interview or it is done as part of a respect agenda, whereby class is another way of being, along with ethnic and gendered subjectivities, which must be acknowledged and valued in the school context. And this latter point leads to another finding by Rampton, namely the by-now much discussed way in which it is extremely difficult to discuss one identity inscription without invoking others. Thus, as Beverley Skeggs has noted over the years, class in modern Britain is inflected by race and ethnicity (e.g. white English) as well as gender (working-class women).

As I stated previously, Rampton's work is not about identity *per se*. However, in his work we see class-inflected subjectivities emerging in the examples of communications between students and teachers which he examines and analyses. Some of the features of Rampton's research, above all his attention to links between 'ordinary experience, and everyday discourses, activities and practices' and 'ideologies, images, and discourses about social groups, about the relations of power between them, and about their different experiences of material conditions and practical activity' (Rampton 2006: 222–3), are useful for future language and identity research focusing on class. However, we need to add to Rampton's work one very important missing element – a political economic layer, as outlined earlier in this chapter. I say this because while Rampton does situate his research sociologically and historically – the title of his 2006 book is, after all, *Language in Late Modernity* – he engages in no discussion of the political economic backdrop of his class-based analysis of language practices, be this diachronic or synchronic in nature.

The framework I propose here would fill this gap in Rampton's work, as it would include discussion and analysis of the high-level macropolitical, social and economic goings on – the world system constantly evolving – and more middle or meso-level fields of social activity – the material structuring bases as well as a range of 'meta-level' representations – and finally, the micro-level of activity and individual experiences of activity (see Block, in preparation, for more detail). If we add to all of this due care in the integration of class with other identity inscriptions such as gender, race, ethnicity, nationality and sexuality, then we have a very promising way forward for class-based research in applied linguistics in neoliberal times.

5

NEOLIBERALISM, CELEBRITY AND 'ASPIRATIONAL CONTENT' IN ENGLISH LANGUAGE TEACHING TEXTBOOKS FOR THE GLOBAL MARKET

JOHN GRAY

Introduction

The British journalist Marina Hyde (2010) reports that in 2008 as the scale of the global economic crisis was becoming clear, the most popular term being keyed into Internet search engines was Britney Spears – a position of pre-eminence the singer had maintained for four consecutive years. For Hyde this fact is emblematic of the hypnotic power of celebrity in contemporary culture and its ability to distract attention from painful and pressing realities. Hyde's book, *Celebrity: How Entertainers Took Over the World and Why We Need an Exit Strategy*, is itself largely an exercise in entertainment and consists mainly of a series of excoriating accounts of the political interventions and pretentions of a host of contemporary celebrities. The book opens with the actor Richard Gere's television message to Palestinian voters on the eve of the 2005 general election in the West Bank and Gaza. Gere's address, which was reported in several media outlets, began with the words: 'Hi, I'm Richard Gere and I'm speaking for the entire world. We're with you during this election time. It's really important. Get out and vote' (ABC News Online 2005). Hyde offers no analysis as to why such celebrity interventions have become commonplace – contemporary celebrities such as Angelina Jolie, Lindsay Lohan, Bruce Willis and Jude Law have all pronounced on the politics of the Middle East, while porn-star turned politician Cicciolina publically offered to have sex with Saddam Hussein in 1991 and 2002 as a way (she explained) of preventing war (Sydney Morning Herald 2002). Neither does Hyde speculate on the cultural meanings that can be attached to such interventions – however, it is clear that she sees them as raising troubling questions about the pervasiveness of celebrity in late modernity.

This chapter shares much of Hyde's disquiet and focuses specifically on the dramatic rise in representations of celebrity in UK-produced ELT textbooks from the late 1970s until the present, a period which coincides with the global expansion of the ELT industry and the spread of neoliberalism across much of the world (see also Gray 2010b). The proliferation of celebrities in contemporary consumer culture can be linked to what has been described as the aestheticisation of everyday life (Featherstone 1991), namely the way in which signs, images and visual messages feature so prominently in all aspects of daily activity; and, at the same time, it parallels the rise of an economy characterised by relentless self-promotion and the need to attract attention (Bauman 2007; Schroeder 2002). The growth of what has been labelled 'celebrity culture' (Friedman 1999: 15) can in fact be seen as integral to the market fundamentalism which lies at the heart of neoliberal ideology. Drawing on work by proponents of self-branding (e.g. Peters 2008) as a response to the challenge of the so-called 'new work order' (Gee *et al.* 1996), this chapter argues that the increasingly pervasive use of celebrity in pedagogic materials is congruent with the values of the neoliberal world-view and is directly traceable to what ELT publishers describe as 'aspirational content'. Such content, focused largely on spectacular personal and professional success, celebrity lifestyles, cosmopolitanism and travel is held by the ELT industry to be inherently motivating for language learners. Given the concerns of this volume as a whole, and given that the teaching of language is a core applied linguistics activity, the manner in which discourses of celebrity are deployed in ELT textbooks clearly warrants scrutiny.

The chapter begins by looking at the ways in which celebrity has been defined and theorised and then moves on to consider the phenomenon specifically in the light of neoliberal ideology. This is followed by an analysis of the use of celebrity in a sample of ELT textbooks, and is accompanied by questionnaire data in which a group of English language teachers, working in a variety of global settings, outline their views on the nature and suitability of such content for language teaching. The chapter concludes with a discussion of the findings and what it sees as the implications for applied linguistics and the specific activity of English language teaching.

Defining celebrity

It is important to state at the outset that celebrity is a problematic concept and deciding what it refers to precisely or indeed who is and who is not a celebrity can be difficult (Turner *et al.* 2008). On an anecdotal level this was brought home to me when a friend mentioned in passing that Barack Obama was clearly a celebrity, whereas Angela Merkel most definitely was not – an assessment I realised I shared. Just what is it about Obama that seems to set him in a different category to that of Merkel? A definition of celebrity, such as that found in the work of Daniel Boorstin (1992: 57), which states that it refers to 'a person who is well-known for their well-knownness', provides little in the way of a satisfactory answer. Equally unsatisfactory is a more contemporary definition given by Anita Biressi and Heather Nunn (2008: 159) who suggest that celebrities are 'people who are objects of pronounced media attention over which they may have only a limited amount of control'. Although both definitions contain elements which many would see as integral to celebrity, some vital aspect that would account for the Obama–Merkel distinction is missing. One clue as to what that might be is provided by Stefan Zweig's (2009: 63) autobiographical memoir in which he describes a number of encounters with public figures in *fin-de-siècle* Vienna:

> Anyone who performed in public as an actor or conductor, anyone who had published a book or wrote in a newspaper, was a star in our firmament ... to have seen Gustav Mahler in the street was an event to be reported to your friends next morning like a personal triumph, and when once, as a boy, I was introduced to Johannes Brahms and he gave me a kindly pat on the shoulder, I was in a state of total confusion for days over this extraordinary event. It is true that, aged twelve, I had only a very vague idea of exactly what Brahms had done, but the mere fact of his fame and his aura of creativity exerted astonishing power over me ... So strongly did we feel the radiance of fame that even if it came at seventh hand, it still awed us; a poor old lady who was a great-niece of Franz Schubert appeared to us a supernatural being, and we looked respectfully at even Joseph Kainz's valet in the street because he was lucky enough to be personally close to that most popular and brilliant of actors.

Despite the fact that pronounced media attention is not referred to by Zweig (although Mahler was the subject of considerable media scrutiny throughout his life), the well-knownness – in the sense of being publicly recognisable – of those he mentions is clearly important. However, what is most interesting in Zweig's account is the way in which it points to the centrality of affect in the phenomenon of celebrity. It is also, as his use of pronouns suggests, an affect which is socially distributed: 'our firmament'; 'So strongly did we feel'; 'it still awed us'; 'appeared to us'; 'we looked respectfully'. This is no interior world of secret adulation – rather Zweig presents us with what Sara Ahmed (2004: 8) refers to as the 'sociality of emotion' whereby objects (such as celebrities) 'become sticky, or saturated with affect' (Ahmed 2004: 11). The capacity to embody and generate affect – whether admiration, desire, envy, fear, loathing – captures what I would argue is a central aspect of celebrity and provides a possible explanation for the Obama–Merkel distinction. Despite being well-known and having a media presence as leader of one of the largest European countries, Merkel is less sticky (to pursue Ahmed's metaphor), less saturated with affect in the way that Obama is (although of course Merkel's celebrity status may be altogether different in the German-speaking world). Part of the reason for this has to do with the way in which both figures are constructed in the media through which they are made known to the public and through which they are used, by those who manage their image or the media themselves, to channel affect. A similar view which implicitly recognises the role of affect is taken by Chris Rojek (2001: 10), who defines celebrity as 'the attribution of glamour or notorious status to an individual within the public sphere'. Citing the Brazilian model Gisele Bundchen as an example of glamour (a quality which John

Berger (1972) suggests has its roots in the stimulation of envy) and the Oklahoma bomber Timothy McVeigh as an example of notoriety (a quality triggered by fear and loathing), Rojek (2001: 10) suggests that what links them together is their cultural impact, and he concludes that 'celebrity = impact on public consciousness'.

The manner in which individuals become culturally impactful has changed considerably since the days of Zweig's adolescent sightings of Mahler. The growth of print media in the twentieth century, the arrival of cinema, television and more recently new media such as the Internet (including YouTube, Twitter and social network sites) mean that the possibilities for individuals to impact on public consciousness have been dramatically increased. In that respect Biressi and Nunn (2008) are right to include media presence in their definition of celebrity, and given that the construction and dissemination of mediatised information about individuals is driven largely by the need to maximise sales of media products (whether directly or indirectly), they are also right to point out that control of what goes into the public domain is in many cases beyond the power of the individuals concerned. Thus, as far as this chapter is concerned, a contemporary celebrity is understood as someone who is well-known (in the sense of being publicly recognisable) as a result of pronounced media attention which is largely commercially motivated and whose impact on public consciousness is as a result of their capacity to embody and generate affect.

At the same time, as the names listed above suggest, celebrities constitute a diverse array of characters comprising creative artists, politicians, actors, porn-stars, models and terrrorists. Rojek usefully categorises these into three main groups, the first of which is *ascribed* celebrity. This group includes those whose status is by virtue of their birth as members of an elite group such as a royal family or a political dynasty (e.g. Windsors, Kennedys or Gandhis). The second group is that of *achieved* celebrity. Here we find those whose status is linked to their achievements (e.g. an Olympic champion or a Pulitzer prize winner). The third group is described as having *attributed* celebrity. This group consists of those whose status is almost entirely the result of intense media attention (and may or may not entail achievement or notoriety). This group includes reality television characters, winners of television talent competitions, footballers' wives and girlfriends, serial killers and members of the public who are recorded as they buttonhole politicians. Those in this group are also referred to by Rojek as *celetoids* – a neologism which seeks to link their celebrity with the tabloid newspapers in which it is largely manufactured and disseminated. Their media life span tends to be shorter than that of those whose celebrity is achieved, although there are exceptions such as Myra Hindley in the UK and Charles Manson in the US – both notorious killers from the 1960s, so saturated with affect that they continue to function in the popular press as embodiments of evil.

Rojek adds a final subcategory to this third group which he calls *celeactors*. These are fictional characters such as Ali G (performed by actor Sasha Baron Cohen), Vicky Pollard (a fictional teenage mother played by comedian Matt Lucas) or the cartoon figure Bart Simpson. Their cultural impact extends beyond the entertainment context in which they first came to public attention. Thus, for example, in 1992 then-president George Bush said that the US needed families more like the Waltons (a wholesome fictional television family) than the Simpsons (a similarly fictional but altogether more fractious and dysfunctional unit). Deployed in this way celeactors can be made to function as cultural reference points in political and media discourse. Overall, Rojek (2001: 29) takes a broadly benign view of what he calls celebrity culture, and celetoids and celeactors in particular, arguing that the former are 'the direct descendants of the revolt against tyranny' (in the sense that the group generally comprises so-called *ordinary people* rather than members of pre-existing elites), while the celeactor 'is a symptom of the decline of ascribed forms of power and a greater equality in the balance of power between social classes'. In the following sections I will argue that this is an unduly optimistic assessment of the role of celebrity in contemporary culture and one which is blind to many of the uses to which celebrity is put.

Theoretical perspectives on celebrity

Given that the rise of the figure of the celebrity throughout the twentieth century is closely linked to the increasingly industrialised production of cultural material, and in particular the rise of cinema and television as forms of mass entertainment, it is hardly surprising that most theorising initially focused on its mass-produced nature. In fact, the figure of the celebrity (and in particular the figure whose celebrity is achieved) is not perceived to be the problem – rather it is the manner in which celebrity is manufactured. Thus, in 1923, we find the poet and critic T. S. Eliot assessing favourably the achievement of the then-recently deceased music-hall artist, and example of early modern celebrity, Marie Lloyd. For Eliot (1963: 225), Lloyd was an embodiment of authentic working-class culture and her death was a reminder that the cultural decline he associated with increasing mass production was gathering speed:

> With the decay of the music-hall, with the encroachment of the cheap and rapid-breeding cinema, the lower orders will tend to drop into the same state of protoplasm as the bourgeoisie. The working man who went to the music-hall and saw Marie Lloyd and joined in the chorus was himself performing part of the act; he was engaged in that collaboration of the audience with the artist which is necessary in all art and most obviously in dramatic art. He will now go to the cinema, where his mind is lulled by continuous senseless music and continuous action too rapid for the brain to act upon, and will receive, without giving, in that same listless apathy with which the middle and upper classes regard any entertainment of the nature of art. He will also have lost some of his interest in life.

It will probably come as no great surprise that an essay which starts out as a eulogy to Marie Lloyd drifts, via this indictment of the cinema as a pernicious form of mass entertainment, into a condemnation of gramophones, cars and electrical appliances – namely, the proliferating paraphernalia of the emerging consumer society. Similar views are found at the other end of the political spectrum in the work of the Frankfurt School – a group of neo-Marxist scholars who came together in the 1930s at the University of Frankfurt's Institute for Social Research. In the introduction to *Dialectic of Enlightenment*, Theodor Adorno and Max Horkheimer (1997: pp. xiv–xv) preface their critique of modern mass-produced culture as follows:

> The fallen nature of modern man cannot be separated from social progress. On the one hand the growth of economic productivity furnishes the conditions for a world of greater justice; on the other hand it allows the technical apparatus and the social groups which administer it a disproportionate superiority to the rest of the population. The individual is wholly devalued in relation to the economic powers, which at the same time press the control of society over nature to hitherto unsuspected heights. Even though the individual disappears before the apparatus which he serves, that apparatus provides for him as never before. In an unjust state of life, the impotence and pliability of the masses grow with the quantitative increase in commodities allowed them ... The flood of detailed information and candy-floss entertainment simultaneously instructs and stultifies mankind.

Here too the theme of decline is foremost, although the assessment is altogether differently motivated. While much of Eliot's writing originated in a concern for a past he saw as in danger of being lost, Adorno and Horkheimer's work arises out of a concern for a future they perceived to be at risk of still-birth. Where they share common ground is on the issue of the perceived inauthenticity of mass-produced cultural forms and on the dangers implicit in the rise of the consumer society – in which commercially produced mass entertainment had already begun to play an increasingly important part. From the Adorno-Horkheimer perspective, what they term the 'culture industry' consists in the manufacture of standardised entertainment and pseudo individuality (explained below) which serve ultimately to fetter consumers into an acceptance of the status quo of class society, thereby scuppering or at least seriously weakening the possibility of structural change. Its entertainment products, which are said to bear the 'stigmata of capitalism' (Adorno *et al.* 1977: 123), instruct in that they serve to naturalise and normalise the exploitation inherent in capitalism through the messages they repeatedly convey. Thus, for example, they argue that 'Donald Duck in the cartoons and the unfortunate in real life get their thrashing so that the audience can learn to take their own punishment' (Adorno and Horkheimer 1997: 138). At the same time these products stultify through the stimulation and temporary satisfaction of false appetites.

Given such attitudes, it is not surprising that their perspective on celebrity was also negative. Thus they contend that the 'cult of celebrities (film stars) has a built-in social mechanism to level down everyone who stands out in any way', adding that 'stars are simply a pattern round which the world-embracing garment is cut' (Adorno and Horkheimer 1997: 236). From this perspective, celebrities (and the generic films they star in) are for all their appearance of heightened individuality merely 'vacant spaces' taken up by the powerful industry which produces them (Adorno and Horkheimer 1997: 236). Their individuality is more accurately a pseudo individuality and is, they suggest, of a piece with the products of Chrysler and General Motors – externally having the appearance of difference, but internally being more or less the same.

Similarly critical views are found in the work of French Marxists Edgar Morin (1960), Henri Lefebvre (2002) and Guy Debord (1994). Morin's (1960:98) study of audience responses to celebrity concluded that it is 'the misery of need, the mean and anonymous life that wants to enlarge itself to the dimensions of life in the movies' which lies at the heart of many fans' experience of identification with celebrity. The mean and anonymous life referred to is that of alienated labour, described by Marx (1971) in the *Economic and Philosophical Manuscripts*. From this perspective human beings under capitalism are held to be estranged from their own nature and from one another. For Morin, the identifications fans make with celebrities are projections of their pent-up need for autonomy and sense of agency denied them by the capitalist system. Thus a system which dehumanises is simultaneously held to provide a mechanism for relief, however illusory and temporary this may be. Similar ideas inform the work of Debord (1994) and his concept of late capitalism as the 'society of the spectacle'. From this perspective, the majority of people in the highly mediatised world of mid-twentieth-century consumer society are reduced to the role of 'Homo Spectator'. There is a parallel here with Noam Chomsky's (1991) assessment of Western capitalist democracy as 'spectator democracy' in which voters participate in elections at four-year or five-year intervals and are then expected to observe passively the spectacle played out by those they have elected as it unfolds before them in the media. In such a society, celebrities are seen as 'spectacular representations of living human beings, distilling the essence of the spectacle's banality into images of possible roles' (Debord 1994: 38). In this scenario, Lefebvre (2002: 91) writes:

> We are spared no detail of the everyday lives of princes and queens, of stars and millionaires, since 'great men' and 'bosses' and even 'heroes' have an everyday life on a par with our own. We 'know' their bathrooms almost as well as we know our own, we 'know' their mansions almost as well as we know our own flat, we 'know' their bodies almost as well as we know our own. This 'knowledge', if we can call it that, is spread throughout the world by means of images, and helps to create the attraction or powerful influence these celebrities exert … The humblest farm-hand 'knows' queens, princesses and filmstars. But if he really believes he has attained a 'knowledge' of something, he is being trapped by one of modernity's strangest and most disturbing alienations.

Contemporary theorists of late capitalism tend to be equally negative in their assessment of such forms of celebrity. Zygmunt Bauman (2007) recounts an anecdote told by the singer Corinne Bailey Rae that primary school children taught by her mother frequently say they want to be 'famous' when asked what they want to be when they grow up. Bauman (2007: 13) suggests that underneath this desire for fame is the 'dream of no longer dissolving and staying dissolved in the grey, faceless and insipid mass of commodities, a dream of turning into a notable, noticed and coveted commodity ... a commodity impossible to overlook, to deride, to be dismissed' – an interpretation wholly consonant with that of Morin. Bauman (2000) also points out that the figure of the celebrity, particularly against the backdrop of the individualism integral to the ideology of neoliberalism (discussed below), functions both as a kind of exemplar for survival in disorienting and uncertain times and as a source of advice. As Jock Young (2007: 184) puts it, the role of the stars 'is not merely to shine, they do not simply glisten, they are there to guide'. Hence the role of celebrity-driven chat shows in which the intimate details of personal battles with addictions, relationship problems and struggles of various types are recounted for public consumption. In this way the lives of celebrities in late modernity are presented as instructive spectacles in much the same way that the lives of the saints were on the walls of medieval cathedrals. Pre-modern devotion to the saints is thus replaced with the late modern cult of celebrity. At the same time, it could also be argued, the agency of the celebrity in consumer society is intimately bound up with the power to consume on a spectacular scale. This too is instruction of a particular kind which advertisers repeatedly draw on in their use of celebrity to endorse their products.

While agreeing with much of the thrust of this critique, it is worth pointing out, as Alex Callinicos (1989) has done, that such assessments (and in particular those of the Frankfurt School) run the risk of implying that life in consumer society automatically induces acceptance of the status quo – something which is clearly not the case. It is worthwhile recalling therefore that Herbert Marcuse's (1964) *One Dimensional Man: Studies in the Ideology of Advanced Industrial Society* (a key Frankfurt School text) was followed in 1968, only four years after its publication, with some of the largest mass strikes the industrialised world had seen – to say nothing of the burgeoning anti-Vietnam War movement, the civil rights movement, campaigns for homosexual law reform and what came to be known as the second wave of feminism. Collectively these might be said to challenge the hypothesis of the numbing effects of the society of the spectacle on the 'consciousness of servitude' (Marcuse 1964: 7) on which liberation was held to depend – or at least its ability to numb permanently. There is no reason to assume that the culture industry's meanings are straightforwardly accepted or that they remain uncontested by those to whom they are directed – nor indeed that all identifications audiences may make are necessarily those suggested by Morin and Bauman. Richard Dyer's (1986) work on the identifications made by gay men with Judy Garland in the 1950s and 1960s argues convincingly that these revolved around the recognition of mutual alienation rather than fantasy or escapism. This in turn was shown to have very real implications for an emerging sense of gay community.

That said, the industrial production of cultural material and the ideological function such material can seek to perform is a reality. In fact the term culture industry remains a useful blanket descriptor for the ways in which mediatised entertainment, news and comment are currently produced and disseminated. Indeed, the UK ELT industry itself can usefully be seen as a type of culture industry in which core products such as standardised textbooks aimed at the global market perform the ideological task of reinforcing the link between English and professional success, one form of which is the spectacular success achieved by some celebrities, in which their power to consume lavishly and the lifestyles they can afford feature prominently. In the following section I will suggest that the proliferation of celebrity culture, particularly over the last 30 years, is closely linked to the nature and functioning of neoliberal ideology.

Celebrity and neoliberalism

The point of connection between celebrity and neoliberalism is the concept of individualism. This has been described as the 'mainspring of bourgeois/capitalist philosophy' (O'Sullivan *et al.* 1994: 149) and 'a theory not only of abstract individuals but of the primacy of individual states and interests' (Williams 1976: 165). The figure of the celebrity can in many ways be seen as the individual writ large and it attracts and beguiles in many ways, in large part because of the agency which celebrities appear to possess. Despite a range of philosophical challenges to the concept of the wholly agentive individual from the mid-nineteenth century onward, individualism remains a necessary fiction for capitalism and may be said to lie at the heart of manufactured celebrity. In *The Road to Serfdom*, the Austrian economist and political philosopher Friedrich von Hayek (2001), whose ideas prefigured contemporary neoliberal thinking, argued (against a background of the Second World War) that individualism and collectivism were the two alternatives facing the world. Both socialism and fascism were seen as forms of collectivism leading to tyranny, while capitalist individualism alone was said to offer the prospect of freedom. As Hayek's ideas on free-market capitalism and his repudiation of welfare statism were taken up across the Anglophone world following the financial crisis of the 1970s (Holborow 2007), discourses of individualism became increasingly prevalent, particularly with regard to work – and ELT textbooks were no exception.

As we saw in Chapter 2, the concept of 'new capitalism' suggested that a transformation of the system had taken place as the so-called knowledge economy purportedly replaced the previously existing industrial model. While rejecting the notion of any structural change, Kevin Doogan (2009: p. x) argues persuasively that capitalism took 'a more irrational and intensely ideological form' from the 1970s onwards and that one of the features of this was the manufacture of uncertainty among employees with regard to job security. One spin-off from this was the proliferation of self-help literature throughout the 1990s by management gurus such as Tom Peters which purported to enable people to survive in times of uncertainty. Peters's 1994 volume *The Tom Peters Seminar* begins with a quotation from the CEO of Intel, 'Only the paranoid survive', a line which sets the tone for much of what follows, in which looking out for yourself and standing clear of the herd is the main message. In *The Brand You 50: Fifty Ways to Transform Yourself from an 'Employee' into a Brand that Shouts Distinction, Commitment and Passion!* Peters (2008) argues that the only way to survive in what he calls the 'new world economic order' is for individuals to brand themselves in such a way that they command attention in the marketplace (see Gray 2010b for detailed discussion). 'Selfishness' in such a climate he argues, 'is not only a virtue, it's a necessity' (Peters 2008: 15–16). From the perspective of this chapter what is interesting about Peters's approach is the way in which he draws repeatedly on celebrity to make his points. The book is dedicated to 'M J, Oprah, and Martha*, inventors of modern Brand You' (Peters 2008: p. v). The asterisk leads to a footnote which reads 'For the one-in-a-hundred-thousand who doesn't "get it": Jordan, Winfrey, and Stewart. (Real Brand Yous don't need full names)' (Peters 2008: p. v). All three are, of course, well-known contemporary US celebrities from the world of sport and television chat shows. In learning how to become what he refers to as 'CEO of your own life', Peters urges his readers to avoid cynicism and to learn from the example of these and other successfully branded individuals:

> Do you think M. Jordan is cynical about basketball ... M. McGwire about baseball ... S. Spielberg about movies ... P. Lynch about mutual funds ... Oprah W. about television? NO WAY! They are true believers all!
>
> (Peters 2008: 42)

> Most of us – save Martha Stewart and a handful of others – don't think of ourselves as 'a package'. Mistake! Everybody is a package.
>
> (Peters 2008: 46)

> We can't all be 'great.' Can't all glide like Michael Jordan. Or empathize like Oprah Winfrey. But we ... can ... aspire ... to achieve ... distinction ...of some sort.
>
> (Peters 2008: 101)

And so it continues. The celebrities Peters refers to are all in the achieved category and their deployment is a powerful reminder of the ideological function celebrity can be made to serve. At the same time, the rise of celebrity parallels the marginalisation of class referred to in Chapter 4 and performs important ideological work in its celebration of individualism. First, with the rise of mass-audience television programmes such as *Big Brother*, *Pop Idol*, *Britain's Got Talent* and *The Apprentice* (to name but a few examples of the celebrity-manufacturing genres that have mushroomed over the period in which neoliberalism has become established), celebrity assumes the appearance of being brought within the reach of all. Seemingly ordinary people, who audiences can relate to, achieve spectacular success for themselves in environments of brutal competition. As Adorno and Horkheimer (1997: 137) suggest – and not improbably – '[a]musement under late capitalism is the prolongation of work. It is sought after as an escape from the mechanised work process, and to recruit strength in order to be able to cope with it again'. Although all reality show participants cannot be winners, these programmes revolve around the premise of a level playing field in which those competing appear to have an equal chance of winning, an ideologically convenient message for the neoliberal times in which we live. The very term *reality* television is in fact an indicator of the ideological work such programmes seek to perform. Secondly, as society is held to have moved from one of producers to one of consumers, so class-based identity is said to be eclipsed by consumer-based identities in which the wealth concomitant with celebrity is fetishised – in the Marxist sense of not being recognised for what it is. Writing about the effects of celebrity culture and its association with wealth, Lawrence Friedman (1999: 46) puts it thus:

> Not many people, it seems, connect their own suffering and privations, their own hunger and longings, with the wealth they see all around them. To the contrary, the money of the rich smells sweet to them. For Marxists, capitalist wealth was blood money, money squeezed from the sweat and muscles of starving workers, money poisoned by poverty, disease and death; money was greed, exploitation; it was man's oppression of man. Contemporary money is radically different; magically it has been washed clean of these bad associations. The public mind connects it with fun: with the world of sports and entertainment. The new (and glamorous) rich are movie stars, rock-and-roll musicians, baseball and soccer players, heroes of TV sitcoms. These are indeed the most visible rich. They breed no resentment. Indeed, the masses seem all too eager to contribute their share of the rents and the tributes.

While I would suggest Friedman overstates his case in his assessment of the public mind (or at least sections of it), he is right to draw attention to the way in which the visible wealth of the celebrity may be seen or presented as somehow the natural accompaniment and result of individual merit. By implication such visibly 'merited' wealth serves to justify the system that permits its accumulation – a point similar to that made by Slavoj Žižek (2008) in his assessment of the ideological function of the philanthropic interventions of capitalists such as Bill Gates and George Soros.[1]

In the following sections I explore the way in which celebrity has featured in UK-produced ELT textbooks from the late 1970s until the present – a period which is more or less coterminous with the emergence of the intensely ideological form of capitalism which is central to this volume.

The textbook sample: criteria for selection and methodology

The textbooks analysed are an amalgamation of two samples used in previous studies (Gray 2010a, 2010b) with the addition of a further three books from the best selling Headway series. Two of these Headway books have appeared since the second study was carried out and one, the first book in the series, was not included in the original study. In the first study I looked at the intermediate-level book in the four top-selling courses published in the UK since the late 1970s – the Streamline, Strategies, Cambridge English and Headway courses (Gray 2010a). In the follow-up study I added a further set of books from the successful Headway series – solely on the basis of its extraordinary global success, attested by booksellers and publishers alike (Gray 2010b). I also included two books from the Cutting Edge series, another popular contemporary course. With the additions mentioned for this chapter, the current sample comprises fifteen titles.[2]

As in the earlier studies I began by adopting a content analysis approach. I counted the units (the term generally used in ELT publishing for textbook chapters) in which a celebrity, whether real or fictional, was profiled in a listening, reading, writing, speaking or grammar-based activity. I also counted the number of celebrities profiled per unit in these activities and recorded the category each one fell into according to Rojek's (2001) taxonomy (see Table 5.1). However, I did not count the plethora of celebrities whose names and photographs pepper the textbooks but who are not profiled as such – although I do refer to some of these on occasion in my discussion below. This was then followed by a more qualitative analysis in which I discuss the changes in the representation and treatment of celebrity over the period.

The treatment of celebrity in ELT materials

Any discussion of textbooks needs to be situated within the bigger picture of the ELT industry. As pointed out in Chapter 1 UK ELT textbook production is a multimillion-pound activity. The British Council's 2009–10 annual report estimates that when industrial testing such as IELTS (International English Language Testing Systems) and ELT services generally are also taken into consideration, the industry is worth £3–4 billion a year to the British economy. Not surprisingly this industry repeatedly makes the case for English as a language worth learning in terms of the economic benefits it can bring to countries and to individual speakers; and with regard to developing world countries it repeatedly equates both development and education with English. Thus the British Council's current involvement in the politically motivated Rwandan Government's switch from French-medium to English-medium education is presented as synonymous with post-genocide development, while the export of the Cambridge Teaching Knowledge Test to Sudan has, it is claimed, 'provided teachers from Darfur to Khartoum with the first step on the road to becoming better qualified and *better able to meet the demands of rebuilding their country*' (British Council 2010: 17; emphasis added). However, the precise nature of the way in which English and such development are linked is not spelled out. Euromonitor International's (2010) report for the British Council entitled *The Benefits of the English Language for Individuals and Societies: Quantitative Indicators from Cameroon, Nigeria, Rwanda, Bangladesh and Pakistan* makes for interesting reading in this respect. Here the suggestion is made that what is referred to as 'linguistic unity' – the report's term for country-wide use of English for business purposes – results in 'a competitive advantage globally' (Euromonitor International 2010: 8). The executive summary concludes as follows:

> Education is a long-term investment for each government, but a citizen's individual ambition is the prime motivator. Interviews with companies indicate that individuals regard education as the best way to escape poverty, and believe that learning English in particular offers great opportunities for career advancement ... and it is broadly accepted in each country that a good degree and strong language skills lead to economic prosperity and individual wealth.
>
> (Euromonitor International 2010: 14)

The report is based in part on interview data with locals in which such ideologies about English are taken at face value. However, as Eddie Williams (2011) points out, UNICEF statistics for 2010 show there is no evidence to suggest that the use of exoglossic languages such as English or French in such settings has in any material way contributed to actual development. The point I wish to underline here is that ideologies associated with English which take it as self-evident that it is perforce the language of economic prosperity and individual wealth are also those of the ELT industry itself (see e.g. British Council annual reports at www.britishcouncil. org). And these ideologies, I will suggest, are repeatedly reproduced in textbooks in a variety of ways, not least through the deployment of celebrity-based content and the associations this seeks to create.

As I have pointed out elsewhere (Gray 2010a), celebrities only begin to proliferate in textbooks in the late 1970s. Initially, they serve a number of limited functions related to students' assumed schematic knowledge. For example, in *Streamline Connections* (Hartley and Viney 1979) students are presented with the question 'Do you work as hard as your boss?', and are then asked to make new questions using elements which include 'drive fast / James Hunt' – the latter a then internationally well-known racing car driver. Other celebrities from the world of sport and pop music feature in similar ways – thus a television interviewer's work schedule lists a meeting with Paul McCartney as a way of underlining his wife's point that his day will be interesting, while hers, spent at home looking after their baby, will not. At the same time, the textbook features a small cast of invented celebrities whose function appears to be mainly for entertainment purposes – for example, a trainee reporter interviews a champion boxer named 'Brutus Cray' (whose voice on the accompanying tape sounds like that of Cassius Clay/Muhammad Ali) and a pop singer called 'Elton Kash'. The textbook also features a lengthy (for *Streamline Connections*) one-page profile of Elvis Presley, accompanied by seven photographs of the singer at different stages of his career. The focus is on his achievement (record sales, earnings, adulation) and his impact on US popular culture. In the accompanying comprehension questions, students are simply asked to retrieve information about this from the text – a conventional textbook approach to reading practice. This reading text is the first detailed portrait of a real celebrity in any book of the period that I am familiar with, and it represents the beginning of a trend which would see celebrities (both real and fictional) becoming an established feature of textbooks and one in which they also come to feature as role models.

From the 1980s onwards the incidence and extended treatment of celebrity increases dramatically. *Cambridge English 2* (Swan and Walter 1990) is the one exception to this trend and is the only book in the sample without a profile of any celebrity figure. Two units out of a total of thirty-six refer to celebrity – but only in passing and the references are at the level of assumed schematic knowledge, as in the James Hunt example above. As a consequence of the absence of celebrity profiling, this textbook has a more educational flavour in terms of thematic content than any of the other books in the sample. In contrast, all the other books feature celebrity in between half and all their units. This occurs at the sentence level (as instanced above) and at the level of artwork (in many cases with no corresponding written text), but increasingly it entails more detailed profiles of celebrities. As stated above, Table 5.1 only records the instances where celebrities are profiled. However, it is important to be aware that, although a textbook such as *New Cutting Edge Upper Intermediate* (Cunningham and Moor 2005a) is shown to contain five units (out of twelve) in which a total of thirteen celebrities are profiled, the book itself contains dozens more who pepper the text and feature in the artwork, but receive no explicit treatment.

It is immediately clear from Table 5.1 that the kind of celebrity most featured is of the achieved kind. The few examples of ascribed celebrity are mainly members of the British royal family, while those in the attributed category tend to be eccentric real-life characters who are somehow notable for their individualism and who have captured the attention of the media (e.g. a retired woman who has travelled the world in a caravan), those who have made money in their business ventures, along with a number of child prodigies of various kinds (e.g. gifted musicians and painters). In the following discussion, I will focus mainly on achieved celebrity, given that it predominates, and the way in which this has changed over time – although I will refer to other kinds where relevant to the points I am making.

As I have suggested elsewhere (Gray 2010b) celebrity characters tend to be presented to students as worthy of their approval on account of their single-minded dedication to a chosen path in life and distinction in their field. Early examples from *Building Strategies* (Abbs and Freebairn 1984) feature profiles of real-life celebrities which include the ice skaters Jayne Torvill and Christopher Dean, Elvis Presley and Winnie Mandela, along with profiles of a fictional boxer, a female folk singer and a female novelist. In all cases the focus of attention is on the nature of their achievement (hit records, gold medals, literary prizes) or aspects of their character (dedication, intelligence, bravery) – but in no case is the focus on their wealth. However, with the appearance of the Headway course things begin to change. By the mid to late 1990s there is a noticeable shift towards the deployment of celebrity characters who are typified by their business acumen or by professional success and whose celebrity is altogether more spectacular than anything found in previous books. Thus we find a reading about real-life attributed celebrity Cherry Haines who left England for

TABLE 5.1   Celebrity in textbooks

Textbook	Number of units	Number of units in which celebrity is profiled	Number of celebrities profiled	Type of celebrity
Streamline Connections 1979	80	5	12	11 achieved/ 1 attributed
Building Strategies 1984	16	2	7	7 achieved
Headway Intermediate 1986	14	7	8	2 achieved/ 1 ascribed/ 5 attributed
The New Cambridge English Course 2 1990	36	–	–	–
New Headway Intermediate1996	12	4	7	6 achieved/ 1 attributed
New Headway Upper-Intermediate 1998	12	4	5	4 achieved/ 1 attributed
New Headway Pre-Intermediate 2000a	14	2	3	3 achieved
New Headway Elementary 2000b	14	3	4	1 achieved/ 3 attributed
New Headway Advanced 2003a	12	7	12	11 achieved/ 1 ascribed
New Edition New Headway Intermediate 2003b	12	5	8	6 achieved/ 2 attributed
New Headway Upper-Intermediate 2005	12	4	12	4 achieved/ 2 ascribed/ 6 celeactors
New Cutting Edge Upper-Intermediate 2005a	12	5	13	12 achieved/ 1 attributed
New Cutting Edge Intermediate 2005b	12	1	7	7 achieved
New Headway Intermediate 2009	12	4	7	6 achieved/ 1 ascribed
New Headway Elementary 2011	12	4	9	7 achieved/ 2 ascribed

Australia 'because there wasn't much employment' (Soars and Soars 1998: 38–9) and who, despite starting off with very little money, effortlessly became a multimillionaire. A typical example of spectacular achieved celebrity, which I have commented on elsewhere (Gray 2010a), is found in the profile of fictional pop star Donna Flynn and footballer Terry Wiseman (Soars and Soars 2000a: 58–9). The text is accompanied by four colour photographs of the attractive young couple staring out at the imagined viewer, a technique used to create identification with the viewer through the use of what Erving Goffman (1979: 16) calls a 'summoning look'. The profile is presented in the form of a two-page spread similar to *Hello! Magazine* and begins as follows:

> This is the most famous couple in the country. She is the pop star who has had six number one records – more than any other single artist. He has scored fifty goals for Manchester United, and has played for England over thirty times. Together they earn about £20 million a year. They invited Hi! Magazine into their luxurious home.
>
> (Soars and Soars 2000a: 58)

Thus in addition to distinction in their respective fields, their wealth is also foregrounded. However, as generic lifestyle magazine characters typified by their wealth, success and glamour they are identical to any number of other celebrities – although they are in fact clearly modelled on David and Victoria Beckham. As such, they may be said to exemplify the 'vacant spaces' hypothesised by Adorno and Horkheimer, their (pseudo) individuality cut to a world-embracing pattern which is largely predetermined. Significantly there is no link between the artwork, which predominates on the page, and the actual language being practised. The artwork functions simply to index a particular set of consumerist values and lifestyle which are being grafted onto English. The appearance of the celebrities, the settings in which they are photographed and the content of the reading itself are in fact part of the familiar spectacle of luxury repeatedly mounted by celebrity magazines such as *Hello!* As part of the follow-up to the reading, students are told to buy 'a magazine like *Hi!* and find an interview with a famous couple. Bring it into class and tell the class about it' (Soars and Soars 2000a: 58) – thereby reinforcing the association of English and the experience of learning English with an exploration of the world of celebrity wealth and professional success.

With this in mind, it is revealing to look at the way in which celebrity characters have been updated over various generations of the same textbook. For example, an exercise to practise time expressions in the 1996 version of *Headway Intermediate* revolves around the biography of the fictional writer Joanna Hardy who, the text informs, 'has had an interesting life' (Soars and Soars 1996: 98) – thereby evaluating her positively for the student. High points in her life story include publishing her first collection of poems while still at primary school, followed by winning The Times Literary Award for her second novel while in her twenties and being given The Whitbread Trophy for literary merit at age 40. She is replaced in the 2003 edition by the equally successful if more glamorous and cosmopolitan Astrid Johnsson, a

42-year-old fictional Swedish cellist. The latter in turn is replaced by Calvin Klein in the 2009 edition, whose career high points are more entrepreneurial in flavour and feature the launch of his clothing company at age 26, a subsequent move into sportswear, followed by the creation of his trademark jeans, underwear, perfume and cosmetics ranges. The profile ends with the information that 'His company makes $6 billion every year' (Soars and Soars 2009: 56). In all cases the follow-up exercises encourage students to identify with the interesting life (mentioned in all three editions) by variously imagining leading such a life themselves, making a similar list of the events in their own life and by interviewing/role-playing the celebrity.

Achieved celebrity is always the result of some kind of merit and it is worth pointing out that celebrities from the world of popular culture (particularly the real-world counterparts of those such as Flynn and Wiseman) received official endorsement from the first New Labour government in the UK (1997–2001). Biressi and Nunn (2008) recount how Tony Blair sought to associate himself with a host of celebrities from the world of popular entertainment and sport, many of whom were invited to 10 Downing Street and photographed with the Prime Minister as part of a branding exercise in which the government's new demotic style was emphasised. The aim was to present New Labour as both popular and meritocratic. As emblems of individual achievement and embodiments of aspiration (a point I will return to later) their function was to set the tone for a government which would make much of its commitment to, in Blair's words, 'social justice and economic dynamism, ambition and compassion, fairness and enterprise going together' (in Fairclough 2000: 10). As Owen Jones (2011) has pointed out, meritocracy implies that inequalities remain unaddressed while those with more ability or more accurately (in its Blairite formulation) those with more ambition, more dynamism and more enterprise naturally come to the fore.

The tendency for textbooks to focus on wealth and success continues throughout the first decade of the twenty-first century with another noticeable shift towards a focus on celebrities from the world of entertainment who are also successful entrepreneurs, or entrepreneurs who become celebrities on account of their spectacular achievement in business. Examples of the former are J. K. Rowling, profiled as 'Author and billionaire' (Soars and Soars 2009) and Oprah Winfrey whose life story is told under the heading 'TV Star and Billionaire' (Soars and Soars 2011). The latter's profile begins by telling readers that she is a famous TV star who has apartments in California and Chicago and that she 'is one of the richest women in America', that she 'earns millions of dollars every year', that she donates a lot of money to charity, and that '[l]ast year she earned $260,000,000 (Soars and Soars 2011: 46–7). This celebratory profile, in which her spending power is clearly signalled, is particularly interesting, given that the Winfrey phenomenon has been the subject of a considerable amount of media coverage and scholarly analysis. Janice Peck's (2008) *The Age of Oprah: Cultural Icon for the Neoliberal Era* is an insightful anatomy of the Oprah Winfrey brand, which she concludes revolves around promoting the concept of the 'enterprising self' that is prepared to take responsibility for all kinds of misfortune including poverty, and peddling the idea that 'changing individual attitudes and behaviour rather than addressing structural political inequities' (Peck

2008: 11–12) is the way to address social problems. The Headway profile concludes with the following lines, which underline Winfrey's own agentive taking of responsibility when dealing with poverty as a child:

> In 1998, Oprah started the charity Oprah's Angel Network to help poor children all over the world. In 2007, she opened a special school in Johannesburg, The Oprah Winfrey Academy for Girls. She says, 'When I was a kid, we were poor, and we didn't have much money. So what did I do? I studied hard.' There are 152 girls at the school, and Oprah calls them her daughters – children she didn't have in real life.
>
> (Soars and Soars 2011: 47)

Peck (2008: 211) points out that the 152 girls in question were all selected on the basis of whether or not they had what Winfrey called the 'it' quality and that the academy aims to convey the message that 'you cannot blame apartheid, your parents, your circumstances, because you are not your circumstances. You are your possibilities. If you know that, you can do anything' (from O, The Oprah Winfrey Magazine, in Peck 2008: 212). Peck points out that hostility to the school, where vast sums of Winfrey's money were spent on a very small number of carefully selected children, was such that the South African Government, which had initially considered partnering the project, withdrew in the face of popular hostility. Needless to say, although in the public domain, none of this information appears in the Headway profile of Winfrey. Instead, Winfrey is presented largely on her own terms as a self-made success.

At the same time there are in-depth profiles of Vijay and Bhikhu Patel, the winners of the 2001 Ernst & Young Entrepreneur of the Year award; Anita Roddick, the founder of the Body Shop (Soars and Soars 2003a); the television chef Jamie Oliver and businessman Roman Abramovich (Soars and Soars 2005); the fashion designer Calvin Klein (as previously mentioned) and Prince Charles (Soars and Soars 2009). The profile of Prince Charles is noteworthy because, although he is clearly an example of ascribed celebrity, he is also presented as an entrepreneurial businessman under the heading of 'The life of a hard-working future King' (Soars and Soars 2009: 18):

> The Prince of Wales has his own food company, Duchy Originals. It originally sold biscuits, but is now expanding to become one of Britain's best-known and most successful organic brands, with over 200 different products, including food, drinks, and hair and body care products.
>
> (Soars and Soars 2009: 19)

In this way celebrity and business success are shown to come together in the lives of those profiled. At the same time, students are encouraged to think about their own lives and career paths in the light of celebrity success. Both the *New Headway Advanced* (Soars and Soars 2003a) and *New Cutting Edge Upper Intermediate* (Cunningham and Moor 2005a) have a whole unit each on celebrity, and while both units imply that celebrity can be problematic (in the sense that we can become obsessed with it), they also encourage students to consider ways of becoming celebrities. In *New Headway Advanced* this takes the form of a speaking activity entitled 'How to become an A-list celebrity' (Soars and Soars 2003a: 44). Students work in groups and are given a series of cards by the teacher, each of which contains information which the group has to discuss. When a decision is made, they request another card and continue until they succeed or fail in their endeavour to achieve celebrity status. The first card reads as follows:

> It is time to start your journey on the road to fame and fortune. You want to make it to the big time as quickly as possible. You have identified two routes that could find you a way to join the rich and famous.
>
> Invent an interesting new past for yourself – become a new person! One that could make you newsworthy. Go to 7.
>
> Work your way into the elite groups of famous people by hanging out in the right places. Basically you will party your way to the top. Go to 2.
>
> (Soars and Soars 2003a: 44)

On completion of the speaking activity, the textbook points out that activities such as these are frequently used in management training 'to practice qualities of good leadership' and asks students 'What are the qualities of a good leader?' (Soars and Soars 2003a: 44). In this way the individualism (whether pseudo or not) that lies at the heart of manufactured celebrity is linked to the individualism needed to succeed in the world of work – precisely the point being made by Peters in his self-help manuals.

Earlier I suggested that the ELT industry can be seen as a type of culture industry in the sense that core products such as textbooks are standardised confections, which despite superficial differences, ultimately package the language they are selling in more or less the same way, with the underlying message being that English equates with success. Nowhere is this more evident than in the treatment of celebrity. Although, as I have shown, the treatment of celebrity is subject to minor modification as celebrities themselves change, the result overall, as Adorno and Horkheimer (1997: 134) concluded with regard to Hollywood movies, 'is the constant reproduction of the same thing'. Before concluding this chapter, I turn briefly in the next section to the way in which a group of experienced teachers working in a variety of very different settings globally discuss the proliferation of celebrity in ELT materials.

Teachers' perspectives on celebrity

As part of an initial exploration of how practising teachers view the use of celebrity in ELT textbooks, I asked 15 teachers to whom I had access to complete a short questionnaire on the treatment of celebrity in textbooks (see Appendix). The reason for this consultation is that earlier research suggests that teachers in certain contexts frequently find some aspects of textbook content problematic (Gray 2010a), and in my view the treatment of celebrity merited exploration. These teachers were completing or had recently completed an MA in ELT. None of the teachers consulted was a novice – the least experienced had four years' experience, while the most experienced had been teaching for 30 years. The eleven teachers who responded work in a variety of very different settings: UK, German and Saudi Arabian university language centres, private-sector schools in the UK, Austria, and Japan, and the state-school sector in Slovenia, Switzerland and Taiwan.

As might be expected, teachers working in such diverse settings held very different views, although they did agree on a number of things. In the first place they all took the view that the proliferation of celebrity in textbooks mirrored the explosion of celebrity in the media generally. Thus Peter (10),[3] a British-Irish teacher working in a language centre in a German university, said:

> As media channels have grown in ubiquity their output has come to dominate much of the 'news' in society. Mostly, the media channels are filled (saturated) with celebrity stories ... The coursebooks, under the belief of relevancy or up-to-dateness, hold a mirror to the world they see and make generalised assumptions about what learners will probably identify with.

Similarly Colin (13), a British teacher who works in a UK university language centre, used the same metaphor in his answer: 'I guess it mirrors the explosion of celebrity coverage in the popular media'. Ahmed (4.5), a British ESOL teacher accustomed to working with migrants and currently working in a private language school in the UK, agreed but nuanced this somewhat by linking the use of celebrity in textbooks with advertising more generally:

> In all forms of mass media, consumers are bombarded with constant streams of advertising. Much of this advertising tends to feature celebrities or is endorsed by celebrities in some way. It's a symbiotic relationship between the media and celebrities. Without celebrity endorsement, a product is said to be bland and lifeless. The use of celebrities gives certain credibility to a product. If a product is used/endorsed by a high profile celebrity, then in the eyes of the consumer, it must be good ... I suppose these advertising techniques have caught the interest of ELT material designers and publishers. It creates a certain brand image, a reputation, more attention, better consumer recall, etc. All of which ultimately means more sales for publishers. Unfortunately, it all comes down to money. Money makes the world go round!

The implication of this comment is that specific textbooks or courses seek to present themselves as if they were endorsed by the kinds of celebrities deployed on their pages – a practice which, he suggests, is designed to promote sales, maintain interest and retain customers. In fact, all informants took the view that textbook use of celebrity was broadly similar to the use of celebrity by the mass media generally.

With regard to the deployment of celebrities of the kind referred to in the previous sections, several informants gave their approval. Ana (30), a Slovenian state-school teacher, was the most enthusiastic of all informants and took the view that:

> Celebrities are mainly individuals that our students see on TV, at the cinema or hear on the radio. So, often enough they tend to be people with whom our students can identify, people that they want to talk about because they idolize them and want to become them. I applaud celebrities in my teaching because it adds that spark needed for motivation to get the students talking, commenting.

However, most informants tended to nuance their comments, particularly with regard to educational context. For example, Ann Marie (26), a British-Austrian teacher working in Austria said that celebrity-based content was suitable for 'westernised, young, up and coming, middle-class teenagers and young couples with relatively high self-esteem', but she suggested that in 'countries where many students are poor' such material would be 'a slap in the face for those whose problems revolve around having enough to eat'. Like Ana, Ann Marie was also convinced of the motivating potential of such material and stated that 'Celebrities represent what "could be yours" if you better your English – and why not?', before adding 'If using celebrities motivates students to learn English then – bring them on'. It is interesting to note that Ann Marie's reservations are related to what she understands to be the potential inappropriateness of celebrity-based material in certain developing world contexts, rather than any qualms about the values associated with such content. In similar vein Billy (22), who works in a private Japanese school, while elsewhere making the case for materials-free teaching, took the view that what could be interpreted as the overtly ideological nature of such content was of little concern if it got students interested and he was sceptical of the possibility that any negative effects could be predicted. In response to the *Hi! Magazine* text described above, he gave his opinion as follows:

> Well, I suppose many opponents of this style of textbook will point to a political bias in that such imagery endorses the perception of the excellence of westernised ideals and is consequently an endorsement of globalisation (or a somewhat surreptitious attempt by publishers and other connections to advertise globalisation). However, there may be some teachers (myself included) who are more than happy to adopt anything legal that makes the act of studying English as attractive as possible to students. The impact of these photographs on students will probably vary according to their situation although it may be somewhat naïve and condescending to assume that students from developing countries will be 'victims' of the 'Learning English = Road to Riches' equation.

The 'anything legal' remark is a reminder that, for many teachers in a range of ELT contexts, pedagogy is understood as an essentially apolitical activity in which the only goal is getting students motivated. Such views resonate with Žižek's (1989) assessment of the ways in which cynicism and ideology come together. In such cases he argues 'one knows the falsehood very well, one is well aware of a particular interest hidden behind an ideological universality, but still one does not renounce it' (Žižek

1989: 26). Interestingly, Billy's final remarks are contradicted by the Euromonitor International report referred to above where developing world informants did indeed confirm their subscription to the dominant ideology emanating from the ELT industry which seeks to link English with economic development and the acquisition of personal wealth.

Liz (16), a Scottish teacher working in the Taiwanese state-school sector saw positive and negative aspects in the use of celebrity-based material in her context. On the negative side she mentioned that not all students are interested in the lives of Western celebrities or even know who they are (a point I will return to below), while on the positive side she suggested:

> Using celebrities usually promotes lively discussion among students. It gives students a chance to freely express opinion without worrying too much about the structure of their language (the need to communicate overcomes the worry about making mistakes, which can be a good thing). There are lots of fun activities based around the topic of celebrities. This topic also allows for introducing music and music videos or film video clips into the classroom.

Fun was also mentioned by Susan (19), a British ESOL teacher who, although largely critical of celebrity-based material, suggested that content can be made to look 'more sexy' and 'fun' through the use of celebrity. Fun was indirectly referred to by Wadud (9), a British teacher working in a Saudi Arabian university language centre, when he suggested that the inclusion of celebrity represented an attempt on the part of publishers 'to make studying language less boring'. The emphasis on fun and games in ELT pedagogy is in fact well established. Titles such as *Play Games with English* (Granger 1993), *Intermediate Communication Games* (Hadfield 2000) and *Easy English Vocabulary Games* (Schinke-Llano 1992) are just a few of the many which are available, all of which testify to this trend within ELT. This tendency has been plausibly linked by Christopher Anderson (2002) to the marketisation of education whereby students are reconstrued as a customers who, as I have suggested elsewhere, are increasingly understood to be 'in need of content which is maximally entertaining' (Gray 2010a: 70). Indeed, as has been pointed out by another of the authors of this book, one of the features of neoliberalism has been the widespread repositioning of individuals as customers across an ever expanding range of domains within the public sphere (Holborow 2007). And of course celebrity-based content can also be linked to this entertainment imperative, given that the manufacture of celebrity is a key feature of the culture industry more generally.

Overall there was no outright rejection of celebrity *per se* – with teachers generally taking the view that it was a question of getting the celebrities right. Those selected for inclusion in textbooks were frequently badly chosen, according to Peter, who outlined his view on the use of celebrities generally as follows:

> I have a number of difficulties with their use. Firstly, overuse of celebrities in the materials and often an erroneous assumption that they (celebrities) help

in some way to engage interest or to be worthwhile topics of discussion or that we care about them. Secondly, they appear to legitimise or standardise the notion that we should be interested in this type of content. Thirdly, even if they are good materials, the transient nature of celebrity means the materials can date very quickly (good business model for the publisher's second, third, fourth, etc. edition, but not good for the pockets of learners, schools or colleges). Lastly and with regard to ELT materials, without fail 95+% are anglocentric celebrities, be it music, actors, business people, etc. Where are all the other people in the world?

His suggestion that the inclusion of celebrity was linked to built-in obsolescence which works to the publishers' advantage was a point also made by Billy, while his comment about Anglocentricity was echoed by many teachers who felt those producing the materials frequently miscalculated in their attempts to identify characters that students might be interested in. The most critical voice in this small database was that of Ahmed. Writing very much from the perspective of British ESOL, his position no doubt reflects the unavoidably political nature of migrant education, particularly in the current climate:

> The vast majority of immigrants in the UK choose to learn English for study, employment and to make a decent living. The life of a celebrity is so far removed from reality and how most 'ordinary' people live in the UK. It is a dishonest portrayal of life in the UK. It creates false dreams and aspirations in the minds of language learners. Instead, I would argue for use of more realistic characters, like the average Joe and what he has to go through in everyday life to feed his family. This is particularly relevant given the current economic situation in the UK and the fact that the country is run by a bunch of toffs and wannabe celebrities completely oblivious to the plight of ordinary people.

But of course most books are produced for the lucrative global market rather than for the sector in which Ahmed works. That said, textbooks are not produced in a vacuum and while they can be said to reproduce dominant ideologies, the ELT industry is also sensitive to challenges to those ideologies – as we shall see in the final section.

Conclusion

In the light of what has been written so far, a number of questions suggest themselves: Why do ELT textbooks take the form they do with regard to celebrity and neoliberalism? Why do some teachers view the representations of the kind described above with equanimity? And finally, with regard to the theme of the present volume, what are the implications for the field generally?

To begin with, it is important to state that there is necessarily a degree of overlap between any answers that can be given and that some hints have already been provided. With regard to the first question a possible explanation can be found in David Harvey's (2005: 3) assertion that neoliberalism has become 'hegemonic as a mode of discourse'. It has, he suggests, 'pervasive effects on ways of thought to the point where it has become incorporated into the common-sense way many of us interpret, live in, and understand the world' (Harvey 2005: 3). For ELT publishers and many teachers alike it may simply reflect how the world now appears to be. As Ann Marie put it:

> The westernised world lives in a world of consumerism and materialism. To deny these facts in materials' contents would be to deny that which our students can see around them in everyday life, that which interests them and that to which they can relate.

Another possible answer to the first question is that many ELT textbooks originate in the highly marketised commercial sector and that, as Scott Thornbury (2010) suggests, 'ELT itself is increasingly seen, by its practitioners, as an entrepreneurial culture, offering plentiful opportunities for self-realisation and, even, fame.' From this perspective the world created in textbooks is very like the world in which those producing them actually live.

And finally, as has already been suggested by some of the teachers, such content may reflect what some students themselves aspire to – although there is no research-based evidence to suggest that this is so. However, ELT publishers do see such content as designed to tap into students' aspirations – something which was confirmed in interviews I carried out with four senior figures in a major ELT publishing house (Gray 2010a). The problem with the ELT industry's view of aspiration is that it is thoroughly individualistic in orientation. Jones (2011) argues convincingly that the world ushered in by successive Thatcher governments was one in which aspiration was re-semanticised to exclude any sense of collective aspiration. On the subject of aspiration and the sale of public housing, he writes:

> the policy was part and parcel of Thatcher's determination to make us think of ourselves as individuals who looked after ourselves above all else. Only that would make people feel responsible for their successes and failures. Thatcherism was fostering a new culture where success was measured by what you owned. Those who did not adapt were to be despised. Aspiration was no longer about people working together to improve their communities; it was being redefined as getting more for yourself as an individual, regardless of the social costs.
>
> (Jones 2011: 61)

This is precisely the kind of aspiration which is found in ELT materials and which I would argue needs to be challenged – such content may be 'legal' as Billy suggested, but that should not mean we automatically subscribe to its limited world-view. That said, change may be in the offing. It is interesting to note how the current crisis in neoliberal ideology appears to have triggered a degree of media disquiet on the topic of celebrity, of the kind found in the Hyde book referred to in the introduction to this chapter. Certain sectors of the ELT industry now appear to share this – although it is too early to say what the consequences of this might be. Global, a new course launched in 2010 by Macmillan, claims to eschew celebrity-based content. Lindsay Clanfield (2010), one of the authors, explains that there are three reasons for this. In the first place, echoing the views of some of the teachers in the previous section, he points out that many supposedly international celebrities are not well-known to students and, by implication, may not trigger the interest they are intended to. Second, the facts about them keep changing in such a way as to complicate the activity of materials production:

> As a coursebook writer, this point was brought home to me in 2005, the year that Brad Pitt and Jennifer Anniston got divorced. I wasn't personally distressed at the break-up of such a nice-looking Hollywood couple, nor was I caught up in the whole Angelina Jolie angle. No, this event was of significance to me as a writer because that very same year a coursebook of mine was coming out that used Brad and Jennifer as an example of 'a married couple'. Everything had to be changed and it was very stressful.
>
> (Clanfield 2010: 4)

Third, there is the recognition that teachers in many contexts have misgivings about the appropriateness of celebrity-based content, particularly those working in settings where English is seen as part of education as opposed to mere skill acquisition:

> There is also a more ideological reason, and it's simply that this kind of material does not conform to many educators' ideas of what education is about. It's what gets English coursebooks criticised for being vapid and, as one fellow teacher remarked to me once, 'so light that if I don't hold on tightly it will just float away'.
>
> (Clanfield 2010: 4)

That the ELT industry appears to be considering such perspectives – and textbook publishing is very cautious about taking risks with regard to tried and tested formulas – is suggestive that changing economic times brought about by the ongoing global financial crisis may be seen to require a rethink with regard to the nature of content.

As to why some teachers featured in this chapter appear to regard celebrity content with a degree of equanimity, I have already suggested that in many settings teaching is viewed as an apolitical activity. In this respect the increasing marketisation of education is crucial as initial teacher training is progressively reconfigured along narrowly defined lines (see Chapter 6 for detailed discussion). There is also the fact that those teachers working in the private sector are positioned overwhelmingly as service providers and their students are seen as customers. This too serves to divorce language teaching from education more generally.

What then are the implications for the field? Elsewhere (Gray 2010a) I have argued that teachers need to become more sociopolitically active in making the case for alternative articulations of English. This is still my view and one of the ways that we can begin to go about this is through engagement with the kind of interdisciplinary thinking being argued for in this book. Such a perspective takes the view that ELT, regardless of the context in which it occurs, is perforce a political activity and it is therefore incumbent on us as teachers, as teacher educators and as applied linguists to understand the nature of this activity and in particular the nature of the tools we use to carry it out. In addition to work of this kind, those of us who are convinced of the necessity for change need to make the case for, and become involved in, the production and dissemination materials which embody values other than those expressed by the ELT industry. It is important to recall that while English may be the language of global capitalism, it has also been, and continues to be, one of the languages of global resistance.

Appendix: Celebrity and ELT materials questionnaire

Please feel free to write as much as you like in all sections.

Personal details

1   What nationality are you?

2   How old are you?

3   Are you male or female?

4   How many years have you been teaching English?

5   What qualifications do you have? (e.g. CELTA, BA, MA, etc.)

6   What country are you currently based in?

7   How long have you been there?

8   What type of institution do you currently work in?

9   What other kinds of institutions have you worked in?

10 What kinds of materials do you use? (e.g. UK-produced materials such as global coursebooks; locally produced materials; self made, etc.)

Celebrity in ELT materials

Celebrities of different types feature increasingly in ELT global coursebooks. To give you an example, Corder's (1960) *An Intermediate English Practice Book* contains no reference to any celebrity of the period and O'Neill's (1970) *English in Situations* refers only indirectly and infrequently to celebrity. However, by the late 1970s explicit references to celebrity are much more common. The following celebrities are featured in *Streamline Connections* (Hartley and Viney 1979) either in the written text and/or the artwork:

Miklos Nemeth; Alberto Juantorena; Bob Beamon; Annegret Richter; Rosemarie Ackermann; David Wilkie; Vasily Alexeev; Paul McCartney; James Hunt; UK Queen; J. F. Kennedy; Elvis Presley

The following celebrities are featured in New Cutting Edge Upper Intermediate (Cunningham and Moor 2005a) either in the written text and/or the artwork:

Jackson 5; Osmonds; Bee Gees; Corrs; Oasis; Boom Kat; Britney Spears; Eminem; Ozzy Osborne; Kelly Osborne; Brian May; Freddie Mercury; Rowan Atkinson; Halle Berry; Paul McCartney; Ringo Star; Steve Redgrave; Ghandi; Martin Luther King; Evana Trump; Bill Gates; John Kennedy Jnr; Jade Jagger; Princess Diana; Liz Hurley; Oprah Winfrey; Tom Cruise; Robbie Williams; Woody Allen; Marilyn Munroe; Arnold Schwarzenegger; Alan Alda; Fred Allen; Harrison Ford; Brad Pitt; David Beckham; George Clooney; Jennifer Lopez; Tony Blair; Madonna; Nicole Kidman; Steven Spielberg; Ricky Martin; John Lennon; Jennifer Aniston; Ralph Fiennes; Hillary Clinton; Elvis Presley; Kiera Knightley; Parminda Nagra; Gurinder Chadha; Roman Polanski; Nirvana

Contemporary coursebooks also often contain fictional celebrities not listed here.

1   Why do you think the presence of celebrities has increased in ELT materials?

2   As a teacher, what are your views on the increased presence of celebrities in ELT materials?

Impact on students

This is an extract from a two-page interview with two fictional celebrities from a fictional celebrity magazine call *Hi!* Magazine from *New Headway Pre-Intermediate* (Soars and Soars 2000a: 59). The language work contrasts the past simple with the present perfect.

1   Why do you think the artwork occupies so much space on the page?

2   Why do you think the publishers have chosen to approach a language point in this way through the use of fictional celebrities?

3   What do think the impact (if any) of such imagery is on students?

[Artwork not reproduced here]

Other comments

Add any other comments you wish to on the use of celebrity in coursebooks you are familiar with, whether produced in the UK or any other country – or indeed any thoughts you may have on the topic in general.

Thank you for your cooperation.

6

THE MARKETISATION OF LANGUAGE TEACHER EDUCATION AND NEOLIBERALISM

CHARACTERISTICS, CONSEQUENCES AND FUTURE PROSPECTS

JOHN GRAY AND DAVID BLOCK

Introduction

What has been described as the knowledge 'fit for teachers' (Cowen 1995: 18), and the manner in which this knowledge is determined and acquired raise issues which Donald Freeman and Karen Johnson (1998) suggest are both epistemological and political. Indeed, the epistemological and the political may be said to form the double helix of language teacher education, in the sense that these interwoven strands combine to determine the nature of this particular activity at any given historical moment. The concern of this chapter is the necessarily dynamic relation between these strands and the precise form this relation has taken in the neoliberal times in which we live. With regard to the epistemological strand, there has been a shift in recent language teacher education literature towards a broadly sociocultural conceptualisation of the field (e.g. Freeman and Johnson 1998; Ellis, Edwards and Smagorinsky 2009; Johnson 2009). However, when we examine in detail teacher education programmes in a range of contexts, both in terms of their planning and their execution, it becomes clear that this sociocultural turn has occurred alongside other developments in the political strand which serve to create tension in the overall activity. As stated elsewhere in this volume, neoliberalism entails not only government intervention to maintain the conditions that guarantee a free market for goods and services, it also involves the deliberate creation of markets and the implementation of market principles where none had previously existed. As we shall see, such principles have made serious inroads into educational practices, in effect colonising domains of activity which previously had been organised along very different lines (Apple 2006; Ball 2007, 2008; Spring 1998, 2004, 2009). Indeed, they may be said to contradict, if not completely negate, the thrust of the sociocultural turn.

As a way into a discussion of this contradiction and its implications for our field, the chapter begins with a brief overview of the history of language teacher education.

This is followed by a specific focus on teacher cognition and the recent rise of a sociocultural perspective on language teacher education. We then discuss the social backdrop of this shift in emphasis, the neoliberal challenge and the McDonaldisation of teacher education in modern foreign languages in the UK. In the final part of the chapter, we shift to a focus on how neoliberalism plays out in the context of a Cambridge ESOL teacher preparation course. In the light of the challenges we describe, the chapter concludes by suggesting that as applied linguists we need to engage more fully with the precise nature of the political strand in language teacher education. In doing so, we argue that discussions about the knowledge base of the field that fail to consider the ideological, economic and political forces (as understood in this volume) which impact upon that knowledge base, and the manner in which it is constructed, are limited by their narrowness of focus.

Language teacher education

The initial problem with any attempt to historicise any field of academic inquiry is deciding where to begin. Ideas about the precise nature of teaching and learning and the manner in which these activities should be conducted are in many ways cyclical in character – one only has to read Plato's *The Meno* to be reminded that contemporary concepts such as 'exploratory talk' (Mercer 2000) and 'instructional conversation' (Tharp and Gallimore 1991), both of which are associated with the sociocultural perspective, are part of a long history in which dialogue and the learner's existing experience and understandings are seen as fundamental in the acquisition/construction of new knowledge. However, for the purposes of this chapter our historical perspective is concerned with language teacher education in the twentieth and early twenty-first centuries and in particular with the aforementioned sociocultural turn and specifically language teacher education as it has been conceptualised and practised in the English-speaking world.

Michael Wallace (1991), writing from the specific perspective of British TESOL, suggests that this history can be seen as falling into three main periods in which three different models of pedagogic expertise have predominated. That said, it is important to point out that this is very much a broad-brush categorisation and that features of individual models are not always specific to one period only. The first period (starting in the nineteenth century) is said to last until the end of the Second World War and is typified by what he calls the 'craft' model. This is a school-based apprenticeship model of teacher education whereby the novice is inducted into what today would be called a 'community of practice' – a 'group ... of people who share a concern or a passion for something they do and learn how to do it better as they interact regularly' (Wenger 2006) – through prolonged observation of old timers and initially supervised performance. It is, as Jack Richards and Graham Crookes (1988) point out, one of the oldest models of teacher education but, as Wallace explains, it came under severe criticism in the immediate post-war period for what was seen as its essential conservatism – in the sense that its aim was to reproduce in the novice an already existing and established set of behaviours. Such an imitative model was held to be inadequate to meet the needs of post-war societies in which schools were seen as instrumental in preparing students for life in a rapidly changing world.

The post-war period saw a move towards a greater professionalisation of state-school teachers in Britain and the USA and was characterised by what Wallace refers to as the 'applied science' model. This has also been referred to as the positivist tradition of teacher education (Wideen *et al.* 1998) in which 'learning to teach is seen as an additive process in which the beginning teacher is provided with knowledge about teaching ... and is then expected to integrate and implement this knowledge in the classroom' (Morton *et al.* 2006: 21) – regardless of the specificities of the context of instruction. Integral to this model of teacher preparation is the concept of *good practice* which is universally applicable. In the case of second language teacher education, the two pillars of this emerging professional base were scientific knowledge of language as understood in disciplines such as linguistics, psycholinguistics, sociolinguistics and SLA (Richards 1998), and knowledge of pedagogy emanating from the study of methods and so-called 'process-product' research which attempted to correlate the identifiable behaviours of supposedly effective teachers with student achievement (Richards and Nunan 1990; Freeman and Johnson 1998).

Although subsequently much maligned (for reasons outlined below), it is important to bear in mind that the applied science model (or at least certain versions of it) presupposed an educated teacher who had a solid grounding in social scientific theory. Bob Cowen (1995: 22–3) explains that during the so-called foundations movement, as the applied science model was known in Britain during the 1960s, the British Government and higher education were in agreement that

> teachers should be given access to philosophy of education, sociology of education, psychology, history of education and ... principles of comparative education, ... administration and management of education, so that they might ... reflect on the relationships between society and the schooling systems in which they worked.

Even earlier in the century, John Dewey had made a similar case for a model of the teacher as a socially necessary kind of thinker who was required to engage in 'reflective action' (Dewey 1933: 9; cited in Gore and Zeichner 1991: 120) – defined as 'active, persistent and careful consideration of any belief or supposed form of knowledge in light of the grounds that support it and the further consequences to which it leads'. Despite this, and despite the fact that reflection is clearly highlighted in these understandings of it, the applied science model came under attack from the 1980s onwards and led, in Wallace's formulation, to the emergence of (or at the very least the case for) what he calls the reflective model in which practical knowledge of teaching occupied a substantially increased role.

Initially the reflective challenge was spearheaded by educationalists influenced by Donald Schön (1983), whose work was concerned with the education of professionals in general. Schön argued that the applied science model led to a hierarchy of knowledge in which that of the university-based expert was permanently privileged over that of the practitioner. His work on reflection and its central role in the way professionals think 'on the job' made the case for recognising the importance of 'experiential knowledge' (gained in the execution of practice) alongside 'received knowledge' (gained through subject-specific study prior to beginning professional life, or in time spent away from practice) in all forms of professional activity (Wallace 1991: 13). This shift in emphasis towards a re-evaluation of the importance of experiential knowledge resonated with many working in the field of teacher education and with teachers themselves because it seemed to address the context-specific nature of practical decision-making. As Johnson (2000: 4) has argued, learning to teach is a 'situated experience' and it is incumbent on teacher educators to 'recognize how specific contexts shape the process of learning to teach' – a view which she sees as also having clear implications for a less top–down approach to second language teacher education:

> Learning to teach is ultimately a reflective process, but it is also extremely complex. When teachers and teacher educators honestly and openly engage in deliberate reflection on and critical inquiry into their own experiences and practices, they become open to true learning ...

And indeed Jan Bengtsson (1995) shows how the theme of reflection came to dominate the teacher education literature in the 1990s, with many initial teacher education courses incorporating the use of tools such as reflective journals, diaries, peer observation, and guided lesson planning as a means of encouraging reflection (Thornbury 1991; Pennington 1996; Gray 1998). The long-term aim was to produce *reflective practitioners* who would be capable of subjecting their post-course practice to constant scrutiny (through the ongoing use of reflective journals, cycles of action research, continuing professional development, etc.). But as Ardra Cole (1997) has argued, post-course reflective practice is time-consuming – and potentially costly – and many beginning teachers find themselves working in settings (whether in the public or the private sector) which are not conducive to its development due to lack of institutional support, absence of funding, heavy teaching loads, and so on. In this chapter we will argue that this is equally true of many second language teacher education programmes which, while purporting to facilitate the development of reflective practice, do so within the context of institutional constraints in which opportunities for reflection and *crucially* the learning opportunities such reflection might afford are severely restricted (Borg 2002; Morton and Gray 2008, 2010).

However, from the perspective of the second language teacher education literature, the re-evaluation of the importance of experiential knowledge has meant that the context-specific nature of teaching and learning has been increasingly accepted. This has resulted in a view of the language teacher as an 'apprentice ethnographer' (Day 1990; Holliday 1994; Golombek 1998) capable of researching a plurality of contexts of instruction, and the concept of appropriate methodology becoming established in the field (Holliday 1994; Kramsch and O'Sullivan 1996; Ellis 1996). This climate of reassessment has also been conducive to the recognition that the findings of SLA research do not always translate in a straightforward fashion (if at all) into recipes for teaching (Johnson 2000; Block 2000; Kumaravadivelu 2003), although some SLA researchers have argued that they can (Lightbown 1985, 2000; Pica 1994, 1997). From the perspective of the reflective model, activities such as the observation of experienced teachers or demonstration lessons by teacher educators as part of initial teacher preparation could be reconstrued as opportunities for reflection, rather than as models to be imitated – something which could also be extended to the findings of SLA.

Concomitant with the case for the reflective model of teacher education are two related developments: the growth of research on teacher cognition (Elbaz 1983; Golombek 1998; Borg 2006; Korthagen 2010), whereby teachers' professional decision-making is seen as being guided by their 'experiential' and 'embodied' *personal practical knowledge* (Connelly and Clandinin 1985: 183), and the epistemological location of all such work within a broadly sociocultural paradigm (Freeman and Johnson, 1998; Johnson 2000, 2009). In Johnson's (2000: 3) view, this has amounted to nothing less than a 'quiet revolution', although we will suggest this is an overly optimistic assessment of second language teacher education in the neoliberal climate.

Teacher cognition and the sociocultural perspective

Research into teacher cognition has been traced to attempts in the 1980s to address some of the limitations of the applied science model and was characterised by a shift away 'from determining what beginning teachers should know and how they should best be trained to know it to attempting to understand what they actually do know and how that knowledge is acquired' (Wideen *et al.* 1998: 133). As Simon Borg (2006) explains, it highlighted a move towards a more constructivist view of learning to teach in which the role of prior beliefs and tacit understandings were recognised as being important. On this orientation, the 'apprenticeship of observation' (Lortie 1975) – that is, the accumulation of a trainee teacher's experience of a lifetime of learning – is explored and made explicit as part of the teacher education process. In addition, the teacher cognition movement took the view that cognition is not an exclusively mental phenomenon but one which is intimately connected with the practice of teaching and the context in which it occurs – that is, it is an essentially *social* psychological phenomenon (Cross 2006, 2010). Central to this is F. Michael Connelly and Jean Clandinin's (1985) previously mentioned concept of personal practical knowledge, which has been described as

> an interpretative framework through which teachers make sense of their lived reality in classrooms. It consists of knowledge of the self, knowledge of subject matter, knowledge of instruction, and knowledge of context, and has important moral and affective dimensions. Teachers use this knowledge both to shape and interpret their practices in the classroom, and its consequences

for themselves and their learners, often through images and narratives of classroom practice and events.

(Morton *et al.* 2006: 23)

Paula Golombek (1998) has argued that such socially constructed knowledge must be explicitly drawn on by teacher educators so that it provides a conceptual hook for 'received knowledge' on teacher education courses. Theory, she adds, must be filtered through 'experiential knowledge' and teachers in preparation should be encouraged to 'assess their values ... write autobiographies ... and identify images of teaching ... as a means of constructing understandings of teaching and learning as students and teachers' (Golombek 1998: 461). Such a view may be said to imply a more dialogic and exploratory approach to second language teacher education than that found in the applied science model.

The case for the application of such a perspective to language teacher education has been made consistently by Freeman and Johnson since the late 1990s. Their starting position is that the argument for a sociocultural orientation is perforce an argument against what Freeman (2002) calls the 'technicist epistemology' of the applied science model in which, as Johnson (2000: 3) states, teachers are viewed as 'technicians who simply act as conduits for the implementation of theories, methods, and curricular efforts that come down from theorists and researchers who remain far removed from classroom life'. They also argue that learning to teach is a reflective process which is facilitated by dialogic inquiry with peers and teacher educators, a process which ideally provides multiple 'theorising opportunities' (Johnson 2000: 6) – thereby underlining their view of the teacher as a thinker capable of theorising her own socially situated teaching context. Such a view of the language teacher aligns Freeman and Johnson with other scholars whose model of the teacher is essentially that of a theorising practitioner (e.g. Prabhu 1990; Pennycook 1989) – someone whose practice is informed by theory which is accepted or rejected on the basis of its contextual relevance and the teacher's own practice-informed sense of plausibility.

Their fundamental argument is that teaching and learning to teach are institutionally situated, inherently social activities and that, as Johnson (2000: 13) says, 'knowing, thinking, and understanding come from participating in the social practices of learning and teaching in specific classroom and school situations'. From this perspective, the knowledge base of language teacher education is *language teaching* rather than *language,* a position which is outlined as follows:

Our proposal is an epistemological framework that focuses on the activity of teaching itself – who does it, where it is done, and how it is done. Our intention is to redefine what stands at the core of language teacher education. Thus we argue that, for the purposes of educating teachers, any theory of SLA, any classroom methodology, or any description of that [sic] English language as content must be understood against the backdrop of teachers' professional lives, within the settings where they work, and within the circumstances of that work.

(Freeman and Johnson 1998: 405)

Their framework for a recalibrated knowledge base for second language teacher education consists of three domains: the nature of the teacher-learner (understood as a learner of language teaching rather than a learner of language); the nature of schools and schooling (understood as the micro (institutional) and macro (political) cultural and historical contexts within which teaching occurs); and finally, the nature of language teaching (which includes knowledge of subject, classrooms and learning). Although the precise details of what such a teacher education course would look like are not spelled out, it is clear that teaching practice would be central to it and that it would be typified by multiple opportunities for dialogue, reflection and opportunities for theorising.

We now turn in the next section to the political and economic background against which this 'quiet revolution' is said to have taken place. As we shall see, it is one in which language teaching and language teacher education are *in practice* increasingly shaped by neoliberal ideology and exposure to market forces – pressures which we suggest may be said to undermine the case for the reflective model of the teacher.

The neoliberal challenge to teacher professionalism

With the arrival of neoliberal governments in many parts of the world in the late 1970s and 1980s teacher education became a key site of ideological battle (Furlong *et al.* 2000). This is hardly surprising, given that the purpose of education from the neoliberal perspective is to service the economy through the production of 'human capital' (see Chapter 3). In other words, education is reconstrued as ultimately being about the production of workers with the skills and the dispositions necessary to compete in the global economy. Forming the kind of teacher required to facilitate this function has entailed the recalibration of teacher education and teacher professionalism along lines quite unlike those presupposed by both the applied science and the reflective models. In Britain changes to initial teacher education programmes from the 1980s onwards have been designed 'to construct a new generation of teachers with different forms of knowledge, different skills and different professional values' to those predating the neoliberal period (Furlong *et al.* 2000: 6). Such an overhaul has meant the removal of subjects such as the philosophy and the sociology of education from pre-service programmes (integral to the foundations movement), alongside a move towards a more school-based induction in which reflective practice, as understood by the teacher cognition movement, plays little or no part. Rather, the focus has been redirected towards subject knowledge and the skills required for effective delivery of the curriculum in an environment increasingly dominated by government-run inspection regimes. A key part of this recalibration has been the implementation of frequent testing of pupils from age 7 onwards with the purported aim of 'raising standards' (a key neoliberal mantra). In turn this has allowed for the creation of league tables (discussed below) which serve to keep teachers focused on the business of being accountable.

Despite the blow which the financial meltdown of 2008 presupposed for neoliberalism (Mason 2009), education in Britain continues to be subjected to 'reforms' which are consistent with the ideological thrust of neoliberalism. At the time of writing (2011), teacher education in Britain is yet again in turmoil as more initial teacher education is set to be transferred to schools away from the universities, who will now have to compete in the education marketplace if they are to retain a role in ensuring that government-set standards are met by those schools responsible for the induction of novice teachers. Such a move resonates with earlier assessments that '[i]n the field of initial teacher education, there has been a recurrent assertion among neo-liberals that initial teacher training is unnecessary, even harmful [and] that teacher training courses actually diminish the effectiveness of teachers (Furlong *et al*. 2000: 10). To understand these changes more fully we need to step back and look at the particular form in which education has been marketised by neoliberal practice and ideology.

The marketisation of education represents a major frame shift in different contexts around the world. In those countries where education operated in a manner relatively free from government interference (e.g. Britain prior to the Thatcher era), with professional accountability of teachers at a minimum and professional autonomy at a maximum, there is now a dominant managerial ethos leading to ever greater government control and increased accountability of all professionals involved. In those parts of the world where education has always been centrally controlled, still greater government control has been introduced (e.g. South Korea). In such an educational climate, students are increasingly seen as customers seeking a service and schools and teachers are, as a consequence, seen as service providers. As this metaphorical frame has been imposed (and accepted by sufficient numbers of key players in education, the media and beyond) the *semantic stretching* of keywords from the world of business referred to earlier has become commonplace (see Chapter 3). Thus terms such as 'outcomes', 'value added', 'knowledge transfer', 'the knowledge economy' and above all 'accountability' have become part of the day-to-day vocabulary of education.

It is important to recall here, as Liz Gordon and Geoff Whitty (1997: 455) point out, that the 'neoliberal project' is profoundly 'contradictory' and 'dualistic' in nature. Hence, there is the deployment (by governments and their allies in the media) of a recurrent rhetoric berating 'big government' and state interference, alongside the institution of regimes of state monitoring in education which are entirely managerialist and bureaucratic in orientation. Here the work of George Ritzer on bureaucracy, although not explicitly concerned with neoliberalism *per se*, has the potential to shed much light on these changes – and it is to this that we now turn.

McDonaldisation as an analytical framework

In a long list of publications appearing over several decades, Ritzer (e.g. 1996, 1998, 2007b, 2011) has developed a theory (or thesis, as he has preferred to call it) for understanding how the dominance of instrumental rationalism as a driving force in our lives has meant the colonisation of an ever increasing number of our activities by organisational mechanisms already in place in the business, in particular in the fast-food sector. He calls this colonisation *McDonaldisation*, defined succinctly as 'the process by which the principles of the fast-food restaurant are coming to dominate more and more sectors of American society as well as the rest of the world' (Ritzer 2011: 1). Some of the sectors dominated by such principles are national and private health services, the service economy in general and, relevant to this chapter, education. Ritzer sees McDonald's, fast-food restaurants in general and all of the McDoctor's, McShopping Malls and McUniversities which have sprung up all over the world as examples of mini-bureaucracies.

For Ritzer, this particular type of bureaucracy is a creation of Western capitalism and his theoretical stance owes much to the thinking of Max Weber. In his work, Weber (1968) describes a process whereby Western society makes the move towards rationalisation, towards domination by systems of organisation which are more efficient, predictable, calculable and which are controlled either internally or externally or both. Efficiency is about having 'the optimum means to whatever end is chosen' (Ritzer 2007b: 24). The assembly line is not only the best concrete example of this characteristic of McDonaldisation, it is also a metaphor for all systems of organisation which can handle a large number of tasks in such a way that there is minimal expense of human and technical resources and money. Calculability means that success can be gauged or counted. Here what is valued is the number of units despatched and the price that it costs to despatch them; thus quality comes to be seen through the blinkers of quantity. Predictability means that the system of organisation provides the assurance that tasks will be done in a uniform manner and that results will be similar if not the same, no matter who is responsible for carrying them out. In other words, it is worker-proof. Finally, the previous three characteristics of rationalised systems of organisation together constitute the fourth characteristic, control. Control may be exercised via the use of both human and technological resources which assure that the system of organisation works in a smooth fashion and that individuals behave in such a way that they reproduce it, perhaps on occasion modify it, but ideally never subvert it. One of the more remarkable characteristics of rationalised systems is that they come to generate irrationalities, defined by Ritzer (1999: 93) as 'the paradoxical outcome of efforts to be completely rational … [whereby] rationalism can be viewed as leading to inefficiency, unpredictability, incalculability and loss of control'.

The four characteristics of systems of organisation, making up a veritable template for uniformity, lead to a situation where human beings, as individuals, are important mainly for their instrumental value, and as a consequence, they are dehumanised and ultimately fall under the control of the bureaucracies which initially were created with the ostensible, though questionable, aim of making their lives easier. This portrayal of rationalised systems of organisation leading to irrationalities is reminiscent of Harry Braverman's account of the state of industrial relations in the post-Second World War industrialised economies of the world. In his classic book *Labour and Monopoly Capital*, Braverman (1974) examines the modes of 'scientific' industrial management, labour processes in industrial settings and the effects of technological change on industrial management and labour processes. Early in the book, Braverman presents the work of William Taylor, the originator of 'Taylorism'. Taylorism is the philosophical basis for Fordism, or assembly line management, and it embodies the key characteristics of McDonaldisation – efficiency, calculability, predictability and control. The basis of Taylorism was 'scientific management', defined by Braverman as follows:

> Scientific management … is an attempt to apply the methods of science to the increasingly complex problems of the control of labor in rapidly growing capitalist enterprises. It lacks the characteristics of true science because its assumptions reflect nothing more than the outlook of the capitalist with regard to the conditions of production. It starts, despite occasional protestations to the contrary, not from the human point of view but from the capitalist point of view … it investigates not labor in general, but the adaptation of labor to the needs of capital. It enters the workplace not as the representative of science, but as the representative of management masquerading in the trappings of science.
>
> (Braverman 1974: 86)

Braverman further writes about changing orientations to the skilling of workers which comes with Taylorism as follows:

> For the worker, the concept of skill is traditionally bound up with craft mastery – that is to say, the combination of knowledge of materials and processes with the practiced manual dexterities required to carry on a specific branch of production. The breakup of craft skills and the reconstruction of production as a collective or social process have destroyed the traditional conception of skill and opened up only one way for mastery of labor process to develop: in and through scientific, technical, and engineering knowledge.
>
> (Braverman 1974: 443)

In the process described by Braverman, skills move from the workers to management and training comes to be about how to operate machinery or carry out orders. Thus, craft knowledge, which entailed workers knowing a great deal about production processes, gives way to the technical scientific model whereby knowledge is held exclusively by management. The result is a systematic deskilling of workers.

The move to more rationalised systems of organisation and the movement from a craft orientation to a technical scientific one together have negative consequences which are not just limited to the control of human agency by social structures and hardware of human creation. Ritzer (1998) draws on the work of Karl Mannheim (1935) to make the point that what is lost in McDonaldisation is what he terms *substantive rationalism*, which encompasses the basic human ability to think intelligently, as well as the possibility of self-transformation through self-observation

– that is, the ability to reflect on oneself and one's actions with a view to individual personal and professional development (activities which, as we have already outlined, are integral to the reflective turn in language teacher education). With so much control, efficiency and predictability in their lives, individuals live disenchanted lives. They become, in effect, trapped in what translators of Weber have termed the 'iron cage' of bureaucracy, which they themselves have helped to build and maintain. As Weber (1968: 987–8) so vividly explained:

> The individual bureaucrat cannot squirm out of the apparatus into which he has been harnessed ... the professional bureaucrat is chained to his activity in his entire economic and ideological existence. In the great majority of cases, he is only a small cog in a ceaselessly moving mechanism which prescribes to him an essentially fixed route of march. The official is entrusted with specialized tasks, and normally the mechanism cannot be put into motion or arrested by him, but only from the very top.[1]

Thus, in Braverman's account of Taylorism, we see how from a management perspective the deskilling of workers may be the road to efficiency, calculability, predictability and control. However, for workers it is the way to a colder, alienating state of affairs, as they are separated from a direct relationship to the means of production by 'scientific, technical, and engineering knowledge', a point made by Marx (1976) in *Capital 1*.

Examining the discussion thus far, one could argue that the free-market ideology integral to neoliberalism is very explicitly about individualism rather than mass production, and therefore it could be seen in some way as the opposite of McDonaldisation (and indeed, Taylorism as described by Braverman). However, one could also question whether this is a valid point given that the kind of individualism that we are talking about here is linked to mass consumerism and the rather conformist type of self-realisation which it leads to (see Chapter 5 for more detailed discussion of this point). One could also argue that the connection between McDonaldisation and neoliberalism is not obvious. Indeed, the two could be seen to be in conflict, given that one common claim made about the 'free' markets which result from greater liberalisation is that they mean a curtailing of bureaucracy. However, a close examination of the complexities of the current worldwide banking system (e.g. Callinicos 2010) shows how it is filled with layers of processes, all of which have to be administered. A bigger related question is how Ritzer's critique of McDonaldisation articulates with the critique of neoliberalism which is foundational to this book.

An answer to this question is to be found in the particular way in which Ritzer conceptualises globalisation and how he sees capitalism and McDonaldisation as part of it. Ritzer (2007b, 2011) invents the term 'grobalisation' to capture how McDonaldisation intersects with neoliberalism (ideologies, policies and practices). The former, as we have seen, is rooted in a Weberian view of society, while the latter is rooted in a Marxist view of capitalism. Ritzer defines grobalisation as the imperialist ambition of nations, corporations, organizations, and the like and their desire to, indeed, their need, to impose themselves on various geographic areas. Their main interest is seeing their power, influence, and in some cases profits grow (hence the term grobalization) throughout the world.

(Ritzer 2011: 169–70)

As for the Marxist basis of his views, and more specifically his critique of neoliberalism, Ritzer writes the following:

One of the major driving forces behind grobalization is the corporate need in capitalism to show increasing profitability through more, and more far reaching, economic imperialism. … Another driving force is the need for cooperation and the states and other institutions (media, education) that buttress them to support efforts at enhancing profitability by increasing their cultural hegemony nationally and ultimately throughout the world.

(Ritzer 2007b: 16)

This view of the current state of the world is very much in line with what authors from Marx to Callinicos and Harvey have written about capitalism, as well as what has been written in the other chapters of this volume.[2]

Over the years, Ritzer's work has been criticised with some justification for its essential pessimism (e.g. Smart 1999), although given the state of the world one might wonder how an overly optimistic view is in any way appropriate. The McDonaldisation thesis has also been seen by many as highly essentialist and deterministic: agents seem to be passive in the face of McDonaldisation in their lives. However, as noted elsewhere (Block 2012a, in preparation), there is good reason to question the overemphasis on individual agency which has characterised so much research in applied linguistics in recent years, and Ritzer's work may be seen as a healthy argument in favour of social structure and how it constrains individual agency. Finally, there is Ritzer's tendency to invent new terms, such as the aforementioned 'grobalisation', when perhaps this is not always obviously necessary. While cognizant of these and other limitations in Ritzer's work over the years, we nevertheless believe that the McDonaldisation thesis is a convenient and effective heuristic for analysing many of the phenomena which we encounter on a day-to-day basis in neoliberal times – and language teacher education is one such phenomenon.

Elsewhere, one of the authors of this chapter has noted how McDonaldisation processes have been at work in understandings of communication, both in language teaching and second language acquisition research (Block 2002). Here, we consider how teacher training has been taken over by notions of technical rationality and concomitant notions of efficiency, calculability, predictability and control. However, we do this within the broader framework of neoliberalism and the subsequent skilling discourses which have become common currency in so many domains of activity. We begin by framing initial teacher training in Britain as a McDonaldised system which is controlled at all levels to ensure that is efficient, calculable and predictable. In doing so, we draw on interviews with two trainee teachers completing the Postgraduate Certificate of Education (PGCE) in Modern Foreign Languages (MFL). This certificate confers *qualified teacher status* and allows those who are certificated to teach in the British state-school system.[3] From there we move to a different teacher education context, a Cambridge ESOL course. Here we examine in detail interactions taking place as part of a guided lesson planning session on a pre-service Certificate in English Language to Adults (CELTA) course in a British university. Our analysis and interpretation of this dataset serve to illustrate the extent to which courses of this type, offered by one of the main commercial providers of English language teaching qualifications globally, position student teachers in ways which are ultimately incommensurate with the thrust of the sociocultural turn, while congruent overall with a technicist epistemology more suited to the neoliberal climate.

Before proceeding further, it is worth noting that we are all too aware of the pitfalls inherent in the grouping together of two very different language education contexts in our discussion. The MFL context in the UK is very different in many obvious ways from the CELTA/ELT context, not least because it is far more philological and country-specific in its origins than the latter, which has always been about serving a global market, specifically one which involves the sale of the English language as a commodity. However, we believe that the two examples which we examine in subsequent sections serve to show how pervasive the infiltration of neoliberal thinking has become in language education across very different contexts.

The PGCE as a McDonaldised system

The PGCE is one-year course leading to the required professional qualification (that of qualified teacher) for individuals who wish to teach in state schools in England, Wales and Northern Ireland. Traditionally, the course has been taught at a university and involves a combination of sessions of educational theory and a teaching practicum. The latter is the most substantial part of the course and it means that candidates spend a great deal of time on school placements. Over the past 30 years, the course has undergone a series of changes, most of which have led to greater bureaucratisation of the type outlined in the work of Ritzer: effectively, the PGCE has, to some extent, become McDonaldised. We now explain how, touching on each of the three main tenets of McDonaldisation and how they lead to control.

Efficiency

The National Curriculum reforms for primary and secondary education beginning in the 1980s and continuing until the present have meant a move towards an increasingly technocratic model of teaching (see Barber 1996, for an account of how the change took place in the 1980s). This model embodies some of the features of Wallace's 'applied sciences model described above, as well as Freeman's technicist epistemology. Following this model, one first establishes desired aims, objectives and outcomes and then proceeds backwards to the specification of content. This approach leads to strict control over content which excludes to a great extent anything deemed impractical (e.g. if an item does not appear in the syllabus, it need not be covered). In addition, one specifies in detail what 'good' or 'best' practice consists of, and then sets up mechanisms to monitor teachers' classroom behaviour. With the pre-specification of criteria for best practice, teaching in Britain has moved from what was termed a *professional contextualist* conception of teaching to the *technocratic-reductionist* conception (Whitty and Power 1998). The *professional contextualist* conception, which became dominant in progressive education circles from the 1980s onward, framed teaching and learning as process oriented and took it as axiomatic that education entailed more than imparting subject knowledge and skill transmission. Precisely the same trajectory is noticeable in ideas about curriculum design for language teaching (Breen and Candlin 1980) and the subsequent case for a more sociocultural orientation to language teacher education (Freeman and Johnson 1998). Meanwhile, the technocratic-reductionist conception derives from the application of marketing principles to education. It frames teaching as product oriented and values the acquisition of instrumental skills and knowledge. The main features of these two conceptions are outlined in Table 6.1.

The streamlined and well-defined technocratic-reductionist curriculum was designed to ensure the control of quality and to clearly establish accountability for results, whether good or bad. During the government of New Labour (1997–2010), and continuing with the Conservative–Liberal coalition government (from May 2010 onwards), it has been a common practice to announce publicly that certain schools are 'failing' (i.e. their examination results are below national averages) and then to send in quality-control 'hit squads' consisting of individuals assigned the title of 'experts', who are expected to put procedures in place which will guarantee desired and measurable outcomes.

TABLE 6.1   The move from professional contextualist to technocratic-reductionist (based on Whitty, Power and Halpin 1998: 65)

Dimension	Professional contextualist	Technocratic-reductionist
Role model	Reflexive practitioner	Skilled technician
Criterion of good practice	Integrity	Competence
Pedagogical aim	Development of diverse human capabilities	Attainment of specific learning outcomes
Administrative context	Professional leadership (collaborative)	Efficient management (hierarchical)
Type of motivation	Intrinsic	Extrinsic
Form of accountability	Professional commitment	Contractual compliance

Calculability

The drive to make schools accountable to their clients necessitated a system to monitor outputs. This system came in the form of what are known as league tables. A league table is the listing of all of the educational institutions in a particular sector (e.g. primary school, secondary school, universities, etc.) along with the criteria used for assessing their quality. The best-known example of such tables in Britain is the secondary school league table for General Certificate of Secondary Education (GCSE) examination results, which are published annually. On the day of publication, newspapers carry special sections where all of the schools in England and Wales are listed, along with the numbers and percentages of students receiving five or more pass marks (A–C) and five or more grades of any kind (A–G) on the examinations sat by year 11 students (generally 16 year olds) at the end of the previous academic year.

Predictability

With centralised control over content and the institutionalisation of calculating the worth of schools through their examination results, predictability of lesson content and school performance is increased. This is assured through the specification of content on PGCE courses as well as the inspection system run by the Office for Standards in Education (OFSTED), which requires inspectors to observe teachers during official inspections. The inspector is expected to grade teachers according to how well they meet specifically defined performance criteria, around issues such as how teachers foster 'good' learning attitudes and behaviours in their students, how they use assessment to support learning processes and how they cater for different abilities across a group of students (see OFSTED 2009 for details). In the same way that there is a washback effect from examination to what teachers teach, with guidelines as specific as these there is a washback effect from teacher evaluation criteria to how teachers are taught to teach on PGCE courses and how teachers teach on the day that they are observed by an OFSTED inspector.

Once in place, this rational system, with its efficiency, calculability and predictability, all combining as means of control, generates irrationalities. For example, while efficient organisation might be expected to work in the teacher's favour, what one finds is the continuous deskilling of teachers as so much of what they have to do is decided well in advance by examinations boards and inspectors who come to inspections with a clear profile of what constitutes good teaching. Accountability systems lead to greater bureaucratisation, with the trend towards more frequent and more in-depth controls. Every form of quality control takes time and money, with the result that proportionately greater human and financial resources are spent controlling the system in detriment to the system itself.

Given this system of maximum surveillance and increased workloads, it is perhaps not surprising that teacher shortages in key areas such as science, mathematics and MFL have become an increasing problem over the past three decades. One solution to this problem has been the incorporation of non–British nationals into the educational system. In the case of MFL, this has meant, above all, EU nationals from France, Germany and Spain (Whitehead and Taylor 1998; Block 2001). One question of interest is how these German, French and Spanish nationals adapt to the British educational system, first during their PGCE course, and later when they take up full-time posts, which in most cases are in secondary schools. As part of a longitudinal study designed to explore this issue (carried out by one of the authors of this chapter, David Block, between 1999 and 2003), 16 French, German and Spanish nationals taking the PGCE course were followed and monitored via periodic interviews as they moved from their PGCE courses to NQT (newly qualified teacher) status to experienced teacher status. Some of the comments taken from an early interview with two enthusiastic and highly motivated Spanish nationals, Elena and Almudena,[4] are worth revisiting here as they serve to illustrate the impact of neoliberal-inspired changes made to PGCE courses in Britain on the attitudes and motivations of teachers. (Quoted sections from this interview are presented in boxes with the original words in Spanish on the left and the English translations on the right. Transcription conventions can be found in the appendix at the end of this chapter.)

Both interviewees already had teaching experience in Britain and both had decided to do the PGCE so that they could seek full-time work in a secondary school as teachers of Spanish and French. When asked about why she had decided to leave an academic post at Cambridge in order to do the PGCE, Elena had the following to say:

Original in Spanish	*English translation*
al final de mi primer año en Cambridge decidí / o más que decidir me di cuenta de que no quería seguir investigando la lingüística / no quería seguir hasta hacer un *PhD* en el uso imperativo o la pragmática de las expresiones derivadas del Griego / porque me parecía demasiado abstracto / demasiado absolutamente no relacionado con nada / solo pensaba que me estaba cavando un agujero realmente muy grande y que me iba a meter ahí y jamás salir de él / y entonces (.5) empecé a pensar en todas las cosas que quisiera hacer / porque siempre me había disfrutado mucho enseñando los idiomas / porque siempre había sido un estudiante en clases de idiomas (.5) de todos los idiomas desde	at the end of my first year in Cambridge I decided / or more than decided I realised that I didn't want to carry on doing research in linguistics / I didn't want to go on to do a PhD in the use of the imperative or the pragmatics of expressions derived from Greek / because it just seemed too abstract / too absolutely not related to anything / I just thought I was digging a really big hole and I was going to get into it and never get out of it / and so / I started thinking about all the things I would like to do / because I had always enjoyed the teaching of languages a lot / because I had always been a student in language classes / of every language since the age of four / I really knew

| los cuatro anos / sabia realmente lo que me gustaba en el aula / y tenia muchas ideas y disfrutaba mucho con aquello / entonces pues decidí que el próximo paso necesariamente había de ser el *PGCE* (.5) realmente echaba de menos aquella experiencia práctica / | what I liked in the classroom / and I had lots of ideas and I really enjoyed that / so well I decided the next step necessarily had to be a PGCE (.5) I really missed that practical experience / |

(Elena, 28 Sept. 1999)

When asked why she had decided to become a teacher in Britain, Almudena said the following:

Original in Spanish	*English translation*
De los muchos trabajos que he probado / enseñar es el que me hacer sentir estupenda / sabes / acabo la clase y voy / *I can't believe I'm getting paid for this, I'm having fun'* / y me encanta trabajar con la gente / y no soy una persona que podría fácilmente estar detrás de una mesa / necesito mezclarme con la gente /	Out of the many jobs that I've tried / teaching is the one that makes me feel great / you know / I just finish the class and I go / *I can't believe I'm getting paid for this, I'm having fun* / and I love working with people / and I'm not a person who could happily be behind a desk / I need to mix with people/

(Almudena, 28 Sept. 1999)

These interviews took place early in the first term of the PGCE and what we see in both extracts is clear enthusiasm for teaching – a feature which was present throughout the initial interviews. While Elena frames a teaching job as far more interesting than an academic career, Almudena sees it as a way to self-realisation as a person who likes mixing and working with people.

Already at this early stage in their PGCE course, Elena and Almudena had been on school placements in London, where they had observed teachers and begun their practice teaching. When asked how they felt about this experience, they both responded positively. At the same time, the two women had grasped two negative aspects of a trainee teacher's life in Britain: the bureaucracy and creeping managerialism. One aspect of this bureaucracy was the requirement that trainees provide evidence of their learning about teaching. Elena spoke about this issue as follows:

Original in Spanish	*English translation*
yo me pasé un día entero la semana pasada escribiendo la *evidence* / que son cosas de siete frases de decir *today I*	I spent a whole day last week writing the *evidence* / which consists of seven sentences stating *today I realised this and*

realised this and bla bla bla / pero como está *evidence based* / en realidad (.5) podría perfectamente no haber hecho estas cosas y escribirlo igual (.5) te están pidiendo que crees la evidencia de la nada (.5) pero es totalmente posible / porque es una lista tan brutal / y lo dije a mi mentor / y me dijo / *well, do it / if you think by the end of the year you haven't produced evidence for everything / just fake it:*	bla bla bla / But because it's *evidence based* / actually (.5) I could very well not have done these things and written it [that I had] anyway / (.5) they're asking you to create the evidence out of nothing (.5) but it's completely possible / because it's such a long list / and I told my mentor that / and he said / *well do it / if you think by the end of the year you haven't produced evidence for everything / just fake it:*

(Elena, 28 Sept. 1999)

Elena's explanation of how she felt overwhelmed by requirements to document her learning in ways which had no face validity for her (given the ease with which 'evidence' can be falsified) was echoed by Almudena who admitted that she had already left such book-keeping exercises to one side. What we see here is in fact institutional lip-service being paid to the ideal of reflection in which the production of 'evidence' required by the bureaucratised system is really what is required and valued. In this way the reflective turn referred to earlier in this chapter is subverted and trivialised at the very moment when genuine opportunities for reflection might be useful. In effect, organised reflection comes to be a burden and therefore fertile ground for the questioning of the technocratic reductionism of school bureaucracy rather than an opportunity for reflection.

Later in the conversation, another absurdity of a teacher's existence arose, as the following exchange shows (E= Elena, D = David Block, A = Almudena):

Original in Spanish	English translation
E: ahora hay *posters*! /	E: now there are *posters*! /
{said with false earnestness}	{said with false earnestness}
D: ¿de que clase? /	D: what kind? /
A: *motivational posters* /	A: *motivational posters*/
{said in dramatic tone}	{said in dramatic tone}
E: *posters* como (.5) *the man hanging off a cliff*=	E: *posters* like (.5) *the man hanging off a cliff*=
{extending arms upwards as if hanging}	{extending arms upwards as if hanging}
A: =no dos delfines!=	A: = no two dolphins!=
{making a sweeping motion with her right hand}	{making a sweeping motion with her right hand}
E: =y una frase que dice *you can do it*= {speaking hurriedly with false earnestness }	E: =and a sentence that says *you can do it*= {speaking hurriedly with false earnestness}

A: =no *group work leads to success* / o algo así /	A: =no *group work leads to success* / or something like that /
{speaking hurriedly with false earnestness }	{speaking hurriedly with false earnestness }
E: los hacen empresas [que	E: they're done by companies [that
A: [me guardé uno para enviar a mis amigos [en España] /	A: [I kept one to send to my friends [in Spain] /

(Almudena and Elena, 28 Sept. 1999)

The focus of this short exchange is motivational posters, which began to be used in business environments in the US from the 1970s onwards, as a supposedly subtle way of getting workers psychologically prepared for whatever tasks might await them. Here we see their intrusion into a domain in which they would have been foreign in Britain until the 1990s – schools. Motivational posters generally centre on a picture of someone in an adverse situation, often an extreme one (Elena's example of the man hanging from a cliff), although some present the opposite extreme of a happy scene from the natural world (Almudena's example of dolphins swimming in the sea). Whatever their orientation, such posters have become the object of much derision on internet sites where they are often ridiculed as silly and naïve.

In the transcription presented here, we attempt to reproduce not only what was said but how it was said and inflected with a view to conveying to the reader the sarcasm coming from the two women as they ridicule the use of motivational posters in the schools where they have had placements. Very obviously 'doubters' as regards this practice, Elena and Almudena not only express in words their disdain but also they embody it with their voice inflections and body language, via feigned dramatic and earnest tones and exaggerated body movements (Elena imitating the man hanging from a cliff and Almudena's sweeping hand movement when talking about dolphins). The code switching into English might be interpreted as further distancing from the posters as the two women do not bother to translate into Spanish the term 'motivational' or, with the exception of Almudena's *dos delfines*, the slogans on the posters ('the man hanging off a cliff'; 'you can do it'; 'group work leads to success').

As noted elsewhere (Block 2010), the two women's expressed resistance to motivational posters, and indeed their ridiculing of the very idea that they are present in schools, perhaps points to clashing of education cultures. After all, Almudena and Elena are Spanish and one could argue that they are just beginning to learn how education works in Britain and adapting to motivational posters is just a part of the process. However there is obviously a bigger point here, namely that the posters are yet another example of the encroachment of marketing and business-like principles and technical rationality on a domain in which they were previously absent. Further indications of this encroachment are to be found in the following section, as we examine interaction in a micro-context on a Cambridge ESOL programme in which a trainee teacher works with an experienced teacher trainer to plan a lesson. These data are supplemented by data from stimulated recall in which the trainee and the trainer discuss the nature of the interaction.

CELTA (Certificate in Teaching English to Speakers of Other Languages)

The CELTA course is an initial teaching qualification awarded by Cambridge ESOL and is regarded by the English Language Teaching (ELT) industry globally as the first step on the way to becoming a fully qualified English language teacher. It also forms part of the National Qualifications Framework for England. The CELTA indicates a basic level of proficiency in lesson planning and delivery and functions as an accepted indicator of employability in the largely deregulated global commercial sector. Over 10,000 people around the world are said to complete such courses each year (www.cambridgeesol.org/teaching/celta.htm).

CELTA courses are short and consist of a minimum of 120 hours, of which six are taken up with assessed teaching practice. These six hours are crucial as they provide candidates with the opportunity to demonstrate 'convincingly and consistently' their ability to meet a total of 42 assessment criteria for teaching practice (Cambridge ESOL 2010: 15). Given the number of criteria to be met within such a short timescale, opportunities to reflect on practice and to learn from mistakes are necessarily limited. Despite suggestions that the course is congruent with a reflective model of teacher education (Barduhn 1998), and despite specific requirements for candidates to demonstrate their ability to reflect before, during and after practice, we will suggest that the CELTA is perforce overwhelmingly technocratic-reductionist in orientation and consists largely in the inculcation of a predetermined set of methodological practices.

This particular CELTA was offered part-time over a period of three months.[5] Trainees attended sessions on ELT methodology and basic language analysis twice a week for the whole period, punctuated with breaks for teaching practice. This cycle took place in two two-week blocs – the first after the trainees had received four weeks of input and the second towards the end of the three-month period. The twelve trainees on this course were divided into two groups of six for teaching practice lessons. These lessons lasted for two hours, with three members of each group teaching for 40 minutes each. The data reproduced here were recorded in the second week of teaching practice when trainees were still very new to teaching and were getting more help in guided lesson planning than they would towards the end of the course. Each day's practice lessons were followed by a feedback session in which the trainees discussed their lessons in depth with the trainer. These sessions lasted for about 45 minutes and were followed by a similar amount of time on guided lesson planning for the following day.[6] The trainers (who included John Gray, one of the present authors) took the view that guided lesson planning was ideally an opportunity for exploratory talk about learning to teach. However, given the time constraints in operation on such courses and the stressful learning environment these constraints tended to create, interpretation of the data suggests that trainers' over-riding concerns relate to the production of pass lessons – with the result of limited opportunities for meaningful reflection among trainees (Morton and Gray 2008).

In the following extracts of recorded interaction, the teacher trainer is working with a trainee Gill who is doing the final teaching slot. The trainee had been assigned a set of work-related vocabulary exercises designed to build on a reading about a job interview and an interview role play to be done by other members of the teaching practice group. The interaction revolves around a piece of material taken from a textbook. This is reproduced in Figure 6.1, with a view to making the discussion easier to follow.

The session gets off to an unsteady start with Gill explaining that she has not been able to prepare in detail for the planning session.

Excerpt 1[7]

1   T: ok and then who's last?
2   G: me /
3   T: ok G / what are you doing?
4   G: uh well / I only found (.5) I wasn't here on Friday / so I only found this out this morning [from Jean{Another fellow trainee}
5   T: [this is an excuse {laughing}/
6   G: what I'm meant to do it's not =
7   H: = the function is excuse /
8   G: I'm doing this vocabulary bit here on page 41 /
9   T: ah ha / right / ok /

First of all, it is worthwhile to see this interaction in terms of how the participants position themselves and one another. According to Bronwyn Davies and Rom Harré (1999: 37), '[p]ositioning is the discursive process whereby people are located in conversations as observably and subjectively coherent participants in jointly produced storylines'. By 'discursive process', the authors mean the day-to-day participation in communicative events involving one or more other individuals, drawing not only on language but also other forms of semiotic activity such as direction of gaze and body movements. Being 'located … as observably and subjectively coherent' relates, on the one hand, to the kind of image management engaged in by individuals in conversations – how, for example, individuals draw on a range of communicative resources to portray themselves as particular types of people (Gee 2008). At the same time, Harré (2004: 4) points out that positioning theory also entails 'the study of the way rights and duties are taken up and laid down, ascribed and appropriated, refused and defended in the fine grain of the encounters of daily lives', which we suggest makes it particularly appropriate for the study of the type of interaction found in teacher trainer–trainee teacher encounters.

Vocabulary 1

JOBS AND DUTIES

1 Work in pairs to complete the following chart. Use your dictionary if necessary.

Job	Duties
traffic warden	_____
_____	repairs electrical apparatus
undertaker	_____
_____	performs medical operations
accountant	_____
_____	flies planes
solicitor	_____
_____	designs machines
plumber	_____
_____	cuts hair
_____	digs for coal

2 Divide the 'duty' verbs in the chart above into those with the final sound /s/ (e.g. cuts) and those with the final sound /z/ (e.g. repairs).

3 Choose an ending from the box to show what field of work the following people are in. Use your dictionary to help you if necessary.

–ing	–ure	–ancy	–ics	–ry	–ism

a)   banker   banking
b)   accountant
c)   actor
d)   psychiatrist
e)   journalist
f)   architect
g)   economist

(Bell and Gower 1992).

FIGURE 6.1   Textbook vocabulary activity

All the trainees were aware of the rights and duties associated with this particular communicative event – one of the duties being that they were expected to come to guided lesson planning sessions having already thought about how to teach the material they had been allocated previously. Gill's explanation in turn 4 can be seen as an initial attempt to position herself as legitimately underprepared – she had been absent (with permission from the course tutor) when the material was allocated at the end of the first week of teaching practice. The trainer's response in turn 5, although mitigated by laughter, could be seen as a more authoritative repositioning of Gill as someone who has failed to comply with the duties incumbent on trainees and as a challenge to the storyline of responsible course member that she seeks to invoke. However, Gill's choice of 'meant to' in turn 6 is a clear positioning of herself as a trainee who is aware of her obligations.

Having positioned herself thusly, Gill continues in excerpt 2 below by articulating her initial ideas about the textbook material and some photographs she has also brought along – clear evidence of some degree of prior thinking about the lesson. However, it is apparent from the length of turn 5 below that her ideas are as yet unclear.

Excerpt 2

1   G: erm and I think that's =
2   T: = this has got a nice jobs [sort of (.5)
3   G: [yeah (.5)
4   T: theme running through it =
5   G: = but erm yes / so {laughing} / help me on this one / erm / OK what I thought first of all would be / it's kind of like I / I I'm wondering whether there's a bit of overlapping / just having heard / erm / you know / what everyone else is doing as well / but I've kind of got these photographs of different jobs / and they're not very clear like that {showing them} / so I would just like start off so you know there's (.5) I would split them into three different groups / and so that's like a traffic warden a hairdresser and doctor nurse kind of thing / and then just get them erm to describe what this job is like / what it is where it is / and how that person would do that job / erm /   but because my main focus is on vocabulary you see / I was thinking I could do vocabulary / and you know say ok so vocabulary / erm / ticket car / uh machine / do you know what I mean? but I mean I can't go into it like that [at all /
6   T: [uh huh /
7   G: so I think I think the main the main vocabulary / I've just got to concentrate
8   on / is just different jobs and what those jobs involve /
9   T: yes I mean look it seems to me / it's really straightforward here Gill/ you've got a (.5) there's a wee slot / that's two clear bits to it / bit one jobs and their duties / bit two write a job description

We suggest that an approach to guided lesson planning that took – or had the time to take – the concept of exploratory talk seriously would have encouraged the trainee (possibly through questioning) to clarify her thinking about the textbook material and the possible uses of the photographs. However, the trainer immediately adopts a more technocratic-reductionist orientation to the activity. The textbook material is positively evaluated twice by the trainer, first in turns 2 and 4 and later in turn 8. This can be seen as an attempt to push Gill, as someone expected to become more like the trainer, to see its value – an interpretation which is backed up by his stimulated recall on this part of the interaction:

> Well I think at this stage I've actually picked up on the fact that she is not happy with the material as it is in the book, erm I think the materials as it is in the book is probably quite straightforward, I'm thinking about the level of the students and I suppose when I say the word straightforward what I'm trying to do, is to suggest to her is that erm this material as it is may be quite useable and quite straightforward and there's no need for her to see it as problematic, possibly I'm thinking, and it's something I encountered with the group before, that when they didn't like material or they thought it was too difficult to teach then they wanted to change it erm I was in some instances trying to discourage them from doing that – obviously as a trainer I want them to be critical of material and to jettison things that I think are flawed or not appropriate or whatever, I think we're all trying to do that – however, erm I don't think that, I mean I wasn't happy with them sometimes saying 'Oh well, we're not going to do that' and I looked at it and thought well actually that's probably quite a useful thing for them to be doing with students at that level and they possibly should be doing that, erm so perhaps what I'm doing is to say 'Look, I want you to do this but it's not difficult'.

The storyline being produced here is that of the CELTA trainer ('obviously as a trainer' is a clear invocation of the speaker's institutional role) who knows what language learners at a particular level need and who understands his role as being endowed with the authority to enforce certain practices – in this case using material adjudged 'useful' which reluctant trainees might initially find 'difficult' to teach. It is also important to point out that trainees would have been aware that one of the learning outcomes for the course was to show that they were able to learn from the tutor in these sessions. The current version of the syllabus states that successful candidates can 'evaluate their own lesson preparation ... *by taking note of comments from tutors*' (Cambridge ESOL 2010: 10; emphasis added). Not surprisingly, the effect of the trainer's evaluative comments was to close down the opportunity for exploratory talk on the issue. Gill's stimulated recall sheds light on this:

> I was thinking about using these photographs and I had them kind of ready and he obviously just kind of thought not, not, you know, such a good idea it should just be quite simple like what it is here, because we hadn't been following the book at all ... so I think when he just kind of, in a nice way, he kind of just you know dismissed what I'd just said, erm and said it's actually

quite simple, I think I was a bit more like erm (laughing) OK, but I mean you know, that, that was the way I was wanting to approach, him telling me you know how to do the lesson … 'cause I was looking for help erm, so but at the same time I had a kind of structure in my mind and it wasn't really the structure that he thought would work.

That the kind of structure Gill had in mind does not emerge in the interaction is indicative of the shortcomings of the technocratic-reductionist view of teacher education contained in these extracts and is clearly at odds with the thrust of the sociocultural reflective turn. In fact this closing down of opportunities to theorise or explore problems typifies the entire interaction.

Having established that the textbook material is to be used as the basis for the lesson Gill goes on to explain her feelings about some of the specific exercises in the textbook material and to express her wish to drop exercise 2 (see Figure 6.1). The following excerpt and the associated stimulated recall show how delicate 'facework' (Goffman 1967) is a key element in this kind of communicative event as both parties seek to position each other and themselves. They also serve to raise more troubling concerns about this approach to initial teacher preparation.

Excerpt 3

1   G: I mean I'm just sorry / but I wasn't just wasn't too sure / I don't like number two at all / I don't think I could =

2   T: = number two is just sticking something in for the sake of sticking it in / I think you're right to drop that / [it's

3   G: [yeah

Here we see Gill's wish to drop one activity being evaluated by the trainer as a wise decision. This evaluative move reminds us that, while being situated by others, individuals may find themselves the subjects of structuring and disciplining discourses. An early example of what structuring and disciplining discourses might mean is to be found in Marx's (1976) *Capital 1,* where in the chapter 'The working day' Marx describes in great detail the ways in which factory owners are able to subject workers to their will via their control over time and space. As regards time, the day is measured to the minute and workers are kept to pre-established timetables, as there are continuous attempts to extract more work for the same pay. As regards space, control is exerted by how factories are constructed and operated. As David Harvey (2010b) notes, the principle here is not just about time and space but discipline and control and indeed punishment.

For Harvey, a more sophisticated and detailed version of Marx's ideas about discipline and control from power was developed much later by Michel Foucault (1973). Harvey believes that Foucault must have read and been influenced by Marx's account of the working day when he famously wrote about the rise of disciplining discourses in modern societies.[8] In the case of his work on the clinic, Foucault charts a shift from a medical profession which relied purely and strictly on academic knowledge to cure patients, to one which additionally took on the role of deciding what was normal and what was abnormal, what was legitimate and what was illegitimate. The key to effectuating this normative behaviour in medical practices is their right to 'gaze'. Gaze is a technical term used by Foucault in reference to how observation is not just about taking in and documenting what is happening before the observer's eyes; it is also about categorising and shaping others according to dominant discourses of normativity.

We see much of this categorising and shaping others according to dominant discourses of normativity at work in the trainer's actions, in this excerpt and in previous interventions. Importantly, as Lionel Boxer (2003) notes, the gaze is about power residing in institutions as discursive fields. It is a discursive resource as opposed to an individually held right or entitlement, even if individuals are invested with the right and entitlement to gaze by virtue of occupying social positions of which the gaze is one of many constituent features. Thus Cambridge ESOL, and ultimately the CELTA course, may be seen to provide the trainer with the discursive resources through which he is able to position Gill in a general sense as a trainee, but more specifically to categorise and shape her according to the dominant discourses of normativity in English language teaching as understood by Cambridge ESOL. It is also a shaping that revolves around the near universal practice on such courses of basing lesson planning on the use of the globally marketed textbooks produced by the UK ELT industry. However, where there is gaze, there is potential for resistance, usefully defined by Susan Seymour as follows:

> In a context of differential power relationships, resistance refers to intentional, and hence conscious, acts of defiance or opposition by a subordinate individual or group of individuals against a superior individual or set of individuals. Such acts are counter-hegemonic but may not succeed in effecting change. They can range from relatively small acts [to large acts.]
>
> (Seymour 2006: 305)

In this case, we see just such a small act as, in the stimulated recall, Gill explains that her apparent apology ('I'm just sorry') is in fact an attempt to resist the supervisory CELTA gaze directed on her by the trainer:

> I had taken the assertive position to cut something out ... I had decided and I didn't really want to change my mind about doing number two so I didn't really want him to say erm no but I think two would be a good idea, so I was kind of like erm sorry I apologise if you're just about to say this but I don't want to do number two so I was kind of pre-empting maybe him saying number two would have been a good idea.

Gill's act of resistance appears to work − the trainer's initial comment (turn 2 in excerpt 3) in fact questions the pedagogic value of the exercise and endorses her decision. However, his stimulated recall for this exchange reveals that this too is a positioning move on his part – one which is more 'calculating', another characteristic of Foucault's gaze:

> My alarm bell has gone off already, she's now said something I agree with so what I want to do is reassure her and, and sort of, I suppose what I'm trying to do there I mean that's totally unnecessary where I say 'it's just stuck in there for the sake of sticking it in' etc., I'm trying to show her I agree with the way she's cast a critical eye over this material ... I'm trying to show erm that I think she's on the right path yeah, erm I think she's erm made a wise decision erm ... and I'm making an issue of it so that I can get her to do the thing I now know she doesn't want to do.

Having ceded ground over exercise 2, the trainer here hopes to be able to make sure Gill does not also try and drop exercise 3. He had in fact guessed correctly that exercise 3 was troubling Gill. However, Gill is given no opportunity to give voice to her problems and the session concludes with an 'agreed' lesson plan in which exercise 3 remains unchanged and unexplored. In fact, when Gill taught the lesson the following day she did not do exercise 3 (although it appears on her lesson plan). Her stimulated recall explains why:

> I think with number three ... I remember thinking I wasn't really too sure how I would even explain you know because I mean some of the endings become like psychiatrist becomes psychiatry, journalist becomes journalism, but there's no dead set rule like -'ist' becomes something, so I was unsure about how I would cope with something like that if they had problems.

In this way, we can see that problems which trainee teachers have with material and specific language points are not necessarily addressed in this approach to lesson planning. This serves to raise questions as to why a course which purports explicitly to value reflection can proceed in this way. It has been suggested (Morton and Gray 2008) that the reason lies in the nature of the CELTA itself and in particular the shortness of the course which does not allow for the kind of exploration and reflection that the sociocultural-reflective turn requires. Even if the amount of time available were to be reallocated to allow greater space for teaching practice, it is difficult to see how other aspects of the syllabus could be covered adequately. It is also important to recall that the CELTA is the current incarnation of an initial training course which had its origins in the explosion of commercial English language teaching in the 1970s. As Joel Spring (2009: 11) points out:

> The global demand for educational credentials has resulted in the worldwide growth of 'shadow' education systems which include for-profit companies offering tutoring services and preparation for high-stakes testing (exams for entering and exiting institutions, such as university and secondary entrance exams and secondary exit exams).

This for-profit sector is serviced by a largely casualised workforce in many parts of the world by young migrant teachers with qualifications such as the CELTA. Thus the CELTA too can be seen as a McDonaldised system designed to produce teachers capable of using basic tools of the trade such as textbooks in ways which are efficient, calculable and predictable and which guarantee the delivery of a standardised product into the educational marketplace. In many cases, as Pennycook (1994) has pointed out, reflective theorising practitioners are not at all what this sector requires. The requirement is more frequently for service providers, capable of delivering language skills to fee-paying customers. Indeed, reflective theorising practitioners (as opposed to minimally trained service providers) can be seen by the commercial sector as having the potential effect 'on the running of a school as would drops of water in oil for the running of an engine' (Bamforth 1993: 4; cited in Pennycook 1994: 166).

Conclusion

We began this chapter with a historical overview of change in language teacher education which much of the literature sees largely in terms of transformation from a craft model to a scientific one, with the eventual eclipse of this by the current model which is deemed to be reflective. This trajectory, as we saw earlier, has been understood by some colleagues who make the case for a sociocultural perspective on language teacher education as amounting to a 'quiet revolution' (Johnson 2000). However, as the examples of the PGCE and the CELTA suggest, we see this as an excessively optimistic assessment of the changes that have actually taken place. Part of the problem with the 'quiet revolution' interpretation of events is that it is not simply about making the case for a more sociocultural understanding of the nature of teacher knowledge; it is also part of an attempt to carve out an autonomous academic space for TESOL and language teacher education which is less reliant on parent disciplines such as linguistics. In this Freeman and Johnson do have a point and we could certainly agree that, for example, descriptions of language do not necessarily translate into prescriptions for teaching. However, we take issue with them when they argue their case for a reconceptualisation of the field in ways which serve to narrow its scope:

> To date, the field of TESOL and indeed language teaching generally, has not pursued and defined its own forms of knowledge. Instead, the field has depended on the familiar forms of research and documentation of its parent disciplines in the social sciences (Freeman 1998). This has created a somewhat conservative hegemony of forms of social science research in the creation of knowledge in the field. These forms have largely failed to penetrate the domain of the classroom and thus remain largely dysfunctional to teachers themselves.
>
> (Freeman and Johnson 1998: 404)

Our own view is that the knowledge base of language teacher education – precisely because of its location at the interstices of a range of disciplines which include linguistics, education, philosophy and sociology – needs to be informed by insights and theory from the social sciences. Failure to explore common ground with the social sciences, we suggest, ultimately runs the risk of intellectually impoverishing the field and weakening it politically. The fact that technocratic-reductionist models of teacher education may in fact predominate should not entail the repudiation of the role of the social sciences in our field; rather, they serve to underline the need for interdisciplinary perspectives (e.g. as found in the UK foundations movement, which although falling within the applied science model presupposed an educated teacher). We conclude this chapter with two thoughts occasioned by this point.

First of all, we think it important to return to the earlier discussion of McDonaldisation, and the work of Braverman which was introduced at that point. If we adapt Braverman's statement about industrial capitalism to education and teaching, we see reflected some of the processes and changes in education and specifically language teaching which have taken place over the past several decades. Thus the technocratic-reductionist approach to education pays far more allegiance to neoliberal capitalism than it does to a genuine and deep interest in applying educational research to educational policy and teaching practice. Indeed, all of the talk about education being research and evidence driven, which has accompanied the implantation of the technocratic-reductionist approach, comes to look a great deal like what Braverman (1974: 86) terms 'management masquerading in the trappings of science'. In addition, teachers like Almudena and Elena apparently have no trouble seeing through this masquerade, judging by their comments about some of its manifestations which they encountered while doing their PGCE course. Just as the rationalised processes described by Ritzer ultimately generate irrationalities, so a technocratic-reductionist model of education, ostensibly set up to make teaching better, leads to the alienation of the workforce.

Second, although we are in sympathy with the thrust of the reflective turn and sociocultural notions of how language teachers might acquire the knowledge and skills that they need to teach, we take the view that the much-needed rejection of 'management masquerading in the trappings of science' which typifies so much teacher education in the neoliberal climate cannot occur unless the reconceptualisation of the knowledge base of language teacher education is broadly, rather than narrowly, focused. Our view of the teacher is one of a theorising practitioner whose practice is informed by theory (rather than just subject knowledge and skills in effective delivery of lessons); and as someone who is capable of reflecting on practice in ways that allow for the genuine education of students. Such a model of the teacher does not see education as being about the production of human capital or as serving the economy in any narrowly construed instrumental way. Taking a view of the teacher as a socially necessary kind of thinker, and in line with Chapters 3–5, where we proposed a number of changes to thinking in applied linguistics, we would argue that teacher education requires an interdisciplinary knowledge base firmly rooted in the social sciences, in which political economy (as described in Chapter 1) is given due consideration. Such a model does not imply any kind of subservience to parent disciplines, rather it takes the view that education is integral to political economy and that initial teacher education which neglects such an understanding of education runs the risk of giving teachers an apolitical view of teaching, by denying them the opportunity to locate the practice of teaching within larger social and theoretical frameworks. At the same time, such an approach would not seek to deny the relevance of situated and experiential learning and the centrality of reflection in teacher education – quite the contrary. However, for reflection to be meaningful, we argue that it not only requires sufficient time and opportunities for exploratory talk but crucially that it is facilitated by the use of theoretical tools and concepts which excessively school-based models such as the PGCE or the CELTA are unlikely to provide.

Appendix: Transcription conventions for PGCE data

/	indicates the minimal but clear pause between phrases/sentences in normally paced speech.
(.5)	indicates pause of half a second
(1)	indicates pause of one second
?	indicates rising intonation (including questions)
[xxx	indicates overlapping speech
[zzz	
=	indicates that the utterance latches with (i.e. occurs seamlessly after) the next utterance
italics	indicates words that were produced in English in the original version
!	indicates raised intonation, exclamation
{xxx}	comments describing aspects of extra-linguistic communication, such as voice inflection, laughter, facial expressions, gaze, hand movements, etc.

NOTES

1   Introduction

1   We do not mean to suggest that Rampton was the first scholar to make such a call for an interdisciplinary applied linguistics. He surely was not. Applied linguistics has always been framed by applied linguists themselves as interdisciplinary. Indeed, years earlier, Michael Halliday wrote about a 'transdisciplinary' applied linguistics, one which would move beyond 'interdisciplinarity' or 'multidisciplinarity' towards 'new forms of activity which are thematic rather than disciplinary in their orientation' (Halliday 1990: 8). However, we have chosen Rampton's article as a starting point for our discussion of applied linguistics and interdisciplinarity because of its significance (it is often cited in discussions of applied linguistics as a field) and its timing (it was published at a time when more and more applied linguists were seeking ideas and frameworks in the social sciences – anthropology, sociology, geography, etc.).

2   In their discussion of globalisation and neoliberalism Ritzer and Atalay (2010: 73–116) include what they term a 'neoliberal' economist although the economist in question in the reading they select offers a Hayekian revamping of economic freedom against 'farcical collectivism'. Other contributors in the section agree that the term is used as a code word for overweening American power and unregulated financial flows.

2   What is neoliberalism?

1   These figures are from the Bank of England *Quarterly Bulletin* (2004): <http://www.bankofengland.co.uk/publications/quarterlybulletin/qb040304.pdf>.

2   In the UK public sector workers make up around 40% of the workforce. See *Observer Fact File UK Economy,* 25 April 2010.

3   See Fine (1980) for an account of how neo-classical economics relies on appearances.

4   Hardt and Negri (2005) and Laclau and Mouffe (1985) recognise their debt to Foucault as do Fairclough and Pennycook in applied linguistics (see Torfing 1999). Joseph (2006: 355) also concurs with Foucault's view that what is knowable is curtailed by power operating through language.

5   Foucault's *Les Mots et les choses* was translated into English as *The Order of Things.*

6   The question of how everything in a capitalist market economy becomes a commodity, and how this affects ideology, will be dealt with in more detail in Ch. 5.

7   Madeleine Bunting, *Guardian,* 6 Oct. 2008.

3   Neoliberal keywords and the contradictions of an ideology

1   The photo is *Bread line during the Louisville Flood Kentucky* taken in 1937 by Margaret Bourke White: see Rubin 1999: 56–7; also at <http://www.masters-of-photography. com/images/full/bourke-white/b-w_living.jpg>.
2   See Holborow (1999) for a fuller account of Volosinov's view of the relationship between language and ideology.
3   See *The Economist,* 14 Oct. 2004.
4   The *Sunday Tribune*, in 'Great minds think alike?', in its Business Section, 4 April 2007, reported that the American Chamber of Commerce (AmCham) and the Department of Finance (DoF) used exactly the same text, word for word, to relay to journalists their views on tax policy.
5   These concordance patterns are available at <http://www.natcorp.ox.ac.uk/index. xml>. Negative descriptors (e.g. *unchecked, ultimate, massive* deregulation) slightly outweigh positive descriptors (e.g. increase *in passenger numbers*) in the BNC sample of 50 solutions from 437 found.
6   Google, Facebook and Microsoft all took advantage of Ireland's lax tax regime. Google e.g. channelled 92% of its profits through Dublin, paying the Irish Government €21 million in total (Toynbee 2010).
7   Fine (2002) and Fine and Lapavitsas (2004) provide a useful critique of the notion of social capital and human capital in the social sciences.
8   The National Development Plan is also available on websites of various Irish ministries – e.g. the Department of Trade and Innovation (DETI 2009). It also appears on the Science Foundation Ireland's website as its own strategy document <http://www.sfi. ie/news-events/publications/orgnisational-publications>, which highlights the degree to which Irish public policy is sourced from advisory committees consisting of people from the corporate sector, whether set up under the auspices of the American Chamber of Commerce in Ireland, or global corporate think-tanks such as the OECD.
9   *Irish Independent,* 30 March 2010.

4   Economising globalisation and identity in applied linguistics in neoliberal times

1   As Marx explained matters: 'In the social production of their existence, men inevitably enter into definite relations, which are independent of their will, namely relations of production appropriate to a given stage in the development of their material forces of production. The totality of these relations of production constitutes the economic structure of society, the real foundation, on which arises a legal and political superstructure and to which correspond definite forms of social consciousness. The mode of production of material life conditions the general process of social, political and intellectual life. It is not the consciousness of men that determines their existence, but their social existence that determines their consciousness' (Marx 1976: 3).
2   An exception is an article I have recently published about second language learning research and class (Block 2012b).
3   Although instead of 'Cockney', Rampton might have used 'slang', a term by now in wide circulation among young Londoners to describe their day-to-day speech (Preece 2010). Posh refers not so much to RP (Received Prounciation) as to a more generalised educated pronunciation of English. Slang refers to the emergent post-Estuary English vernacular of young people in London, which includes traditional cockney pronunciation features – such as glottal stops (e.g. wa/?/er), h-dropping (e.g. 'appy), voiced labiodental fricatives for more standard voiced dental fricatives (e.g. 'bruver' for 'brother') and voiceless labiodental fricatives for more standard voiceless dental fricatives (e.g. 'fing' for 'thing'), but also manifests other influences, such as Caribbean Englishes and African American Vernacular English.

5   Neoliberalism, celebrity and 'aspirational content' in English language teaching textbooks for the global market

1   Žižek (2008) suggests that the philanthropy of such individuals allows capitalism to assume a more human face than it in fact possesses.
2   Titles in Gray (2010b): *Streamline Connections* (Hartley and Viney 1979); *Building Strategies* (Abbs and Freebairn 1984); *The New Cambridge English Course 2* (Swan and Walter 1990); and *The New Edition New Headway Intermediate* (Soars and Soars 2003b). Titles in Gray (2010a): *New Headway Intermediate* (Soars and Soars 1996); *New Headway Upper-Intermediate* (Soars and Soars 1998); *New Headway Pre-Intermediate* (Soars and Soars 2000a); *New Headway Elementary* (Soars and Soars 2000b); *New Headway Advanced* (Soars and Soars 2003a); *New Headway Upper-Intermediate* (Soars and Soars 2005); *New Cutting Edge Upper-Intermediate* (Cunningham and Moor 2005a); *New Cutting Edge Intermediate* (Cunningham and Moor 2005b). Additional titles for this chapter: *Headway Intermediate* (Soars and Soars 1986); *New Headway Intermediate* (Soars and Soars 2009); *New Headway Elementary* (Soars and Soars 2011).
3   Pseudonyms have been used throughout and names on first mention are followed with the number of years of teaching experience.

6   The marketisation of language teacher education and neoliberalism: characteristics, consequences and future prospects

1   Weber's words resonate with what Antonio Gramsci wrote about Taylorism: 'Taylor is in fact expressing with brutal cynicism the purpose of American society – developing in the worker to the highest degree automatic and mechanical attitudes, breaking up the old psycho-physical nexus of qualified professional work, which demands a certain active participation of intelligence, fantasy and initiative on the part of the worker, and reducing productive operations exclusively to the mechanical physical aspect' (Gramsci 1971: 302).
2   This is an interesting position for Ritzer to be taking, given that in just about everything that he has written over the years, he has shown himself to be a hard-core Weberian with little proclivity for a Marxist analysis of society.
3   The progressive transfer of the PGCE from the universities to the schools got under way in 2011.
4   The names of all trainee teachers in the chapter have been fictionalised.
5   The course took place at Queen's University, Belfast, in 2002. There has been no significant change to the CELTA syllabus or structure since then.
6   Data reproduced here have already been drawn on in Morton and Gray (2008, 2010) – although in neither case is the impact of neoliberalism considered.
7   Transcription conventions for this and subsequent excerpts discussed in this section can be found at the end of this chapter in Appendix 1. In all interactions, the trainer is referenced as T and Gill is referenced as G. Harry, a fellow trainee, appears in the first excerpt as H.
8   Harvey writes that '[a]lthough in his works he departs from what Marxists … were saying, his early fundamental texts about asylums, prisons and clinics should, in my view, be read as continuations of rather than departures from Marx's arguments concerning the rise of disciplinary capitalism in which workers have been socialised and disciplined to accept the spatiotemporal logic of the capitalist labor process' (Harvey 2010b: 149).

REFERENCES

Abbs, B., and Freebairn, I. (1984) *Building Strategies,* Harlow: Longman.

ABC New Online (2005) 'Gere urges Palestinians to vote': <http://www.abc.net.au/news/newsitems/200501/s1277796.htm> (accessed May 2011).

Adorno, T., and Horkheimer, M. (1997 [1944]) *Dialectic of Enlightenment,* London: Verso.

Adorno, T., Benjamin, W., Bloch, E., Brecht, B., and Lukács, G. (1977) *Aesthetics and Politics,* ed. Rodney Taylor. London: NLB.

Ahmed, S. (2004) *The Cultural Politics of Emotion,* Edinburgh: Edinburgh University Press.

Albright, J. (2008) 'Problematics and generative possibilities', in J. Albright and A. Luke (eds), *Pierre Bourdieu and Literacy Education* (pp. 11–32), London: Routledge.

Albrow, M. (1996) *The Global Age: State and Society beyond Modernity,* Cambridge: Polity.

Allen, K. (2007) *The Corporate Takeover of Ireland,* Dublin: Irish Academic Press.

Allen, K. (2009) *Ireland's Economic Crash: A Radical Agenda for Change,* Dublin: Liffey Press.

Althusser, L. (2008 [1971]) *On Ideology,* London: Verso.

American Chamber of Commerce Ireland (2007) *Retuning the Growth Engine: Developing an Innovation Base to Secure Ireland's Future:* http://capitalmarkets.bankofireland.com/fs/doc/wysiwyg/retuning_growth_engine.pdf.

Anderson, C. (2002) 'Deconstructing teaching English to speakers of other language: problematising a professional discourse', unpubl. thesis, Canterbury Christ Church University College.

Appadurai, A. (1990) 'Disjuncture and difference in the global cultural economy', in M. Featherstone (ed.), *Global Culture: Nationalism, Globalization and Modernity* (pp. 295–310), London: Sage.

Appadurai, A. (1996) *Modernity at Large: Cultural Dimensions in Globalization,* Minneapolis, MN: University of Minnesota Press.

Apple, M. W. (2004) 'Creating Difference: Neo-liberalism, Neo-Conservatism, and the Politics of Education Reform', *Educational Policy,* 18(1): 12–44.

Apple, M. W. (2006) *Educating the 'Right' Way,* 2nd edn, London: Routledge.

Apple, M. W., Au, W., and Gandin, L. A. (eds) (2009) *The Routledge Handbook of Critical Education,* New York: Routledge.

Arrighi, G. (2007) *Adam Smith in Beijing: Lineages of the Twenty-First Century,* London: Verso.

Arrighi, G. (2010) *The Long Twentieth Century: Money, Power and the Origins of Our Times*, new edn, London: Verso.

Ball, S. (2007) *Education Plc: Understanding Private Sector Participation in Public Sector Education*, new edn, London: Routledge.

Ball, S. (2008) *The Education Debate: Policy and Politics in the Twenty-First Century*, London: Policy Press.

Bamforth, D. (1993) 'Teaching as marketing', *ELT Management* (Feb.), 2–4.

Barber, M. (1996) *The Learning Game: Arguments for an Education Revolution*, London: Phoenix.

Barduhn, S. (1998) 'Traits and conditions that accelerate teacher learning', unpubl. thesis, Thames Valley University, London.

Barker, M. (2008) 'Analysing Discourse', in Mike Pickering (ed.), *Research Methods for Cultural Studies* (pp. 150–72), Edinburgh: Edinburgh University Press.

Barthes, R. (1973) *Mythologies*, London: Paladin Books.

Bauman, Z. (2000) *Liquid Modernity,* Cambridge: Polity.

Bauman, Z. (2007) *Consuming Life*, Cambridge: Polity.

Becker, G. S. (1962) 'Investment in human capital: a theoretical analysis. Part 2: Investment in human beings', *Journal of Political Economy*, 70(5): 9–49.

Béland, D. (2010) 'Resiliance of state power', in G. Ritzer and Z. Atalay (eds), *Readings in Globalisation* (pp. 175–8), Malden, MA: Wiley Blackwell.

Bell, D. (1973) *The Coming of Post-Industrial Society: A Venture in Social Forecasting*, New York: Basic Books.

Bell, J. and Gower, R. (1992) *Upper Intermediate Matters*, Harlow: Longman.

Bengtsson, J. (1995) 'What is reflection? On reflection in the teaching profession and teacher education', *Teachers and Teaching: Theory and Practice*, 1(1): 23–32.

Bennet, T., Grossberg, L., and Morris M. (2005) *New Keywords: A Revised Vocabulary of Culture and Society,* Malden, MA: Blackwell.

Berger, J. (1972) *Ways of Seeing,* London: BBC/Penguin.

Bernstein, B. (1971) *Class, Codes and Control*, vol. 1, *Theoretical Studies towards a Sociology of Language*, London: Routledge & Kegan Paul.

Bhabha, H. (1994) *The Location of Culture*, London: Routledge.

Birch, K., and Mykhnenko, V. (eds) (2010) *The Rise and Fall of Neo-Liberalism: The Collapse of an Economic Order?*, New York: Zed Books.

Biressi, A., and Nunn, H. (2008) *The Tabloid Culture Reader,* Maidenhead: Open University Press/McGraw-Hill Education.

Block, D. (1996) 'Not so fast! Some thoughts on theory culling, relativism, accepted findings and the heart and soul of SLA', *Applied Linguistics*, 17(1): 65–83.

Block, D. (2000) 'Revisiting the gap between SLA researchers and language teachers', *Links and Letters*, 17: 127–41.

Block, D. (2001) 'Foreign nationals on a PGCE modern languages course: questions of national identity', *European Journal of Teacher Education*, 24: 291–311.

Block, D. (2002) 'Negotiation for meaning as McCommunication: a problem in the frame', in D. Block and D. Cameron (eds), *Globalization and Language Teaching* (pp. 117–33), London: Routledge.

Block, D. (2006) *Multilingual Identities in a Global City: London Stories,* London: Palgrave.

Block, D. (2007) *Second Language Identities,* London: Continuum.

Block, D. (2010) 'Engaging with human sociality: thoughts on communication and embodiment', *Applied Linguistics Review*, 1(1): 45–56.

Block, D. (2012a) 'Unpicking agency in sociolinguistic research with migrants', in M. Martin-Jones and S. Gardner (eds), *Multilingualism, Discourse and Ethnography* (pp. 47–60), London: Routledge.

Block, D. (2012b) 'Class and second language acquisition research', *Language Teaching Research*, 16(2).

Block, D. (in preparation) *Class in Applied Linguistics: A Global Perspective*, London: Routledge.

Block, D., and Cameron, D. (2002) *Globalisation and Language Teaching*, London: Routledge.

Blommaert, J. (ed.) (1999) *Language-Ideological Debates*, Berlin: Mouton de Gruyter.

Blommaert, J. (2005) *Discourse*, Cambridge: Cambridge University Press.

Blommaert, J. (2008) 'Commentary: multi-everything London', *Journal of Language, Identity and Education*, 7(1): 81–9.

Blommaert, J. (2010) *The Sociology of Globalization*. Cambridge: Cambridge University Press.

Boltanski, L., and Chiapello, E. (2007) *The New Spirit of Capitalism*, London: Verso.

Boorstin, D. (1992 [1961]) *The Image: A Guide to Pseudo-Events in America*, New York: Vintage Books.

Borg, M. (2002). 'Learning to teach: exploring trainee teachers' beliefs on a CELTA Course', unpubl. thesis, University of Leeds.

Borg, S. (2006) *Teacher Cognition and Language Education: Research and Practice*, London: Continuum.

Bottero, W. (2005) *Stratification: Social Division and Inequality*, London: Routledge.

Bottomore, T. B. (1965) *Classes in Modern Society*. London: George Allen & Unwin.

Boucher, G., and Graine, C. (2003) 'Having one's cake and being eaten too: Irish neo-liberal Corporatism', *Review of Social Economy*, 61(3): 295–316.

Bourdieu, P. (1977) *Outline of a Theory of Practice*, Cambridge: Cambridge University Press.

Bourdieu, P. (1984) *Distinction*, London: Routledge.

Bourdieu, P. (1986) 'The forms of capital', in J. F. Richardson (ed.), *Handbook of Theory of Research for Sociology of Education* (pp. 241–58), New York: Greenwood Press.

Bourdieu, P (1991) *Language and Symbolic Power*, Cambridge: Polity.

Bourdieu, P. (1998) 'Utopia of endless exploitation: the essence of neo-liberalism': <http://mondediplo.com/1998/12/08bourdieu>.

Bourdieu, P. (2005) *The Social Structures of the Economy*, Cambridge: Cambridge University Press.

Bowles, S., and Gintis, H. (1975) 'The problem of human capital: a Marxian critique', *American Economic Review*, 65(2): 74–82.

Boxer, L. (2003) 'Assessment of quality systems with positioning theory', in R. Harré and F. Moghaddam (eds), *The Self and Others: Positioning Individuals and Groups in Personal, Political, and Cultural Contexts* (pp. 251–78), New York: Praeger.

Boyle, D., and Evans, J. (2007) 'Competition and productivity', in *Perspectives on Irish Productivity*: <http://www.forfas.ie/media/productivity>.

Braudel, F. (1972 [1949]) *The Mediterranean and the Mediterranean World in the Age of Philippe II*, vol. 1, London: Collins.

Braverman, H. (1974) *Labor and Monopoly Capital*, New York: Monthly Review Press.

Breen, M., and Candlin, C. (1980) 'The essentials of a communicative curriculum in language teaching', *Applied Linguistics*, 1(2): 89–112.

Brenner, R. (1977) 'The origins of capitalist development: a critique of neo-Smithian Marxism', *New Left Review*, 104: 25–92.

Brenner, R. (2000) 'The Boom and the bubble', *New Left Review*, NS 6 (Nov.–Dec.): <http://www.newleftreview.org/?view=2286>.

British Council (2010) *Annual Report 2009–10: Working for the UK Where it Matters*, London: British Council.

Brumfit, C. (1991) 'Applied linguistics in higher education: riding the storm', *BAAL Newsletter*, 38: 45–9.

Bruthiaux, P. (2008) 'Dimensions of globalization and applied linguistics', in R. Rubdy and Tam (eds), *Language as Commodity: Global Structures, Local Marketplaces* (pp. 1–30), London: Continuum.

Bunting, M. (2004) *Willing Slaves: How the Overwork Culture is Ruling our Lives*, London: Harper Collins.

Bunting, M. (2008) 'Faith. Belief. Trust. This economic orthodoxy was built on superstition', Guardian, 8 Oct.: <http://www.guardian.co.uk/commentisfree/2008/oct/06/economics.economy>.

Burkitt, I. (2008) Social Selves, London: Sage.

Business and Finance (2007) 'Peter Sutherland, Denis O'Brien and Airtricity founder Eddie O'Connor honoured at Business & Finance Awards Dinner', 14 Dec.: <http://www.findfacts,ie/financenews/article_1012122.shtml>.

Caldas-Coulthard, C. R., and Iedema, R. (eds) (2008) *Identity Trouble Critical Discourse and Contested Identities*, London: Palgrave.

Callinicos, A. (1989) *Against Postmodernism: A Marxist Critique,* Cambridge: Polity.

Callinicos, A. (2009) *Imperialism and Global Political Economy*, Cambridge: Polity.

Callinicos, A. (2010) *Bonfire of Illusions*, Cambridge: Polity.

Cambridge ESOL (2010) *Cambridge English for Teaching: CELTA Syllabus*, Cambridge: University of Cambridge ESOL Examinations; <http://www.cambridgeesol.org/exams/teaching-awards/celta.html> (accessed July 2011).

Cameron, D., Fraser, E., Harvey, P., Rampton, B., and Richardson, K. (1992) *Researching Language: Issues of Power and Method*, London: Routledge.

Canagarajah, Suresh (1999) *Resisting Linguistic Imperialism in English Teaching*, Oxford: Oxford University Press.

Castells, M. (2000) *The Rise of the Network Society: The Information Age: Economy, Society and Culture,* vol. 1, Oxford: Blackwell.

Castells, M. (2009) *Communication Power*, Oxford: Oxford University Press.

Castles, S., and Miller, M. (2009) *The Age of Migration,* 4th edn, London: Palgrave.

Caughey, J. (1984) *Imaginary Social Worlds: A Cultural Approach,* Lincoln, NE: University of Nebraska Press.

Central Bank of Ireland (2010) 'Ensure proper and effective regulation of financial institutions and markets': <http://www.financialregulator.ie/about-s/Pages/default.aspx>.

Chomsky, N. (1991) *Media Control: The Spectacular Achievements of Propaganda,* New York: Seven Stories Press.

Clandinin, D. J., and Connelly, F. M. (1985) 'Personal practical knowledge and the modes of knowing: relevance for teaching and learning', in E. Eisner (ed.), *Learning and Teaching Ways of Knowing: Eighty-Fourth Yearbook of the National Society for the Study of Education, Part II* (pp. 174–98), Chicago, IL: University of Chicago Press.

Clanfield, L. (2010) 'Coursebooks and the curse of celebrity', *Guardian Weekly*, 21 May: 4.

Cohen, N. (2007) *What's Left? How Liberals Lost their Way*, London: Harper Perennial.

Cole, A. L. (1997) 'Impediments to reflective practice: toward a new agenda for research on teaching', *Teachers and Teaching: Theory and Practice*, 3(1): 7–27.

Collins, M. (2004) *The Likes of Us*, London: Granta Books.

Cook, G. (2003) *Applied Linguistics*, Oxford: Oxford University Press.

Corder, S. P. (1960) *An Intermediate English Practice Book,* Harlow: Longman.

Cowen, B. (1995) 'The state and control of teacher education: the knowledge fit for teachers', in R. Gardner (ed.), *Contemporary Crises in Teacher Education* (pp. 18–34), Birmingham: British Association of Teachers and Researchers in Overseas Education.

Coyle, D. (1997) *The Weightless World: Strategies for Managing the Digital Economy,* Oxford: Capstone.

Coyle, D. (2003) *Paradoxes of Prosperity: Why the New Capitalism Benefits All,* London: Texere.

Crompton, R. (2008) *Class and Stratification,* 3rd edn, Cambridge: Polity.

Cross, R. (2006) 'Identity and language teacher education: the potential for sociocultural perspectives in researching language teacher identity', paper presented at the Annual Conference of the Australian Association for Research in Education, Adelaide, Nov.

Cross, R. (2010) 'Language teaching as sociocultural activity: rethinking language teacher practice', *Modern Language Journal,* 94(3): 434–52.

Cunningham, S., and Moor, P. (2005a) *New Cutting Edge / Upper Intermediate,* Harlow: Pearson Longman.

Cunningham, S., and Moor, P. (2005b) *Cutting Edge / Intermediate,* Harlow: Pearson Longman.

Davies, A. (2007) *An Introduction to Applied Linguistics: From Practice to Theory,* Edinburgh: Edinburgh University Press.

Davies, A., and Elder, K. (eds) (2005) *The Handbook of Applied Linguistics,* new edn, Oxford: Wiley Blackwell.

Davies, B., and Harré, R. (1999) 'Positioning and personhood', in R. Harré and L. van Langenhove (eds), *Positioning Theory* (pp. 32–52), London: Sage.

Day, R. R. (1990) 'Teacher observation in second language teacher education', in J. C. Richards and D. Nunan (eds), *Second Language Teacher Education* (pp. 43–61), Cambridge: Cambridge University Press.

Debord, G. (1994 [1967]) *The Society of the Spectacle,* New York: Zone Books.

Deem, R., and Brehony, K. J. (2005) 'Management as ideology: the case of "new managerialism" in higher education', *Oxford Review of Education,* 31(2): 217–35.

De Fina, A., Schiffrin, D., and Bamberg, M. (eds) (2006) *Discourse and Identity,* Cambridge: Cambridge University Press.

Denning, M. (1997) *The Cultural Front: The Laboring of American Culture in the Twentieth Century,* New York: Verso.

Department of the Taoiseach (2006) 'Regulatory reform in Ireland': <http://www.Taoiseach.gov.ie/eng/Publications_Archive/publications_2006>.

Department of the Taoiseach (2010) 'Government White Paper on better regulation': <http://www.betterreuglation.ie/eng>.

Department of Trade and Employment (2005) 'Irish electricity market principle challenges': <http://www.deti.ie/publications/trade/2005/electricitymarket.pdf>.

Department of Trade and Innovation (DETI) (2009) *Powering the Smart Economy: Strategy 2009–2013:* <http://www.deti.ie/publications/trade/2005/electricitymarket.pdf>.

Dewey, J. (1933) *How we Think,* Buffalo, NY: Prometheus Books.

Doogan, K. (2009) *New Capitalism? The Transformation of Work,* Cambridge: Polity.

Dublin City University (2004) *Commercialisation Handbook:* <http://www.dcu.ie/chemistry/asg/commercialisationhandbook.pdf>.

Duménil, G., and Lévy, D. (2005) 'The neoliberal (counter-)revolution', in A. Saad-Filho and D. Johnston (eds), *Neoliberalism: A Critical Reader* (pp. 9–19), London: Pluto Press.

Duménil, G., and Lévy, D. (2009) 'Thirty years of neoliberalism under US hegemony': <http://www.jourdan.ens.fr/levy/dle2009b.htm>.

Dunn, B. (2009a) *Global Political Economy: A Marxist Critique,* London: Pluto Press.

Dunn, B. (2009b) 'Myths of globalisation and the new economy', *International Socialism,* 121: 75–97: <http://www.isj.org.uk/index.php4?id=509&issue=121>.

Durkheim, E. (1984 [1893]) *The Division of Labor in Society,* New York: Free Press.

Dyer, R. (1986) *Heavenly Bodies: Film Stars and Society,* London: Macmillan.

Eagleton, T. (1996) *The Illusions of Postmodernism,* Oxford: Blackwell.

Eagleton, T. (2007) *Ideology: An Introduction,* London: Verso.

Edge, J. (2006) *(Re)locating TESOL in an Age of Empire,* London: Palgrave.

Elbaz, F. (1983) *Teacher Thinking: A Study of Practical Knowledge,* New York: Nichols Publishing Co.

Eliot, T. S. (1963) *Selected Prose,* ed. John Hayward, London: Penguin Books/Faber & Faber.

Ellis, G. (1996) 'How culturally appropriate is the communicative approach?', *ELT Journal,* 50(3): 213–18.

Ellis, V., Edwards, A., and Smagorinsky, P. (eds) (2009) *Learning Teaching: Cultural Historical Perspectives on Teacher Education and Development,* London: Routledge.

Ernst & Young (2006) 'Entrepreneur of the Year 2006': <http://ey.mobi/IE/EN/Home>.

Ernst & Young (2010) 'In the spotlight: social entrepreneurship': <http://www.ey.com/GL/EN/Home>.

Euromonitor International (2010) *English Language Quantitative Indicators: Cameroon, Nigeria, Rwanda, Bangladesh and Pakistan. A Custom Report Compiled by Euromonitor International for the British Council,* London: Euromonitor International Ltd.

Evans, M. (2004) *Killing Thinking: The Death of Universities,* London: Continuum.

Fairclough, N. (1992) *Discourse and Social Change,* Cambridge: Polity.

Fairclough, N. (1995) *Critical Discourse Analysis,* London: Longman.

Fairclough, N. (2000) *New Labour, New Language?,* London: Routledge.

Fairclough, N. (2002) 'Language in new capitalism', *Discourse and Society,* 13(2): 163–6.

Fairclough, N. (2004) 'Critical discourse analysis in researching language in the new capitalism: overdetermination, transdisciplinarity and textual analysis', in L. Young and C. Harrison (eds), *Systemic Functional Linguistics and Critical Discourse Analysis* (pp. 103–22), London: Continuum.

Fairclough, N. (2006) *Language and Globalization,* London: Routledge.

Fairclough, N., and Graham, P. (2002) 'Marx as critical discourse analysis: the genesis of a critical method and its relevance to the critique of global capital', *Estudios de Sociolinguistica,* 3(1): 185–229.

Featherstone, M. (1991) *Consumer Culture and Postmodernism,* London: Sage.

Fine, B. (1980) *Economic Theory and Ideology,* London: Edward Arnold.

Fine. B. (2002) 'It ain't social, it ain't capital and it ain't Africa', *Studia Africana,* 13: 18–33: <http://eprints.soas.ac.uk/2334/>.

Fine, B. (2010) '*Zombieconomics*: the living death of the dismal science', in K. Birch and V. Mykhnenko (eds), *The Rise and Fall of Neoliberalism: The Collapse of an Economic Order?* (pp. 53–70), New York: Zed Books.

Fine, B., and Lapavitsas, C. (2004) 'Social capital and capitalist economies', *South Eastern Journal of Economics,* 1: 17–34.

Firth, A., and Wagner, J. (1997) 'On discourse, communication, and (some) fundamental concepts in SLA Research', *Modern Language Journal,* 81(3): 286–300.

Fisher, M. (2009) *Capitalist Realism: Is there No Alternative?,* Winchester: O Books.

Foucault, M. (1973) *The Birth of the Clinic: An Archaeology of Medical Perception,* London: Routledge.

Foucault, M. (2002a) *Power: Essential Works of Foucault 1954–1984,* ed. James D. Faubion, Harmondsworth: Penguin.

Foucault, M. (2002b) *The Order of Things,* London: Routledge.

Fraser, N. (2003) 'Social justice in the age of identity politics: redistribution, recognition, and participation', in N. Fraser and A. Honneth, *Redistribution or Recognition? A Political-Philosophical Exchange* (pp. 7–109), London: Verso.

Freeden, M. (2003) *Ideology: A Very Short Introduction,* Oxford: Oxford University Press.

Freeman, D. (2002) 'The hidden side of the work: teacher knowledge and learning to teach. A perspective from North American educational research on teacher education in English language teaching', *Language Teaching,* 35: 1–13.

Freeman, D., and Johnson, K. (1998) 'Reconceptualizing the knowledge base of language teacher education', *TESOL Quarterly,* 32(3): 397–417.

Friedman, L. M. (1999) *The Horizontal Society,* New Haven, CT: Yale University Press.

Fuchs, C. (2009) 'Some reflections on Manuel Castells' book "Communication Power"', *TripleC,* 7(1): 94–108.

Furlong, J., Barton, L., Miles, S., Whiting, C., and Whitty, G. (2000) *Teacher Education in Transition: Re-forming Professionalism?,* Buckingham: Open University Press,

Gee, J. P. (2008) *Social Linguistics and Literacies: Ideology in Discourses,* 3rd edn, London: Falmer.

Gee, J. P., Hull, G., and Lankshear, C. (1996) *The New Work Order: Behind the Language of the New Capitalism,* Cambridge: Polity.

Giddens, A. (1973) *The Class Structure of Advanced Societies,* London: Hutchinson.

Giddens, A. (1985) *The Nation-State and Violence,* vol. 2 of *A Contemporary Critique of Historical Materialism,* Cambridge: Polity.

Giddens, A. (2000) *Runaway World: How Globalization is Reshaping our Lives,* 2nd edn, London: Routledge.

Giroux, H. A. (2004a) *The Terror of Neoliberalism: Authoritarianism and the Eclipse of Democracy,* Boulder, CO: Paradigm Publishers.

Giroux, H. A. (2004b) 'Neoliberalism and the demise of democracy: resurrecting hope in dark times', *Dissident Voice,* 7 Aug.: <http://dissidentvoice.org/Aug04/Giroux/0807.html>.

Giulianotti, R., and Robertson, R. (2007) 'Forms of glocalization: globalization and the migration strategies of Scottish football fans in North America', *Sociology,* 41(1): 133–52.

Goffman, E. (1967) *Interaction Ritual.* New York: Pantheon.

Goffman, E. (1979) *Gender Advertisements,* London: Macmillan.

Gokulsing, K. M., and Dissanayake, W. (2004) *Indian Popular Cinema: A Narrative of Cultural Change,* revised edn, London: Trenthan Books.

Goldthorpe, J. H., and Lockwood, D. (1963) 'Affluence and the British class structure', *Sociological Review,* 11(2): 133–63.

Golombek, P. R. (1998) 'A study of language teachers' personal practical knowledge', *TESOL Quarterly,* 32(3): 447–64.

Gordon, L., and Whitty, G. (1997) 'Giving the "hidden hand" a helping hand? The rhetoric and reality of neoliberal education in England and New Zealand', *Comparative Education,* 33: 453–67.

Gore, J. M., and Zeichner, K. M. (1991) 'Action research and reflective teaching in preservice teacher education: a case study from the United States', *Teaching and Teacher Education,* 7(2): 119–36.

Graddol, D. (2006) *English Next,* British Council: <http://britishcouncil.org/learning-research-english-next.pdf>.

Gramsci, A. (1971) *Selections from the Prison Notebooks,* London: Lawrence & Wishart.

Granger, C. (1993) *Play Games with English,* Oxford: Heinemann.

Gray, J. (1998) 'The language learner as teacher: the use of interactive diaries in teacher training', *ELT Journal,* 52(1): 29–37.

Gray, J. (2010a) *The Construction of English: Culture, Consumerism and Promotion in the ELT Global Coursebook,* London: Palgrave.

Gray, J. (2010b) 'The branding of English and the culture of the new capitalism: representations of the world of work in English language textbooks', *Applied Linguistics,* 31(5): 714–33.

Grusky, D., and Galescu, G. (2005) 'Foundations of neo-Durkheimian class analysis', in E. O. Wright (ed.), *Approaches to Class Analysis* (pp. 51–81), Cambridge: Cambridge University Press.

Gumperz, J. (1982) *Discourse Strategies*, Cambridge: Cambridge University Press.

Hadfield, J. (2000) *Intermediate Communication Games*, Harlow: Pearson.

Halliday, M. (1990) 'New ways of meaning: a challenge to applied linguistics', *Journal of Applied Linguistics*, 6: 7–36.

Hardt, M., and Negri, A. (2000) *Empire*. Cambridge, MA: Harvard University Press.

Hardt, M., and Negri, A. (2005) *Multitude: War and Democracy in the Age of Empire*. Harmondsworth: Penguin.

Harman, C. (2007) 'Theorising neoliberalism', *International Socialism*, 117: 87–121.

Harman, C. (2009) *Zombie Capitalism: Global Crisis and the Relevance of Marx*, London: Bookmarks.

Harman, G. (2003) 'Australian academics and prospective academics: adjustment to a more commercial environment', *Higher Education and Management Policy*, 15(3): 105–22.

Harré, R. (2004) 'Positioning theory': <www.massey.ac.nz/~alock/virtual/positioning.doc>.

Hartley, B., and Viney, P. (1979) *Streamline English Connections,* Oxford: Oxford University Press.

Harvey, D. (1989) *The Condition of Postmodernity: An Enquiry into the Origins of Cultural Change*, Oxford: Blackwell.

Harvey, D. (2003) *The New Imperialism*, Oxford: Oxford University Press.

Harvey, D. (2005) *A Brief History of Neoliberalism*, Oxford: Oxford University Press.

Harvey, D. (2006) *Spaces of Global Capitalism: Towards a Theory of Uneven Geographical Development*, London: Verso.

Harvey, D. (2010a) *The Enigma of Capital,* Oxford: Oxford University Press.

Harvey, D. (2010b) *A Companion to Marx's Capital,* London: Verso.

Hasan, R. (2003) 'Globlisation, literacy and ideology', *World Englishes*, 22(4): 433–48.

Hayek, F. A. (2001 [1944]) *The Road to Serfdom,* London: Routledge.

Heath, S. B. (1983) *Ways with Words*, Cambridge: Cambridge University Press.

Held, D., McGrew, A., Goldblatt, D., and Perraton, J. (1999). *Global Transformations: Politics, Economics and Culture*, Cambridge: Polity.

Heller, M. (2011) *Paths to Postnationalism*, Oxford: Oxford University Press.

Higgins, C. (ed.) (2011) *Negotiating the Self in a Second Language: Identity Formation in a Globalizing World*, Berlin: Mouton de Gruyter.

Hill, D., and Kumar, R. (2009) *Global Neoliberalism and Education and its Consequences (Studies in Neoliberalism and Education)*, New York: Routledge

Hirst, P., and Thompson, G. (2009) *Globalization in Question*, 2nd edn, Cambridge: Polity.

Hodge, R., and Kress, G. (1993) *Language as Ideology*, 2nd edn, London: Routledge.

Holborow, M. (1999) *The Politics of English: A Marxist View of Language,* London: Sage.

Holborow, M. (2006) 'Ideology and language: interconnections between neo-liberalism and English', in J. Edge (ed.), *(Re)locating TESOL in an Age of Empire* (pp. 84–103), London: Palgrave.

Holborow, M. (2007) 'Language, ideology and neoliberalism', *Journal of Language and Politics*, 6(1): 51–73.

Holliday, A. (1994) *Appropriate Methodology and Social Context,* Cambridge: Cambridge University Press.

Howarth, D. (2000) *Discourse.* Maidenhead: Open University Press/McGraw Hill Education.

Hyde, M. (2010) *Celebrity: How Entertainers Took Over the World and Why we Need an Exit Strategy,* London: Vintage Books.

Hymes, D. (1974) *Foundations of Sociolinguistics*, London: Tavistock.

Ives, P. (2006) '"Global English": linguistic imperialism or practical lingua franca?', *Studies in Language and Capitalism*, 1: 121–41.

Jaworski, A., and Thurlow, C. (2010) 'Taking an elitist stance: ideology and the discursive production of social distinction', in A. Jaffe (ed.) *Stance: Sociolinguistic Perspectives* (pp. 195–226), Oxford: Oxford University Press.

Jessop, B. (2004) 'Critical semiotic analysis and cultural political economy', *Critical Discourse Studies* 1(2), 159–74.

Johnson, K. (2000) 'Innovations in TESOL teacher education: a quiet revolution', in K. Johnson (ed.), *Teacher Education: Case Studies in Teacher Practice Series* (pp. 1–7), Alexandria, VI: TESOL.

Johnson, K. (2009) *Second Language Teacher Education: A Sociocultural Perspective*, London: Routledge.

Jones, O. (2011) *Chavs: The Demonization of the Working Class*, London: Verso.

Joseph, J. (2006) 'Language and politics' in A. Davies and C. Elder (eds), *The Handbook of Applied Linguistics* (pp 347–366), Oxford: Blackwell Publishing.

Joseph, J., and Taylor, T. (eds) (1990) *Ideologies of Language*, London: Routledge.

Kachru, B. (1986) *The Alchemy of English: The Spread, Functions, and Models of Non-Native Englishes*, London: Pergamon Press.

Kalra, V. S., Kaur, R., and Hutnyk, J. (2005) *Diaspora and Hybridity*, London: Sage.

Kaplan, R. (ed.) (2005) *The Oxford Handbook of Applied Linguistics*, Oxford: Oxford University Press.

Kay, J. (2004) *The Truth about Markets*, Harmondsworth: Penguin.

Keeling, R. (2006) 'The Bologna process and Lisbon research agenda: the European Commission's expanding role in higher education discourse', *European Journal of Education*, 41(2): 203–23.

Kirby, P. (2010) *Celtic Tiger in Collapse: Explaining the Weakness of the Irish Model*, 2nd edn, London: Palgrave.

Klein, N. (2007) *The Shock Doctrine: The Rise of Disaster Capitalism*, New York: Metropolitan Books.

Korthagen, F. A. J. (2010) 'Situated learning theory and the pedagogy of teacher education: towards an integrative view of teacher behavior and teacher learning', *Teaching and Teacher Education*, 26(1): 98–106.

Kramsch, C., and O'Sullivan, P. (1996) 'Appropriate pedagogy', *ELT Journal*, 50(3): 199–212.

Kullman, J. (2003) 'The social construction of learner identity in the U.K.-published ELT coursebook', unpubl. thesis, Canterbury Christ Church University College.

Kumaravadivelu, B. (2003) *Macrostrategies for Language Teaching*, New Haven, CT: Yale University Press.

Kuper, A., and Kuper, J. (2004) *The Social Science Encyclopaedia*, London: Routledge.

Labov, W. (1966) *The Social Stratification of English in New York City*, Washington, DC: Center for Applied Linguistics.

Laclau, E. (2007) 'Discourse', in R. E. Goodlin, P. Petit, and T. Pogge (eds), *A Companion to Contemporary Philosophy*, 2nd edn (pp. 541–7), Oxford: Blackwell.

Laclau, E., and Mouffe, C. (1985) *Hegemony and Socialist Strategy*, London: Verso.

Lakoff, G. (2006) *Whose Freedom?*, New York: Picador.

Lakoff, G., and Johnson, M. (2003 [1980]) *Metaphors we Live by*. Chicago, IL: University of Chicago Press.

Lapavitsas, C. (2005) 'Mainstream economics in the neoliberal era', in A. Saad-Filho and D. Johnston (eds), *Neoliberalism: A Critical Reader*, London: Pluto Press.

Leadbeater, C. (2010) *Cloud Culture: The Future of Global Cultural Relations*, London: British Council: <www.counterpoint-online.org>.

Lee, R. E. (2010) 'Critiques and developments in world-systems analysis: an introduction to the special issue', *Journal of Philosophical Economics*, 4(2) 5–18.

Lefebvre, H. (2002 [1961]) *Critique of Everyday Life: Foundations for a Sociology of the Everyday*, vol. 2, London:Verso.

Li Wei (ed.) (2011) *The Routledge Applied Linguistics Reader*, London: Routledge.

Lightbown, P. (1985) 'Great expectations: second-language acquisition research and classroom teaching', *Applied Linguistics*, 6(2): 173–89.

Lightbown, P. (2000) 'Classroom SLA research and classroom teaching', *Applied Linguistics*, 21(4): 431–62.

Lin, A. (2008a) 'Modernity, postmodernity, and the future of "identity": implications for educators', in A. Lin (ed.), *Problematizing Identity: Struggles in Language, Culture, and Education* (pp. 199–219), London: Lawrence Erlbaum.

Lin, A. (ed.) (2008b) *Problematizing Identity*, Mahwah, NJ: Lawrence Erlbaum.

Llamas, C., and Watt, D. (eds) (2010) *Language and Identities*, Edinburgh: Edinburgh University Press.

Lo Bianco, J. (1999) *Globalisation: Frame Word for Education and Training, Human Capital and Human Development/Rights,* Melbourne: Language Australia (National Languages and Literacy Institute of Australia).

Lortie, D. (1975) *Schoolteacher: A Sociological Study*, Chicago, IL: University of Chicago Press.

Lynch, K. (2006) 'Neo-liberalism and marketisation: the implications for higher education', *European Educational Research Journal*, 5(1): 1–17.

Mannheim, K. (1935) *Man and Society in an Age of Reconstruction*, New York: Harcourt, Brace & World.

Marcuse, H. (1964) *One Dimensional Man: Studies in the Ideology of Advanced Industrial Society,* London: Routledge & Kegan Paul.

Marx, K. (1971 [1844]) 'Economic and philosophical manuscripts', in D. McLellan (ed.), *Early Texts* (pp. 130–83), Oxford: Blackwell.

Marx, K. (1972 [1852]) 'The eighteenth brumaire of Louis Bonaparte', in R. C. Tucker (ed.), *The Marx-Engels Reader* (pp. 432–525), New York: W. C. Norton.

Marx, K. (1974 [1867]) *Capital: A Critique of Political Economy*, vol. 1, London: Lawrence and Wishart.

Marx, K. (1976 [1867]) *Capital: A Critique of Political Economy,* vol. 1, New York: Vintage Books.

Marx, K. (1977 [1859]) *A Contribution to the Critique of Political Economy*, Moscow: Progress Publishers: <http://www.marxists.org/archive/marx/works/1859/critique-pol-economy/preface.htm>.

Marx, K. (1991 [1865]) *Capital,* vol. 3, Harmondsworth: Penguin.

Marx, K. (1995 [1847]) *The Poverty of Philosophy,* Buffalo, NY: Prometheus Books.

Marx, K., and Engels, F. (1967 [1846]) *Communist Manifesto,* Oxford: Oxford University Press.

Marx, K., and Engels, F. (1974 [1846]) *The German Ideology*, London: Lawrence & Wishart.

Mason, P. (2009) *Meltdown: The End of the Age of Greed*, London:Verso.

Maton, K. (2008) 'Habitus', in M. Grenfell (ed.), *Pierre Bourdieu: Key Concepts* (pp. 49–65), Stocksfield: Acumen.

Mautner, G. (2005) 'The entrepreneurial university: a discursive profile of a higher education buzzword', *Critical Discourse Studies*, 2(2): 1–26.

Mautner, G. (2010) *Language and the Market Society: Critical Reflections on Discourse and Dominance,* London: Routledge.

McNally, F. (2010) 'An Irishman's diary', *Irish Times*, 3 September.

Mercer, N. (2000) *Words and Minds: How we Use Language to Think Together*, London: Routledge.

Morin, E. (1960) *The Stars: An Account of the Star-System in Motion Pictures,* New York: Grove Press, Inc.

Morton, T., and Gray, J. (2008) 'The mediating role of talk-in-interaction in guided lesson planning in a pre-service TESOL training course: an ethnomethodological and activity theoretic perspective', paper at Sociocultural Perspectives on Teacher Education and Development conference, Dept of Education, Oxford, Apr.

Morton, T., and Gray, J. (2010) 'Constructing personal practical knowledge and identity in lesson planning conferences in pre-service English language teacher education', *Language Teaching Research*, 14(3): 297–317.

Morton, T., McGuire, T., and Baynham, M. (2006) *A Literature Review on Research on Teacher Education in Adult Literacy, Numeracy and ESOL*, London: NRDC.

Mount, F. (2004) *Mind the Gap: Class in Britain Now*, London: Short Books.

Murphy, A. (1986) *Richard Cantillon: Entrepreneur and Economist*, Oxford: Oxford University Press.

Murphy, D., and Devlin. M. (2009) *Banksters: How a Powerful Elite Squandered Ireland's Wealth*, Dublin: Hachette Books Ireland.

National Development Plan (NDP) 2007 *Transforming Ireland: A Better Quality of Life for All*: <http://www.ndp.ie/docs/NDP_Homepage/1131.htm>.

Nederveen Pieterse, J. (1995) 'Globalization as hybridization', in M. Featherstone, S. Lash, and R. Robertson (eds), *Global Modernities* (pp. 45–68), London: Sage.

Nederveen Pieterse, J. (2009) *Globalization and Culture: Global Mélange*, 2nd edn, Oxford: Rowman & Littlefield.

Negri, A. (2008) *The Porcelain Workshop: For a New Grammar of Politics*, Los Angeles, CA: Semiotext(e).

Nunan, D., and Choi, J. (eds) (2010) *Language and Culture: Reflective Narratives and the Emergence of Identity*, Cambridge: Cambridge University Press.

OFSTED (2009) *The 2009 OFSTED Inspection Framework: Handout for School Governing Bodies.* Online. Available: http://www.derby.gov.uk/NR/rdonlyres/B6BE8D03-4F05-4EE4-BF0F-C97A994CFDA9/0/2009OFSTEDInspectionFrameworkforGovs.pdf.

Omoniyi, T., and White, G. (eds) (2006) *The Sociolinguistics of Identity*, London: Continuum.

O'Neil, J. (2001) 'Oh! My others, there is no other: capital culture, class and other-wiseness', *Theory, Culture and Society*, 18(2/3): 77–90.

O'Neill, R. (1970) *English in Situations*, Oxford: Oxford University Press.

Organisation for Economic Cooperation and Development (OECD) (1998) *Human Capital Investment: An International Comparison*, Paris: OECD.

O'Sullivan, T., Hartley, J., Saunders, D., Montgomery, M., and Fiske, J. (1994) *Key Concepts in Communication and Cultural Studies*, London: Routledge.

O'Toole, F. (2009) *Ship of Fools: How Stupidity and Corruption Sank the Celtic Tiger*, London: Faber & Faber.

Pakulski, J., and Waters, J. (1996) *The Death of Class*, London: Sage.

Peck, J. (2008) *The Age of Oprah: Cultural Icon for the Neoliberal Era*, Boulder, CO: Paradigm Publishers.

Peck, J. (2010) *Constructions of Neoliberal Reason*, Oxford: Oxford University Press.

Pennington, M. (1996) 'The teacher change cycle', *TESOL Quarterly*, 29(4): 705–31.

Pennycook, A. (1989) 'The concept of method, interested knowledge and the politics of language teaching', *TESOL Quarterly*, 23(4): 589–618.

Pennycook, A. (1994) *The Cultural Politics of English as an International Language*, London: Longman.

Pennycook, A. (2007) *Global Englishes and Transcultural Flows*, London: Routledge.

Peters, T. (1994) *The Tom Peters Seminar*, London: Vintage Books.

Peters, T. (2008) *The Brand You 50: Fifty Ways to Transform Yourself from an 'Employee' into a Brand that Shouts Distinction, Commitment, and Passion!*, New York: Alfred A. Knopf.

Phelan, S. (2007) 'The discursive dynamics of neo-liberal consensus: Irish broadsheet editorials and the privatization of Eircom', *Journal of Language and Politics*, 6(1): 7–29.

Phillipson R. (1992) *Linguistic Imperialism,* Oxford: Oxford University Press.

Phillipson R. (2003) *English-Only Europe? Challenging Language Policy,* London: Routledge.

Phillipson, R. (2008a) 'The linguistic imperialism of neoliberal empire', *Critical Enquiry in Language Studies,* 5(1): 1–43.

Phillipson, R. (2008b) 'The new linguistic order: English as an EU *Lingua Franca* or *Lingua Frankensteina*?', *Journal of Irish and Scottish Studies*, 1(2): 189–203.

Phillipson, R. (2009a) *Linguistic Imperialism Continued*, London: Routledge.

Phillipson, R. (2009b) 'Tensions between linguistic diversity and dominant English', in T. Skutnabb-Kangas, R. Phillipson, A. K. Mohant, and P. Minati (eds), *Social Justice through Multilingual Education* (pp. 85–102), Clevedon: Multilingual Matters.

Pica, T. (1994) 'Questions from the language classroom: research perspectives', *TESOL Quarterly,* 28: 49–79.

Pica, T. (1997) 'Second language teaching and research relationships: a North American view', *Language Teaching Research*, 1(1): 48–72.

Polyani, K. (2001 [1944]) *The Great Transformation: The Political and Economic Origins of our Time*, Boston, MA: Beacon Press.

Poole, B. (2010) 'Commitment and criticality: Fairclough's critical discourse analysis evaluated', *International Journal of Applied Linguistics*, 20(2): 137–55.

Prabhu, N. S. (1990) 'There is no best method: why?', *TESOL Quarterly*, 24(2): 161–76.

Preece, S. (2010) *Posh Talk*, London: Palgrave.

Rampton, B. (1997) 'Retuning in applied linguistics', *International Journal of Applied Linguistics*, 7: 3–25.

Rampton, B. (2006) *Language in Late Modernity: Interaction in an Urban School*, Cambridge: Cambridge University Press.

Rampton, B. (2010) 'Social class and sociolinguistics', *Applied Linguistics Review*, 1: 1–21.

Razool, N. (2007) *Global Issues in Language, Education and Development: Perspectives from Postcolonial Societies*, Clevedon: Multilingual Matters.

Reich, R. (1991). *The Work of Nations,* New York: Vintage.

Rex, J., and Tomlinson, S. (1979) *Colonial Immigrants in a British City: A Class Analysis*, London: Routledge & Kegan Paul.

Richards, J. C. (1998) *Beyond Training*, Cambridge: Cambridge University Press.

Richards, J. C., and Crookes, G. (1988) 'The practicum in TESOL', *TESOL Quarterly*, 22(1): 9–27.

Richards, J., and Nunan, D. (eds) (1990) *Second Language Teacher Education*, Cambridge: Cambridge University Press.

Ritzer, G. (1996) *The McDonaldization of Society*, revised edn, Thousand Oaks, CA: Sage.

Ritzer, G. (1998) *The McDonaldization Thesis*, London: Sage.

Ritzer, G. (1999) *Enchanting a Disenchanted World: Revolutionizing the Means of Consumption*, Thousand Oaks, CA: Pine Forge Press.

Ritzer, G. (ed.) (2007a) *The Blackwell Companion to Globalization,* Oxford: Blackwell.

Ritzer, G. (2007b) *The Globlization of Nothing 2,* Thousand Oaks, CA: Pine Forge Press.

Ritzer, G. (2010) *Globalization: A Basic Text,* Oxford: Wiley Blackwell.

Ritzer, G. (2011) *The McDonaldization of Society 6,* London: Sage.

Ritzer, G., and Atalay, Z. (eds) (2010) *Readings in Globalization*, Malden, MA: Wiley Blackwell.

Roberts, K. (2001) *Class in Modern Britain*, London: Palgrave.

Robertson, R. (1995) 'Glocalization: time-space and homogeniety-heterogenity', in M. Featherstone, S. Lash, and R. Robertson (eds), *Global Modernities* (pp. 25–44), London: Sage.

Rojek, C. (2001) *Celebrity*, London: Reaktion Books.

Ross, S. (2009) *The Bankers: How the Banks Brought Ireland to its Knees,* Dublin: Penguin Ireland.

Rubin, S. G. (1999) *Margaret Bourke White: Her Pictures were her Life*, New York: Harry N. Abrams.

Rubinstein, W. D. (1977) 'Wealth, elites, and the class structure of modern Britain', *Past and Present*, 76: 99–126.

Saad-Filhlo, A. (2003) 'Introduction', in A. Saad-Fihlo (ed), *Anti-Capitalism: A Marxist Introduction* (pp. 1–23), London: Pluto Press.

Saad-Filho, A. (2005) 'From Washington to Post-Washington Consensus', in A. Saad-Filho and D. Johnston (eds), *Neoliberalism: A Critical Reader,* London: Pluto Press.

Saad-Filho, A., and Johnston, D. (eds) (2005) *Neoliberalism: A Critical Reader,* London: Pluto Press.

Sachs, J. (1990) 'What is to be done?', *The Economist,* 13 Jan.: 19–24.

Saltman, K. J. (2009) 'Corporatization and the control of schools', in M. W. Apple, W. Au, and L. A. Gandin (eds), *The Routledge Handbook of Critical Education* (pp. 51–63), New York: Routledge.

Samuelson, B., and Freedman, S. (2010) 'Language policy, multilingual education, and power in Rwanda', *Language Policy,* 9: 191–215.

Sassen, S. (2007) *Sociology of Globalization*, New York: W. W. Norton.

Savage, M. (2000) *Class Analysis and Social Transformation*, Buckingham: Open University Press.

Schieffelin, B., Woolard, K., and Kroskrity, P. (eds) (1998) *Language Ideologies: Practice and Theory,* New York: Oxford University Press.

Schinke-Llano, L. (1992) *Easy English Vocabulary Games*, Lincolnwood, CH: Passport Books.

Scholte, J. A. (2000) *Globalization*, London: Macmillan.

Schön, D. (1983) *The Reflective Practitioner*, New York: Basic Books.

Schroeder, J. E. (2002) *Visual Communication*, London: Routledge.

Schuller, T. (2000) "Social and human capital: the search for appropriate technomethodology', *Policy Studies*, 21(1): 25–35: <http://www.ndp.ie.docs/NDP_Homepage/1131.html>.

Science Foundation Ireland (2009) *Powering the Smart Economy: SFI Strategy 2009–2013:* <http://www.sfi.ie/news-events/publications/orgnisational-publications>.

Seymour, S. (2006) 'Resistance', *Anthropological Theory*, 6(3): 303–21.

Simpson, J. (ed.) (2011) *The Routledge Handbook of Applied Linguistics*, London: Routledge.

Skeggs, B. (2004) *Class, Self, Culture*, London: Routledge.

Skeggs, B. (2008) 'Making class through fragmenting culture', in A. Lin (ed.), *Problematizing Identity: Everyday Struggles in Language, Culture, and Education* (pp. 35–50), London: Lawrence Erlbaum,

Sklair, L. (2010) 'Transnational practices', in G. Ritzer and Z. Atalay (eds), *Readings in Globalization* (pp. 185–95), Malden, MA: Wiley Blackwell.

Slaughter, S., and Leslie, L. (1997) *Academic Capitalism, Politics, Policies, and the Entrepreneurial University,* Baltimore, MD: Johns Hopkins University Press.

Smart, B. (ed.) (1999) *Resisting McDonaldization*, Thousand Oaks, CA: Sage.

Smith, P. (1997) *Millennium Dreams*, London: Verso.

Soars, J., and Soars, L. (1986) *Headway*, Oxford: Oxford University Press.

Soars, L., and Soars, J. (1996) *New Headway*, Oxford: Oxford University Press.

Soars, L., and Soars, J. (1998) *New Headway/Upper Intermediate*, Oxford: Oxford University Press.

Soars, L., and Soars, J. (2000a) *New Headway/Pre-Intermediate,* Oxford: Oxford University Press.

Soars, L., and Soars, J. (2000b) *New Headway/Elementary*, Oxford: Oxford University Press.

Soars, L., and Soars, J. (2003a) *New Headway/Advanced*, Oxford: Oxford University Press.

Soars, L., and Soars, J. (2003b) *New Edition New Headway/Intermediate*, Oxford: Oxford University Press.

Soars, L., and Soars, J. (2005) *New Headway/Upper-Intermediate*, Oxford: Oxford University Press.

Soars, L., and Soars, J. (2009) *New Headway/Intermediate*, Oxford: Oxford University Press.

Soars, L., and Soars, J. (2011) *New Headway/Elementary*, Oxford: Oxford University Press.

Sowden, C. (2008) 'There's more to life than politics', *ELT Journal*, 6(2): 284–91.

Spring, J. (1998) *Education and the Rise of the Global Economy*, Mahwah, NJ: Lawrence Erlbaum Associates.

Spring, J. (2004) *How Educational Ideologies are Shaping Global Society: Intergovernmental Organizations, NGOs, and the Decline of the Nation-State*, Mahwah, NJ: Lawrence Erlbaum Associates.

Spring, J. (2008) 'Research on globalization and education', *Review of Educational Research*, 78(2): 330–63.

Spring, J. (2009) *Globalization of Education: An Introduction*, London: Routledge.

Stigliz, J. E. (2010) *Freefall: America, World Markets and the Sinking of the World Economy*, New York: W. W. Norton.

Stockholm International Peace Research Institute (2010) *Stockholm International Peace Research Institute Yearbook 2010*, Oxford: Oxford University Press.

Stubbs, M. (2001) *Words and Phrases: Corpus Studies of Lexical Semantics*, Oxford: Blackwell.

Stuckler, D., King, L., and McKee, M. (2009) 'Mass privatisation and the post-communist mortality crisis: a cross national analysis', *The Lancet*, 373: 399–407.

Swan, M., and Walter, C. (1990) *The New Cambridge English Course/2*, Cambridge: Cambridge University Press.

Sydney Morning Herald (2002) 'Bush and Saddam should duel: Iraq's challenge': <http://www.smh.com.au/articles/2002/10/05/1033538810033.html> (accessed May 2011).

Tharp, R. G., and Gallimore, R. (1991) *The Instructional Conversation: Teaching and Learning in Social Activity*, NCRCDSLL Research Reports, Centre for Research, Diversity and Excellence, Berkeley, CA: UC Berkeley.

Thompson, E. P. (1980 [1963]) *The Making of the English Working Class*, Harmondsworth: Penguin.

Thompson, J. B. (1984) *Studies in the Theory of Ideology*, Cambridge: Polity.

Thompson, J. B. (1990) *Ideology in Modern Culture: Critical Social Theory in the Era of Mass Communication*. Stanford, CA: Stanford University Press.

Thornbury, S. (1991) 'Watching the whites of their eyes: the use of teaching practice logs', *English Language Teaching Journal*, 45(2): 140–6.

Thornbury, S. (2010) 'N is for neoliberalism', *An A–Z of ELT*: <http://scottthornbury.wordpress.com/2010/12/26/n-is-for-neoliberalism> (accessed July 2011).

Todd, I. (2003) *After the Empire: The Breakdown of the American Order*, London: Constable.

Torfing, J. (1999) *New Theories of Discourse: Laclau, Mouffe and Žižek*, Oxford: Blackwell.

Toynbee, P. (2010) 'What is unforgivable is Ireland's shameless status as Europe's greatest tax haven, helping to cheat tax from the world's treasuries for decades', *Irish Times*, 24 Nov.: <http://www.irishtimes.com/newspaper/opinion/2010/1124/1224284018946.html>.

Trudgill, P. (1974) *The Social Differentiation of English in Norwich*, Cambridge: Cambridge University Press.

Turner, G., Bonner, F., and Marshall, P. D. (2008) 'The meaning and significance of celebrity', in A. Biressi and H. Nunn (eds), *The Tabloid Culture Reader* (pp. 141–8), Maidenhead: Open University Press/McGraw-Hill Education.

Vally, S. (2007) 'Higher education in South Africa: market mill or public good?' *JHEA/RESA (Council for the Development of Social Science Research in Africa)*, 5(1): 17–28.

Van Dijk, T. A. (1998) *Ideology: A Multidisciplinary Approach*, London: Sage.

Van Dijk, T. E. (2008) *Discourse and Power*, London: Palgrave.

Van Lier, L. (1994) 'Forks and hope: pursuing understanding in different ways', *Applied Linguistics*, 15: 328–47.

Vertovec, S. (2009) *Transnationalism*, London: Routledge.

Volosinov, V. N. (1973) *Marxism and the Philosophy of Language*, New York: Seminar Press.

Wallace, M. J. (1991) *Training Foreign Language Teachers*, Cambridge: Cambridge University Press.

Wallerstein, I. (2004) *World Systems Analysis: An Introduction*, Durham, NC: Durham University Press.

Waters, A. (2009) 'Ideology in applied linguistics for language teaching', *Applied Linguistics*, 30(1): 138–43.

Watkins, S. (2010) 'Shifting Sands' (Editorial), *New Left Review*, 61: 5–27.

Weber, M. (1968 [1924]) *Economy and Society*, vols. 1 and 2, Berkeley, CA: University of California Press.

Wenger, E. (2006) 'Communities of practice: a brief introduction': <http://www.ewenger.com/theory/communities_of_practice_intro.htm>.

Whitehead, J., and Taylor, A. (1998) *Teachers of Modern Foreign Languages: Foreign Native Speakers on Initial Teacher Training Courses in England*, Bristol: Faculty of Education, UWE, Bristol.

Whitty, G., and Power, S. (1998) *Devolution and Choice in Education: The School, the State and the Market*, Buckingham: Open University Press.

Whitty, G., Power, S. and Halpin, D. (1998) *Devolution and Choice in Education. The School, the State and the Market,* Buckingham: Open University Press.

Wideen, M., Mayer-Smith, J., and Moon, B. (1998) 'A critical analysis of the research on learning to teach: making the case for an ecological perspective on enquiry', *Review of Educational Research*, 68(2): 130–78.

Williams, E. (2011) 'Language policy, politics and development in Africa', in H. Coleman (ed.), *Dreams and Realities: Developing Countries and the English Language* (pp. 41–58), London: British Council.

Williams, R. (1976) *Keywords,* London: Fontana.

Williams, R. (1986) *Keywords*, 2nd edn, London: Fontana.

Williams, R. (1977) *Marxism and Literature*, new edn, Oxford: Oxford University Press.

Willis, P. (1977) *Learning to Labour: How Working Class Kids Get Working Class Jobs*, London: Saxon House.

Wills, J., Datta, K., Evans, Y., Herbert, J., May, J., and McIlwaine, C. (2010) *Global Cities at Work: New Migrant Divisions of Labour,* London: Pluto Press.

Woods, E. M. (1998) 'Modernity, postmodernity or capitalism', in R. W. McChesney, E. M. Wood, and J. B. Foster, *Capitalism and the Information Age* (pp. 27–50), New York: Monthly Review Press.

World Bank (2010) *Doing Business Report 2010: Reforming through Difficult Times,* International Bank for Reconstruction and Development/World Bank: <http://go.worldbank.org/DC5JETJPR0> (accessed April 2011).

Wright, E. O. (1985) *Classes*, London: Verso.

Wright, E. O. (ed.) (2005) Approaches *to Class Analysis*, Cambridge: Cambridge University Press.

Young, J. (2007) *The Vertigo of Late Modernity,* London: Sage.

Žižek, S. (1989) *The Sublime Object of Ideology,* London: Verso.

Žižek, S. (2009) *First as Tragedy, then as Farce,* London: Verso.

Zweig, S. (2009 [1942]) *The World of Yesterday,* London: Pushkin Press.

INDEX

Abbs, B. and Freebairn, I. 99
Abramovich, Roman 103
academic entrepreneurship 51–2
accountability 45, 121, 127, 128
Adorno, T. and Horkheimer, M. 91–2, 95–6
Aer Lingus 44
Ahmed, S. 88
Ali G 89
American Chamber of Commerce, Ireland 45, 47
Anderson, C. 107
Anglo Irish Bank 53
Appadurai, A. 58
applied linguistics: as backdrop 2–4; and biases in second language learning research 3; critical discourse analysis 3; and ELT 8–9, 109–11; and globalisation 61–3, 82; identity, class and 70–85; ideology in language studies 3; and individual agency 125; and interdisciplinarity 1–2, 3–4; and language teacher education 142–3; and the political economy 1–2, 4; postcolonial frames of analysis 3; Rampton 1, 2, 3 *see also* Rampton, B.
Arrighi, G. 64, 66–7

Bailey Rae, Corinne 93
banking crisis 5–6
banksters 53
Barthe, R. 31
Bauman, Z. 93
Becker, G. S. 46
Béland, D. 18
Bengtsson, J. 117

Bennet, T. *et al.* 38–9
Berger, J. 88–9
Bernstein, B. 83
Big Society 71
Biressi, A. and Nunn, H. 87, 89, 102
Blair, Tony 23, 71, 81, 102
Blommaert, J. 23, 31, 41, 64–5
Bollywood 68
Bologna process 27
Boorstin, D. 87
Borg, S. 118
Bourdieu, P. 5, 28, 42, 49, 74–5, 78, 79–80
Bourke White, Margaret 34
Boxer, L. 139
Braudel, F. 64
Braverman, H. 122–3, 124, 142
Brazil 68
Brenner, R. 65
BRIC 68
British Council 21, 27, 97, 98
British hegemony 67
Brown, Gordon 56
Brumfit, C. 2, 3
Bruthiaux, P. 62
Building Strategies 99
Bundchen, Gisele 88–9
Burchill, Julie 71
Bush, George H. W. 90
Business and Finance 51

calculability 122, 128
Callinicos, A. 17, 68, 93
Cambridge English 2 99
Cantillon, Richard 50

capital 17, 49; cultural 79; economic 79;
    human 46–50; investment, and social
    power 21; linguistic 27–8; social 49, 79;
    symbolic 79
capitalism: academic 52; amusement
    under late capitalism 95–6; capitalist
    homogenisation 49; capitalist market *see*
    free market; capitalist world-economy
    65; and class relations 34; discourse-led
    transformations of 22; and free-market
    thinking 5 *see also* free market; hegemonies
    of 66–8; late 92–3, 95–6; Marxist view
    of 65–6, 124–5; and McDonaldisation
    122 *see also* McDonaldisation in language
    teacher education; and neoliberalism
    16, 19–22, 94–5; 'new capitalism' and
    neoliberalism 19–22, 94–5; as the 'society
    of the spectacle' 92; structural disorders of
    17; and WSA 65–6
Castells, M. 20
CDA *see* critical discourse analysis
celeactors 89–90
celebrity 86–112; culture 87, 89–90, 91–6;
    and ELT materials questionnaire 111–13;
    and ELT textbooks 87, 96–113; and
    individualism 93; nature and definitions
    of 87–90; and neoliberalism 93,
    94–6; teachers' perspectives on 104–8;
    theoretical perspectives on 90–4
CELTA (Certificate in Teaching English to
    Speakers of Other Languages) 133–41
Charles, Prince of Wales 103
Chicago School of Economics 15, 46
China 17, 66, 68
Chomsky, N. 92
Cicciolina 86
civil rights movement 93
Clanfield, L. 110
class: consciousness 78; habitus, field and 79,
    80; and identity 70–85; and ideology
    40–1; marginalisation of 70, 71–4, 82;
    middle class 71, 80, 81, 84, 106; nature and
    definitions of 74–82; and neoliberalism
    70–1; Rampton 71, 82, 83–5; relations 34;
    working class 57, 66, 72, 80–2, 84, 85, 90
cloud computing 21
coercion 66–7
Cohen, Nick 71
Cohen, Sasha Baron 89
Cole, A. L. 117
collectivism 94
Collins, M. 71
communication power 20–1
communication technologies 20–2
Communist Manifesto 63, 75

Connelly, F. M. and Clandinin, D. J. 118–19
consent 66–7
Conservative–Liberal coalition government
    71, 127
construction business 81
consumerism 68; consumer-based identity
    96; consumer society 90–1, 92, 93
consumption patterns 81
Cowen, B. 116
Coyle, D. 19
critical discourse analysis (CDA) 2, 3, 32; and
    neoliberalism 7, 14–15, 28–9
culture: celebrity 87, 89–90, 91–6; cultural
    capital 79; cultural cycles 64; cultural
    imperialism 68; culturalist views of
    globalisation 61–2; cultural relativism 74;
    industry 91, 93–4, 104, 107; local cultures
    60; Williams 35–40
Cunningham, S. and Moor, P. 99
cyclical processes 64

Davies, B. and Harré, R. 134
Dean, Christopher 99
Debord, G. 92
decorating business 81
Deloitte Touche Ireland 44
Denning, M. 9
deregulation 43–6, 54
Dewey, J. 116
discourse: analysis 23–4 *see also* critical
    discourse analysis (CDA); CDA *see* critical
    discourse analysis; as constitutive of
    social being/society 3, 20; discourse-led
    transformations of capitalism 22; discursive
    performativity 26; discursive practices
    and social relations 33–4; 'discursive
    turn' 3; and ideology 3, 23–4, 26–9,
    31–2, 33–4, 36–41 *see also* neoliberal
    keywords; management discourses 10,
    49; marketisation in 40; neoliberal *see*
    neoliberal discourse; neoliberal ideology
    as a discursive event 23; neoliberal
    keywords *see* neoliberal keywords; and
    the 'new capitalism' 19–20; orders of
    22–3; and power 23, 24–5, 34; and social
    engagement 33–4
Doogan, K. 21, 94
Dublin City University (DCU) 52;
    Commercialisation Handbook 51
Duménil, G. and Lévy, D. 16, 17
Durkheim, E. 76
Dutch nation state 67
Dyer, R. 93

Eagleton, T. 25, 30–1

economic capital 79
economic crises 4, 5–6, 14, 18, 30, 33, 34, 45, 52, 55
economic cycles 64
economic globalisation 18
economic liberalism 5
economic power 65
economic theory, neoliberal 15–19; and economic practice 16
economies: capitalist world-economy 65; an economically/historically grounded view of globalisation 63–8; Irish economy 42, 44–5, 50, 53; knowledge-based 20, 21, 49; and the Washington Consensus 16, 43, 70
education: and class 80; English language teaching see English language teaching (ELT); and the entrepreneurial university 51–2; EU higher education initiatives 27; global privatisation 7; and human capital 48–9; impact of neoliberalism 6–7; language teacher see language teacher education; language teaching see English language teaching (ELT); SLA; TESOL; league tables 120, 128; marketisation of 107, 121; marketisation of language teacher education 114–43; and motivational posters 131–2; National Curriculum reforms 126–7; PGCE see Postgraduate Certificate of Education; pupil testing 120; Rwandan 97; SLA (second language acquisition) 118, 119 see also TESOL; teachers' perspectives on celebrity 104–8
efficiency 122, 126–7
electronic mass media 61–2; internet 21
Eliot, T. S. 90–1
ELT see English language teaching
embourgeosiment thesis 81
employment 5, 56–7, 72; occupation 80, 81
English: and globalisation 16–17, 22; and neoliberalism 26–9; world English 26
English language teaching (ELT) 8–9, 97; celebrity and 'aspirational content' in ELT textbooks 87, 96–113; celebrity and ELT materials questionnaire 111–13; TESOL 27, 115, 141
entrepreneurship 50–4
Ernst & Young 'Entrepreneur of the Year®' 51, 52–3, 103
ethnoscapes 58, 61
Eurocentricism 66
Euromonitor International 97–8, 107
European Central Bank 6, 43
European Union (EU) 43, 52
experiential knowledge 117, 119

Fairclough, N. 7, 18, 19, 20, 22, 23, 24, 25; and Graham, P. 19
fascism 94
Federal Reserve Bank, US 16
feminism, second wave 93
field 79, 80
FitzPatrick, Sean 51, 53
flows 58, 61, 62 see also ideoscapes
Foucault, M. 24–6, 84, 138–9
Frankfurt School 91, 93
Fraser, N. 57
Freeman, D. 119; and Johnson, K. 114, 119, 141
free market: capitalism see capitalism; 'new capitalism'; failure 14, 33 see also economic crises; fundamentalism 38, 61; ideology 29–30, 34, 55, 124; and neoliberalism 4–6, 14, 15–16, 18–19, 42, 46, 55; and privatisation 15 see also privatisation; supply and demand 42; Thatcherism 15
Friedman, L. M. 96
Friedman, Milton 15, 46

Gates, Bill 96
gay community 93
gaze (Foucault) 139–40
Gere, Richard 86
Giddens, A. 61, 66
Giroux, H. A. 16
Giulianotti, R. and Robertson, R. 60
globalisation 58–60; and applied linguistics 61–3; culturalist views of 61–2; economic 18; an economically/historically grounded view of 63–8; and English 16–17, 22; global order of discourse 22–3; and nation states 18; and neoliberalism 16–17, 22–3; and the 'new capitalism' 19; Ritzer 124–5
glocalisation 59–60
Goffman, E. 101
Goldthorpe, J. H. and Lockwood, D. 81
Golombek, P. R. 119
Gordon, L. and Whitty, G. 121
Graddol, D. 20
Gramsci, A. 9, 30, 41
Grusky, D. and Galescu, G. 76
Gumperz, J. 83–4

habitus 79, 80
Haines, Cherry 99–101
Halliday, M. 73
Hardt, M. and Negri, A. 17, 20, 69
Harré, R. 134
Harvey, D. 5, 15, 42, 43, 49, 69, 70, 73, 109, 138
Hasan, R. 38, 73

Hayek, F. A. 50, 93, 94
Headway textbooks 96–7, 99, 101–4
Heath, S. B. 83
hegemony 41, 66–8
Heller, M. 62
Hello! 101
Hindley, Myra 89
hip-hop 61, 68
history 64; an economically/historically
    grounded view of globalisation 63–8
homogenisation 49, 58, 60
homosexual law reform campaigns 93
human capital 46–50, 54
Hunt, James 98
hybridity 59
Hyde, M. 86
Hymes, D. 2, 3

identity 73–4; in applied linguistics
    publications 72–3; class, applied linguistics
    and 70–85; consumer-based 96;
    electronic mass media, virtual realities
    and 61–2; politics 59, 72, 73–4; and
    postmodernism 74; and recognition 57
ideology: and class 40–1; as a discursive
    regime 23, 33; entrepreneurship and
    ideological evaluation 50–4; foundations
    of 24, 29; gap between theory and reality
    in neoliberalism 16–19, 33–4; and human
    capital 46–50; and language/discourse 3,
    23–4, 26–9, 31–2, 33–4, 36–41 *see also*
    neoliberal keywords; market 29–30, 34, 55,
    124; Marxist interpretations of 24, 40–1;
    neoliberal ideology and English 26–9;
    neoliberal ideology as a discursive event
    23; and neoliberalism 29–32, 33–55;
    neoliberal keywords and the contradictions
    of an ideology 33–55; and social relations
    30, 31, 33–4, 40–1; stretching of meaning
    for ideological purposes 46–50; and texts
    23–4; Williams 35–9, 40
ideoscapes 58, 61, 68
IFSC (International Financial Services Centre)
    45
IMF (International Monetary Fund) 6, 7, 16,
    43, 70
imperialism: cultural 68; new 69–70
individualism 34, 39, 50, 70–1, 73–4, 76, 93,
    94, 95, 99, 104, 124; and celebrity 93;
    individual agency 125
information and communication technology
    20–2
information society 19
Intel Ireland 44
interdisciplinarity 1–2, 3–4, 9

International Financial Services Centre (IFSC)
    45
International Monetary Fund (IMF) 6, 7, 16,
    43, 70
internet 21
Ireland 6, 28, 42–3, 44–6, 47–8, 50, 51, 52, 53;
    Irish economy 42, 44–5, 50, 53
IREM 56
Irish bankers 51, 53
Irish Central Bank 45
Irish Independent 53
Irish Times 53

Johnson, K. 117, 119
Jolie, Angelina 86
Jones, O. 71, 81, 102, 109
Jordan, Michael 95
Journal of Language, Identity and Education 72

Kagame, Paul 8
Keynesianism 15
keywords, neoliberal *see* neoliberal keywords
Klein, Calvin 102, 103
Klein, N. 5, 18
knowledge: base, in language teacher
    education 119–20, 141–2; and education
    48; experiential 117, 119; and human
    capital 48 *see also* human capital;
    knowledge-based economy 20, 21, 49; and
    power 24; socially constructed 118–19;
    and teacher cognition 118–20

Labov, W. 72–3, 82
Laclau, E. and Mouffe, C. 20, 31
Lakoff, G. 39; and Johnson, M. 46
language: biases in second language learning
    research 3; discourse *see* discourse;
    English *see* English; generative nature
    of 31; and ideology 3, 23–4, 26–9,
    31–2, 33–4, 36–41 *see also* neoliberal
    keywords; linguistic capital 27–8; linguistic
    diversity 27; linguistic imperialism 15,
    27; neoliberal keywords *see* neoliberal
    keywords; re-semanticisation 38, 46–50,
    55, 121; rights for minority languages 27;
    studies *see* linguistics; teacher training *see*
    language teacher education; teaching *see*
    English language teaching (ELT); TESOL;
    unpredictability of 25
language teacher education 114–43; applied
    science model 116–17; calculability
    122, 128; CELTA 133–41; craft/
    apprenticeship model 115–16; efficiency
    122, 126–7; knowledge base 119–20,
    141–2; McDonaldisation as an analytical

framework 121–6; and motivational posters 131–2; move from professional contextualist to technocratic-reductionist 127, 142; need of social science input 142; neoliberal challenge to teacher professionalism 120–1; neoliberalism and the marketisation of 114–43; overview of history of 115–18; PGCE as a McDonaldised system 126–33; predictability 122, 128; reflective model 116–18; teacher cognition and the sociocultural perspective 118–20

Latin America 17

Law, Jude 86

league tables, educational 120, 128

Lefebvre, H. 92

Lehman Brothers 5

Lin, A. 61–2

linguistic capital 27–8

linguistics: applied *see* applied linguistics; CDA *see* critical discourse analysis; linguistic diversity 27; linguistic imperialism 15, 27; performative 26; socially constituted 2–3

Lisbon Treaty 43, 52

Llamas, C. and Watt, D. 72–3

Lloyd, Marie 90

Lo Bianco, J. 47, 48

local cultures 60

Lohan, Lindsay 86

Lucas, Matt 89

McCartney, Paul 98

McCreevy, Charlie 53

McDonaldisation in language teacher education 121–6; CELTA seen as a McDonaldised system 141 *see also* CELTA (Certificate in Teaching English to Speakers of Other Languages); PGCE as a McDonaldised system 126–33

McVeigh, Timothy 89

Mahler, Gustav 88

management 37; Braverman 123–4, 142; discourses 10, 49; industrial 123; scientific 123; training 104

Mandela, Winnie 99

Mannheim, K. 123

Manson, Charles 89

Marcuse, H. 93

market, free *see* free market

marketisation 40; of education 107, 121; of language teacher education 114–43

Martin, Micheál 51

Marxist theory: of capitalism 65–6, 124–5; of globalisation 63–4; of ideology 24, 40–1

Marx, K. 1, 4, 18, 29, 31–2, 34, 39, 40–1, 75–6, 92, 124, 138; and Engels, F., *Communist Manifesto* 63, 75; and Weber 77–8

Mason, P. 6

Maton, K. 79

Mautner, G. 7, 40, 51

mediascapes 58, 61, 68

meritocracy 71

Merkel, Angela 87, 88

middle classes 71, 80, 81, 84, 106

migration 61, 62

mobility, social 76–7, 82

monetarism 15

Morin, E. 92

Morton, T. *et al.* 118–19

motivational posters 131–2

Mount, F. 71

multiculturalism 73–4

Murphy, D. and Devlin. M. 53

National Curriculum reforms 126–7

nation states: diminishing role of the state 17; and globalisation 18; hegemonies of capitalism 67–8; post-crash state 18; state expenditure 18; state influence/power 18; state intervention 17

Nederveen Pieterse, J. 59

neoliberal discourse: American *neoliberal speak* 42; and discursive practices 22–6, 30, 33–4; and educational privatisation 7; interaction between neoliberalism and discourse 14; keywords *see* neoliberal keywords; and neoliberal ideology as a discursive event 23; and the 'new capitalism' 19–20; re-semanticisation 38, 46–50, 55, 121

neoliberalism: applied linguistics studies of 7; and the banking crisis 5–6; and capitalism 16, 19–22, 94–5; and celebrity 93, 94–6 *see also* celebrity; as a challenge to teacher professionalism 120–1; and class 70–1 *see also* class; and critical discourse analysis 7, 14–15, 28–9; current interest in 4–6; discourse *see* neoliberal discourse; as an economic theory 15–19; effects on health and mortality 5; and English 26–9; and the free market 4–6, 14, 15–16, 18–19, 42, 46, 55 *see also* free market; gap between theory and reality 16–19, 33–4; and globalisation 16–17, 22–3 *see also* globalisation; and identity politics 73–4; and ideology 29–32, 33–55 *see also* ideology; impact on education 6–7; and the individual 26; individualism *see* individualism; and the marketisation of language teacher education 114–43; and multiculturalism 73–4; nature and definitions of 14–32; and the 'new capitalism' 19–22, 94–5; and the new imperialism 69–70; relationship to political economy 2 *see also* political economy; and small government 17; 'There is No Alternative' to 7, 57, 70; Washington Consensus 16, 43, 70

neoliberal keywords: and the contradictions of an ideology 33–55; deregulation 43–6, 54; entrepreneurship and ideological evaluation 50–4; human capital 46–50, 54; and neoliberal meanings and associations 42–6; and the stretching of meaning for ideological purposes 46–50; of Williams 35–40

Netherlands: Dutch nation state 67

networks 20; network society 20–1; social networking 22, 80–1

'new capitalism' 19–22, 94–5

New Cutting Edge Upper Intermediate 99, 103–4

new imperialism 69–70

New Labour 102, 127

Nigeria 28

Obama, Barack 87, 88

occupation 80, 81

OECD (Organisation for Economic Cooperation and Development) 7, 42–3, 47

Office for Standards in Education (OFSTED) 128

Oliver, Jamie 103

O'Neil, J. 74

O'Neill, R. 112

Organisation for Economic Cooperation and Development (OECD) 7, 42–3, 47

O'Toole, F. 6

Pakulski, J. and Waters, J. 71–2

Patel, Vijay and Bhikhu 103

Peck, J. 102, 103

Pennycook, A. 24, 26, 61, 141

performative linguistics 26

Peters, T. 94–5

PGCE *see* Postgraduate Certificate of Education

Phelan, S. 22

Phillipson, R. 7, 26–7, 28–9

Plato, *The Meno* 115

political cycles 64

political economy: and applied linguistics 1–2, 4; and neoliberalism as an economic theory 15–19; relationship to neoliberalism 2; uses and definitions of the term 1–2

Pollard, Vicky (fictional character) 89

Poole, B. 7

Postgraduate Certificate of Education (PGCE): calculability 128; efficiency 126–7; as a McDonaldised system 126–33; and motivational posters 131–2; predictability 128; transcription conventions 143

post-structuralism 24, 61

power: capital investment and social power 21; communication power 20; and discourse 23, 24–5, 34; economic 65; Foucault 24–6; internalising of social power 25–6; and knowledge 24; state power 18

Powering the Smart Economy 50

predictability 122, 128

Presley, Elvis 98, 99

privatisation: educational 7; inefficiencies of 17; of public services 15

pupil testing 120

Quinn, Sean 53

Rampton, B. 1, 2, 3, 71, 82, 83–5

Razool, N. 62

Reaganomics 15

reality television 95–6

recognition 51, 57

regulation 10, 25, 43, 44, 45–6 *see also* deregulation; Rwandan business regulation 8

Reich, R. 69

residency 80

Richards, J. C. and Crookes, G. 115

Ritzer, G. 68, 121–2, 123, 124–5

Roberts, K. 81

Robertson, R. 59, 60

Roddick, Anita 103

Rojek, C. 88–9

Rowling, J. K. 102

RPF (Rwandan Patriotic Front) 8

Rwanda 8–9; education 97

Rwandan Patriotic Front (RPF) 8

Sachs, J. 5

Saltman, K. J. 7

Samuelson, B. and Freedman, S. 8

scapes 58, 61, 68

Schön, Donald 116–17

Schuller, T. 47

Schumpeter, Joseph 50

scientific management 123
second language acquisition (SLA) 118, 119
second language teacher education *see* language teacher education
self-help literature 94–5
Seymour, S. 139
signs 31
Simpson, Bart 89
Skeggs, B. 72, 85
Sklair, L. 17
SLA (second-language acquisition) 118, 119
small government 17
Soars, L. and Soars, J. 101, 102, 103, 104
social capital 49, 79
social democracy 16
social entrepreneurs 52–3 *see also* entrepreneurship
socialism 94
socially constituted linguistics 2–3
social mobility 76–7, 82
social networking 22, 80–1
social relations 19, 22, 31, 33–4, 38, 39–40, 46, 49, 54; and class 78; and discursive practices 33–4; and ideology 30, 31, 33–4, 40–1; and power 25; and technology 21–2
Soros, George 96
Sowden, C. 8, 9
Spears, Britney 86
'spectator democracy' 92
Spring, J. 140
state intervention 17
states, nation *see* nation states
Stewart, Martha 95
Streamline Connections 112
strikes 93
structuralism 3, 24
structural time 64
Stubbs, M. 40
Stuckler, D. *et al.* 5
symbolic behaviour 81
symbolic capital 79

Taylorism 123
Taylor, William 123
teachers: language teacher education *see* language teacher education; neoliberalism as a challenge to teacher professionalism 120–1; perspectives on celebrity 104–8; teacher cognition 118–20
Teaching English to Speakers of Other Languages (TESOL) 27, 115, 141
technology 20–2, 61
TESOL (Teaching English to Speakers of Other Languages) 27, 115, 141 *see also* English language teaching (ELT)

texts 23–4; celebrity and 'aspirational content' in ELT textbooks 87, 96–113
Thatcherism 15, 43, 72
Thatcher, Margaret 70–1
'There is No Alternative' (TINA) 7, 57, 70 *see also* Washington Consensus
Third Way 16
Thompson, E. P. 78–9, 84
Thompson, J. B. 34, 40
Thornbury, S. 109
Torville, Jayne 99
Total 56–7
Toynbee, Polly 71
transnationalism 17
Trudgill, P. 82

unemployment 15, 21, 50, 56
United States of America: American hegemony 67–8; Federal Reserve Bank 16; and Ireland 42–3; 'state manager' diplomacy 68
universities, entrepreneurial 51–2

Vietnam War movement 93
Village 53
virtual realities 61
Volosinov, V. N. 25, 31, 37–8

Wallace, M. J. 115, 116
Wallerstein, I. 64, 65, 66
Washington Consensus 16, 43, 70
Waters, A. 8
wealth 80, 81, 96
Weber, M. 76–8, 122, 124
Wenger, E. 115
Williams, E. 8–9, 98
Williams, R. 35–40, 50, 78, 84
Willis, Bruce 86
Winfrey, Oprah 95, 102–3
Woods, E. M. 21
working classes 57, 66, 72, 80–2, 84, 85, 90
World Bank 8, 16, 70
world hegemony 66–7
world systems analysis (WSA) 64–6
Wright, E. O. 75, 76, 77–8
WSA (world systems analysis) 64–6

Young, J. 93

Žižek, S. 4, 21, 30, 96, 106
'zombies' 53
Zweig, S. 88